CAMBRIDGE TEXTS IN THE
HISTORY OF PHILOSOPHY

———

ETIENNE BONNOT DE CONDILLAC
Essay on the Origin of Human Knowledge

D0140288

CAMBRIDGE TEXTS IN THE HISTORY OF PHILOSOPHY

Series editors

KARL AMERIKS

Professor of Philosophy at the University of Notre Dame

DESMOND M. CLARKE

Professor of Philosophy at University College Cork

The main objective of Cambridge Texts in the History of Philosophy is to expand the range, variety and quality of texts in the history of philosophy which are available in English. The series includes texts by familiar names (such as Descartes and Kant) and also by less well-known authors. Wherever possible, texts are published in complete and unabridged form, and translations are specially commissioned for the series. Each volume contains a critical introduction together with a guide to further reading and any necessary glossaries and textual apparatus. The volumes are designed for student use at undergraduate and postgraduate level and will be of interest not only to students of philosophy, but also to a wider audience of readers in the history of science, the history of theology and the history of ideas.

For a list of titles published in the series, please see end of book.

ETIENNE BONNOT DE CONDILLAC

Essay on the Origin of Human Knowledge

TRANSLATED AND EDITED BY

HANS AARSLEFF
Princeton University

CAMBRIDGE
UNIVERSITY PRESS

CAMBRIDGE UNIVERSITY PRESS
Cambridge, New York, Melbourne, Madrid, Cape Town, Singapore,
São Paulo, Delhi, Dubai, Tokyo

Cambridge University Press
The Edinburgh Building, Cambridge CB2 8RU, UK

Published in the United States of America by Cambridge University Press, New York

www.cambridge.org
Information on this title: www.cambridge.org/9780521585767

First published 2001

A catalogue record for this publication is available from the British Library

Library of Congress Cataloguing in Publication data
Condillac, Etienne Bonnot de, 1714–1780.
[Essai sur l'origine des connaissances humaines. English]
Essay on the origin of human knowledge / Etienne Bonnot de Condillac;
translated and edited by Hans Aarsleff.
p. cm. – (Cambridge texts in the history of philosophy)
Includes bibliographical references and index.
ISBN 0 521 58467 1 – ISBN 0 521 58576 7 (paperback)
1. Psychology – Early works to 1850.
2. Knowledge, Theory of – Early works to 1800.
3. Language and languages – Philosophy – Early works to 1800.
I. Aarsleff, Hans. II. Title. III. Series.
B1983.E88 2 E513 2001
121–dc21   00–054721

ISBN 978-0-521-58467-8 Hardback
ISBN 978-0-521-58576-7 Paperback

Transferred to digital printing 2010

Contents

Contents

Contents

Acknowledgments

It is my great pleasure to acknowledge the advice and support I have at various stages received while working on this translation from the series editor, Professor Desmond M. Clarke; from Dr. John L. Logan, Literature Bibliographer at Princeton; and from Gregory Lyon, also of Princeton. Their cheerful help in the task of moulding a good fit between French and English idiom has greatly advanced the completion of the project. To Gregory I am especially grateful for his expertise in doing the word processing and putting the whole thing on a disk with wonderful accuracy and speed. I am also grateful to the copyeditor, Jane Van Tassel, for her good work in the final stage. Needless to say, I alone am responsible for all the errors and infelicities that print is heir to, though only of course in this book.

Abbreviations

CO   *Œuvres philosophiques de Condillac*, ed. Georges le Roy, 3 vols., Paris, Presses Universitaires de France, 1947–51

Crit. Refl.   Jean-Baptiste Du Bos, *Critical Reflections on Poetry, Painting, and Music*, tr. Thomas Nugent, 3 vols., London, 1748. Reprinted New York, AMS Press, 1978

De oratore   Cicero, *De oratore*, tr. E. W. Sutton and H. Rackham, 2 vols., Loeb Classical Library, Cambridge, MA, Harvard University Press, 1942

Div. Leg.   William Warburton, *The Divine Legation of Moses*, 3 vols., London, 1738–41

E   John Locke, *Essay Concerning Human Understanding*, ed. Peter H. Nidditch, Oxford, Clarendon Press, 1975

EMGL   *Encyclopédie méthodique: Grammaire et littérature*, ed. Nicolas Beauzée and Jean-François Marmontel, 3 vols., Paris, Panckoucke, 1782–6

Encyclopédie *Encyclopédie, ou dictionnaire raisonné des sciences, des arts et des métiers*, ed. Denis Diderot and Jean le Rond d'Alembert, 28 vols., Paris, 1751–72. Supplement, 4 vols., 1776–7

FLS   Hans Aarsleff, *From Locke to Saussure: Essays on the Study of Language and Intellectual History*, Minneapolis, University of Minnesota Press, 1982

Hiérogl.   William Warburton, *Essai sur les hiéroglyphes des égyptiens, où l'on voit l'origine et les progrès du langage et de l'écriture, l'antiquité des sciences en Egypte, et l'origine du culte des animaux*, tr. Marc-Antoine Léonard des Malpeines, Paris,

	1744. Ed. Patrick Tort, Paris, Aubier Collection Palimpseste, 1977 (= *Div. Leg.* 2.66–205)
Orator	Cicero, *Orator*, tr. H. M. Hubbell, Loeb Classical Library, Cambridge, MA, Harvard University Press, 1997 [1939]
Origin	Condillac, *Essai sur l'origine des connaissances humaines* in CO 1.3–118
Quintilian	Quintilian, *Institutio oratoria*, tr. H. E. Butler, 4 vols., Loeb Classical Library, Cambridge, MA, Harvard University Press, 1920–2

Introduction

In the introduction to *Origin*, Condillac explains that his entire argument hinges on two notions: the connection of ideas and the language of action. About the former he believed that it is a fact of experience that the world, both natural and social, is a concatenation of things and events. Of these we may form ideas in the mind, but the world will still remain foreign to us unless we have some way of gaining mastery over ideas so that we can connect them at will to form discursive thinking; knowledge is not possible without the power of recall. Fortunately, ideas connect with signs, "and it is, as I will show, only by this means that they connect among themselves," namely in our minds, in which signs constitute a particular kind of ideas. Thus the connection of ideas is a way of rebuilding, as it were, as much of the world as we can by bringing the outside under inside control. On its first publication *Origin* carried the subtitle "a work in which all that pertains to the human understanding is reduced to a single principle." The introduction makes it clear that this principle is the connection of ideas.

Having assigned this crucial role to signs, Condillac next admitted that he was obliged to show how we have acquired the habit of using signs and gained the aptitude to employ them. He would need to give an account of the origin of speech, and here also he began from the outside with what he called the language of action. By this he meant the spontaneous movements and gestures of both voice and body which Descartes had warned against as posing a threat to the integrity of discursivity when in Part V of his *Discourse on the Method* he wrote that "we must not confuse speech with the natural movements which express the passions and which can be imitated by machines as well as by animals." Condillac's program was designed to do away with the dualism of body and mind. It was relentlessly anti-Cartesian. We shall later return to the connection of ideas and the language of action.

But before proceeding it will be useful to bear in mind two things that have pervasive relevance to our subject. The first concerns how the eighteenth century differed from the seventeenth about the role of social life in human affairs, while the second is about the nature of Condillac's argument. In the Cartesian view, innateness owes no debt to social intercourse. Right reason and knowledge are private achievements, for in the Augustinian sense we do not truly learn anything from anybody. God alone is the teacher. Communication is risky. Seen in this light, it took a contract to ensure social bonding. The eighteenth century took a different view, shown for instance in Hume's and Adam Smith's rejection of contract theory because they had other means of accounting for social cohesion. Hume said it was "needless . . . to ask, why we have humanity and a fellow-feeling with others. It is sufficient, that this is experienced to be a principle in human nature. We must stop somewhere in our examination of causes."[1] What he had in mind was sympathy. This very radical cultural shift toward emphasis on natural sociability is illustrated in the proportions of certain word occurrences in French for the years 1600–1700 and 1701–1800, based on a survey of 334 texts by ninety-three authors for the first of those centuries and 488 texts by a hundred and fifty-six authors for the second. The figures are not directly comparable, but still striking enough to leave no doubt about their lesson. See the accompanying table.[2] It would seem safe to conclude that in such a dramatic shift toward social awareness, the entire range of all means of communication would move toward the center of interest: music, pantomime, dance, ballet, acting, poetry, opera, prose, and the condition of being deaf or blind.

The other thing to bear in mind is this: Condillac's conception of the possibility and growth of knowledge rests on an argument about the origin and progress of language which occurs in a process of develop-

[1] David Hume, *Enquiries Concerning Human Understanding and Concerning the Principles of Morals*, ed. L. A. Selby-Bigge, with text revised and notes by P. H. Nidditch (Oxford, Clarendon Press, 1988), p. 219. Cf. Hume, *Treatise of Human Nature*, ed. Selby-Bigge (Oxford, Clarendon Press, 1955), p. 22: "To explain the ultimate causes of our mental actions is impossible. 'Tis sufficient we can give any satisfactory account of them from experience and analogy."

[2] Daniel Gordon, *Citizens without Sovereignty: Equality and Sociability in French Thought, 1670–1789* (Princeton, NJ, Princeton University Press, 1994), p. 53, in the fine chapter "The Language of Sociability" (pp. 43–85).

Word	1600–1700	1701–1800
Société	620	7,168
Social	8	838
Sociabilité	0	66
Sociable	16	222

ment that requires much repetition, well-formed habits, steady social interaction as in a continuing game, and a very long time. Thus speech and knowledge come to be seen as aspects of our natural history. I think it is true to say that no one before Condillac had so fully and cogently argued that a fundamental human institution is the product of evolving adaptation and functional success over time. This bold conceptualization is a major contribution to theory and knowledge. It readily calls to mind Adam Smith's conception of the invisible hand that stirs individuals into social action without any forethought or intention on their part about ultimate effects. The early formation of speech is not the work of lone creating minds of the private Cartesian sort. Like the market economy, it is not invented; it just comes about in the manner which is illustrated by Hume's beautiful example of how "two men, who pull the oars of a boat, do it by an agreement and convention, though they have never given promises to each other," to which he later in the same paragraph added the observation that "in like manner are languages gradually established by human conventions without any promise" (*Treatise*, p. 490). Adam Smith had read Hume, but I see no likelihood that Condillac had read either of the two Scots. It is surely thought-provoking that Condillac all the same pulled oars with them "without any promise."

Cartesian dualism and language

For Descartes speech was an epistemological obstacle because it was an easy vehicle for the seductive inducements of eloquence and emotive persuasion – hence the denunciations of rhetoric that are so common in Galileo, Descartes, and Locke. By its very nature the expressive uses of language replicated the passion that caused Adam's and thus humanity's loss of the nearly perfect knowledge he demonstrated in the naming of the animals, a naming that characteristically relied not on hearing but on seeing. Let us also remember that in *Paradise Lost* Satan's tempting of Eve succeeds by eloquence. Thus language was split in two, one form being considered naturally cognitive, rational, and the inert means for the communication of ready-made, prior mental discourse; the other active, emotive, and in the strict sense allied with sin and unnatural.[3] As late as the 1760s this dual scheme was, as we shall see, advanced against Condillac's expressivism.

This Cartesian conception amounted to a cognitive appropriation of language that perfectly served the epistemological and descriptive priorities of its parent philosophy. Thus, though the seventeenth century was the great age of French eloquence – now the subject of an important book by Marc Fumaroli[4] – only its philosophical rival had a doctrine about the nature of language, a doctrine that was largely Augustinian and orthodox. It is a puzzling fact that in the matter of language Locke was at his most Cartesian in taking the position that the word-free discourse of the mind is the only guarantor of true knowledge. By the same token, Locke shared the rationalist doctrine that syllogistic is trivial, for "a man knows first, and then he is able to prove syllogistically. So that *syllogism* comes after knowledge, and then a man has little or no need of it" (E 4.17.6). This, I believe, is what Quine in the famous essay "Two Dogmas of Empiricism" called "the impossible term-by-term empiricism of Locke and Hume," though of course that impossible doctrine was taken over from rationalism.

But as we shall see, in the decades around 1700 this situation changed, and soon rhetoric became the source of an altogether new understanding of the nature of language. Now communication was no longer risky but creative, and its study became the best avenue of insight into mind and thought. According to a report by one of his students, this principle was stressed by Adam Smith in his lectures on rhetoric and belles-lettres during the 1750s in these words: "The best method of explaining and illustrating the various powers of the human mind, the most useful part of metaphysics, arises from an examination of the several ways of communicating our thoughts by speech, and from an attention to the

---

[3] On belief in the Adamic language, see Hans Aarsleff, "The Rise and Decline of Adam and His *Ursprache* in Seventeenth-Century Thought" in *The Language of Adam/Die Sprache Adams*, ed. Allison P. Coudert, Wolfenbütteler Forschungen, vol. 84 (1999), 277–95.
[4] Marc Fumaroli, *L'Age de l'éloquence* (Paris, Albin Michel, 1994 [1980]).

principles of those literary compositions which contribute to persuasion and entertainment."[5] To Descartes and Locke that statement would have made no sense at all.

Condillac and Locke

Condillac admired Locke as the best of philosophers because he had studied the operations of the mind without reliance on postulates about its essential nature. The rejection of innate ideas was one aspect of this empirical commitment, and on this as on other points the debt to Locke is too obvious to need explication. On this basis, however, it is still widely believed that Condillac was a mere follower of Locke, even to the extent that one can still in print meet the dogmatic claim that *Origin* is just a short version of Locke's *Essay*. That conception is false. Even a brief look at *Origin* shows that its philosophy differs from Locke's in at least two fundamental ways.

The first is that while Locke in Book III of the *Essay* worked hard to protect his trusted mental discourse from what he called "the cheat of words," Condillac turned the whole thing upside down by making speech and words the condition for discursivity and thus the agency of knowledge and the exercise of reason. This aspect of *Origin* is so obvious that one wonders how it can be missed and why. I have no doubt that the reason lies in the still prestigious opinion that what have been called "the soulless mechanical rationalists of the French Enlightenment" represented a sort of faint but loyal afterglow of seventeenth-century rationalism with its hostility to poetry, expressivism, and the creative energies of language. The mention of the mechanical is astonishing, since the tenor of French thought at the time was overwhelmingly organismic, as clearly shown, for instance, by Condillac's evident preference for organic metaphors.

The second radical difference between Locke and Condillac can be read directly from the table of contents of Part II. "The Prosody of the First Languages," "Progress of the Art of Gesture among the Ancients," "Music," "The Origin of Poetry," "The Genius of Languages," and other chapter headings indicate topics that could have

---

[5] Dugald Stewart, "Account of the Life and Writings of Adam Smith," ed. I. S. Ross in Adam Smith, *Essays on Philosophical Subjects*, ed. W. P. D. Wightman and J. C. Bryce (Indianapolis, IN, Liberty Classics, 1982), p. 274.

had no imaginable relevance to Locke's enterprise. But for Condillac they were the heart of the matter. For him the origin of knowledge begins with sentiment, expression, sympathy, and the mutual benefit of affective responses that arise in social interaction. *Origin* argues that speech is the primal human institution, and that aesthetics comes before epistemology, and imagination before reason. With Hume, he believed that reason is at the service of the passions.

Both George Berkeley and Condillac found that the *Essay*'s argument somehow went awry because Locke treated ideas in Book II before treating "words and language in general" in Book III. If he had reversed the order, they thought, he would have seen that his faith in the Cartesian discourse of the mind clashed with his open admission that words often have an active role in thought, as, for example, when he observed that like children we learn most words before having experiences to provide the appropriate ideas (E 3.5.15; 3.9.9); that the complex ideas of mixed modes would either not exist at all or would lose stability without the words that connect the component ideas under a single name, because, as Locke said, "it is the name that seems to preserve those essences, and give them their lasting duration," a passage Condillac cited against the coherence of Locke's argument (E 3.5.10; *Origin* I, 4, §27); and that we hardly ever engage in pure mental discourse, but use words instead, "even when men think and reason within their own breasts," a passage Condillac also cited against Locke (E 4.6.1; *Origin* I, 4, §27). But this critique was balanced by awareness that the *Essay* was rich in forward-looking notions about language. The *Essay* helped create the climate that favored the coming change.

(1) Locke insisted that there is no natural connection between the sounds of words and what they signify. The dismissal of this common seventeenth-century dogma released words from any imputation of a natural connection and divine origin by virtue of Adam's naming of the animals, thus clearing the way for the only alternative, human origin. (2) Locke gave language a public dimension owing both to its social use and to its continued existence and modification in speaking. Languages, he said, are "suited only to the convenience of communication . . . not to the reality and extent of things" (E 2.28.2), and were "established long before sciences," their "more or less comprehensive terms" having received "their birth and signification from ignorant and illiterate people who sorted and denominated things by those sensible qualities

they found in them" (E 3.6.25). Though Locke never treated the origin of language, he made suggestive remarks about the beginners, the beginning, and the growth of languages.[6] (3) This process of usage will cause change over time, thus giving each language a particular quality and a historical dimension. He noted that even with our great volume of classical scholarship, we still often cannot be certain we get the right sense of ancient authors, and he remarked that much the same was true of the reading and interpretation of Scriptures (E 3.9.10 & 23). His writings on religion show that he was no stranger to hermeneutics. Locke's *Essay* had the effect of expanding thinking about language into the larger issue of the nature of communication in general.

The *Essay* ranged so widely over the nature and workings of language that it went beyond the needs of epistemology, but Locke still found no place for the uses of language on the stage, at the bar, in the pulpit, or in poetry. He was confident that if we wish to "speak of things as they are, we must allow, that all the art of rhetoric . . . all the artificial and figurative application of words eloquence has invented are for nothing else but to insinuate wrong ideas, move the passions, and thereby mislead the judgment" (E 3.10.34). This sounded reassuring, but it was rather like whistling in the dark, for if words did push their way into mental discourse, as Locke admitted they were apt to do, then emotion entering with them would spoil the cognitive appropriation. For Berkeley one problem with that appropriation was that the language of the Bible and religion is not cognitive. This leads to the rhetorical expressivism that took its place; but first we need to pay attention to the full title of *Origin*.

The title of *Origin*

In French, Locke's *Essay* had the title *Essai philosophique concernant l'entendement humain*, in which the last two words stand for "human understanding" in the English title. But Condillac chose to call his work *Essai sur l'origine des connaissances humaines*, which in Thomas Nugent's translation of 1756 became *An Essay on the Origin of Human Knowledge*.

---

[6] See E 2.22.2; 2.28.2; 3.1.5; 3.6.46; 3.6.51. On the social and public nature of language in Locke, see James Tully, *A Discourse on Property: John Locke and His Adversaries* (Cambridge, Cambridge University Press, 1980), pp. 12–16; E. J. Ashworth, "Locke on Language," *Canadian Journal of Philosophy*, 14 (1984), 49–51, 72; Lia Formigari, *Language and Experience in Seventeenth-Century British Philosophy* (Amsterdam, Benjamins, 1988), pp. 135–6.

That comes close if we take it in the sense of "the ways in which human beings acquire knowledge," which of course may be too long for a title. But the point is obvious. Condillac could have called his work "Essai sur l'origine de l'entendement humain," but his not doing so must surely be taken to indicate deliberate choice.

In the penultimate paragraph of the introduction, Condillac leaves no doubt why he finds fault with Locke's notion of the understanding. Since the soul, Condillac there writes,

> does not from the first instant control the exercise of all its operations, it was necessary, in order to give a better explanation of the origin of our knowledge (*pour développer mieux l'origine de nos connaissances*), to show how it acquires that exercise, and what progress it makes in it. It does not appear that Locke addressed that question, or that anyone has ever blamed him for the omission.

Those plain words should decide the issue. But among other reasons for not easily granting that Condillac meant to write on "the origin of human understanding," one can also cite his detailed treatment of the roles of attention, reminiscence, memory, and imagination in the process of gaining knowledge; and note the crucial role given to signs in *Origin*, contrasted with Locke's hard work to protect the understanding against "the cheat of words."

Like Descartes, Locke thought of the understanding as a private endowment, while for Condillac understanding and knowledge are public benefits. It is misleading to give the impression that after Locke had written "concerning human understanding" Condillac got the not very interesting copycat notion of writing "on the origin of human understanding." Such a title also tends to sanction the fatal error of believing that *Origin* is merely "a supplement to Mr. Locke's *Essay*," as it says on the title page of the English translation of 1756. It would be correct to call Condillac's work "an essay on the origin of language and human knowledge," but that possibility is ruled out for the good reason that he did not use that title. His title was and is *Essay on the Origin of Human Knowledge*.

Rhetorical expressivism

In the chapter on the progress of gesture in antiquity, Condillac tells how mimes in the time of Augustus had brought their art to such perfection that they could perform entire plays by gestures alone, thus unawares creating "a language which had been the first that mankind spoke" (II, 1, §34). This was the ultimate progress of expressivism; it was what Condillac called the language of action, which in his argument is the proto-language of the speech that sets humans apart from other animals. But the reaction against the cognitive appropriation had already by 1700 advanced the claim that emotion, passion, and gesture cannot be kept apart from communication.

This claim is best known from Berkeley's identification of what has been called the emotive theory of meaning, in paragraph twenty of his *Treatise on the Principles of Human Knowledge* (1710). It is often said that his theory was altogether new and revolutionary at the time, but that is not correct. It had already been stated with equal force in at least two works with large readerships. The Port-Royal *Logic* (1662)[7] had a chapter on "what words mean in usage," which argued that in addition to the "principal idea" which is its proper signification, a word often "raises several other ideas that we can call accessory (*accessoires*) of which we do not take notice though the mind receives the impression of them." Thus if someone says, "You have lied about it," the sense is not merely "You have said what you know is not true," which pertains to the "truth of things," but also covers the accompanying thoughts of contempt and outrage that pertain to the "truth of usage." The concept of accessory ideas obviously belongs with emotive meaning in Berkeley's sense; even the example of the liar also turns up in Berkeley and in other texts about emotive meaning. The same chapter also made the rhetorical point that accessory ideas need not have their source in custom and usage, but may also be created by the speaker's tone of voice, facial expression, gestures, and "other natural signs that attach a multitude of ideas to words," including the affective deviation from standard syntax, as in the inversion of normal word order.

The second work to anticipate Berkeley was Bernard Lamy's *Rhetoric or the Art of Speaking*, which after its initial publication in 1675 until the author's death in 1715 went through a stream of fifteen steadily expanded and revised French printings that with increasing force and detail expounded the emotive and expressive dimensions of speech.[8]

---

[7] Antoine Arnauld and Pierre Nicole, *La Logique ou l'art de penser*, ed. Pierre Clair and François Girbal (Paris, PUF, 1965), pp. 93–9. This is Ch. 14 in the fifth edition (1683).

[8] Bernard Lamy, *La Rhétorique ou l'art de parler*, 4th ed. revised and enlarged (Amsterdam, 1699).

Lamy followed the Port-Royal *Logic* on the primacy of usage (pp. 66–72), on accessory ideas with the example of the liar (p. 39), and on the use of vocal gestures, for which he cited interjections (or particles, as he called them) that express "admiration, joy, disdain, anger, pain" (pp. 38–9). Lamy boldly claimed that "the passions are good in themselves" (p. 343) and that people hardly ever act on reason but on imagination and sense (p. 367), and declared that his book did something unusual by aiming to uncover the foundations of rhetoric (p. 153). Lamy's *Rhetoric* remained a respected authority for much of the eighteenth century.

At this point oratory begins to blend with sympathy, gestures, and sociability, and in this context Lamy made a timely observation about the foundations of rhetoric, as we shall see in a moment. In its classical formulation the art of oratory had five parts: invention, disposition, expression, memory, and delivery. Traditionally these parts were given roughly equal importance, but toward the end of the seventeenth century delivery began to get the most attention, because it came to be seen as the chief agent of effective persuasion. This change is evident in Fénelon's *Dialogues on Eloquence in General and on That of the Pulpit in Particular*, first published in 1718 (in French of course) but written some forty years earlier.[9] Their thesis is that truth will not prevail without eloquence and persuasion, and their chief target was sermons that tended to present ineffectual philosophical argument. In our present fallen state, wrote Fénelon, with man being "wholly enmeshed in things of sense . . . it is necessary to give physical body to all the instructions one wishes to inject into his soul, and to find images that beguile him," that is by poetry, which, being "the lively portrayal of things, is as it were the soul of eloquence" (p. 94).

Fénelon found the greatest eloquence in the Old and New Testaments, especially in the prophets and the psalms, which for him surpassed Homer and Plato in grandeur, naïveté, liveliness, and sub-

---

The first seven, steadily expanded, issues bore the title *L'Art de parler*, but in 1688 the title was changed to *La Rhétorique ou l'art de parler* to take account of the new orientation of the work. This change also signals a movement away from the strict Cartesianism which Lamy professed earlier in his career.

[9] François de Salignac de la Mothe-Fénelon, *Dialogues on Eloquence*, a translation with an introduction and notes by Wilbur Samuel Howell (Princeton, NJ, Princeton University Press, 1951). This text identifies the many references to Cicero, Quintilian, and Longinus. In the introduction (p. 46), Howell says, rightly I think, that the *Dialogues* are "the earliest statement . . . of what may be said to have become the dominant modern attitude toward rhetoric."

limity (p. 131). The example of David showed that "the oriental nations regarded the dance as a serious art, similar to music and poetry," just as the fact that the ancient Greeks went to war to the sounds of "trumpets and drums that threw them into a state of enthusiasm and a sort of furor they called divine" showed that even in pagan Greece "music, dance, eloquence, poetry had no other purpose but to give expression to the passions and to inspire them in the very act of expressing them" (p. 68). Fénelon paid much attention to the use of gestures in delivery. Citing Cicero, he wrote that the "action of the body" expresses "the sentiments and passions of the soul" (p. 99). The Latin word *actio* was Cicero's and Quintilian's term for delivery.

Both cited Demosthenes in support of their belief that delivery is the heart of oratory. Cicero declared that "nature has assigned to every emotion a particular look and tone of voice and bearing of its own; and the whole of a person's frame and every look on his face and utterance of his voice are like the strings of a harp, and sound according as they are struck by each successive emotion."[10] The body is itself like a musical instrument, with delivery or action being "a sort of eloquence of the body, since it consists in gesticulation as well as speech."[11] "Action," said Cicero, "influences everybody, for the same emotions are felt by all people and they both recognize them in others and manifest them in themselves by the same marks" (*De oratore* III, 223). The gestures of action, both with voice and body, constitute a universal language that advances communication and social cohesion. Classical rhetoric did not have a term for the mysterious something that provides humanity with a means of universal communication, but Lamy suddenly supplied it in the fourth edition of his *Rhetoric*. "Human beings are bound to one another," he wrote, "by a wonderful sympathy (*sympathie*) which naturally makes them communicate their passions." Thus a "person with an expression of sadness on his face causes sadness, just as a sign of joy makes those who notice it share in the joy," and all this, Lamy declared, "is an effect of the wonderful wisdom of God" (pp. 111–12). For support Lamy cited (p. 220) some lines from Horace which Hume also used in the second *Enquiry* to make the same

[10] *De oratore* III, 216; cf. *Origin* II, 1, §42n. On Demosthenes, see *De oratore* III, 213; *Orator*, 56; Quintilian III, iii, 1 and XI, iii, 6. In both of these places Quintilian says that the words *actio* and *pronuntiatio* are synonyms for delivery.

[11] *Orator*, 55: "Est enim actio quasi corporis quaedam eloquentia, cum constet e voce atque motu." This compact statement is quoted often.

point. It is a bit of a puzzle how Lamy came upon the term. It is Greek and its philosophical home was in Stoic philosophy, in which "sympathy" is the name for the cosmic harmony that binds all things together in an organized whole of interconnection that embraces both the physical and the moral worlds. A loan-translation appears in ecclesiastical Latin as *compassio*, which in turn produced other loan-translations such as the German *Mitleid*.

The essential role of sympathy in human affairs calls to mind Hume and Adam Smith, for whom it is the bond that joins individuals together in society owing to "the propensity we have," as Hume said, "to sympathize with others, and to receive by communication their inclinations and sentiments, however different and contrary to our own" (*Treatise*, p. 316). Both stressed that since sympathy, like an instinct, works without deliberation, forethought, or reflection, neither the gestural expression nor the response to it can be false or mistaken. "The passions, upon some occasions," wrote Adam Smith, "may seem to be transfused from one man to another, instantaneously, and antecedent to any knowledge of what excited them in the person principally concerned."[12] This error-free effect of sympathy ensures that the grounds of morality are firm and public. In sympathy we sense the presence of the great agent Adam Smith memorably called "the superintendent of the universe," whose invisible hand guides us to promote ends that do not figure in our intentions.

Sociability grows on sympathy, and the most commonly used illustration of this effect was the reaction to someone else's pain. In his *Critical Reflections*, which was a work well known to Hume and Adam Smith, Du Bos observed that our conduct would be determined by self-interest if nature had not implanted in us the prompt and instant "natural sensibility of the heart . . . as the first foundation of society." The feelings of those who need our help touch us without delay and, as we are moved, "they receive from us what they would never have gained by way of reasoning or persuasion," for "the tears of a stranger move us even before we know what makes him weep; the cries of a person with

---

[12] Adam Smith, *The Theory of Moral Sentiments*, ed. D. D. Raphael and A. L. Macfie (Indianapolis, IN, Liberty Classics, 1982), p. 11. The passage continues with the introduction of the spectator: "Grief and joy, for example, strongly expressed in the look and gestures of any one, at once affect the spectator with some degree of a like painful or agreeable emotion." Cf. Hume, *Treatise*, p. 317: "When any affection is infused by sympathy, it is at first known only by its effects."

whom we share nothing but our humanity make us rush to assistance by an involuntary movement that precedes all deliberation."[13] Most of this passage was quoted verbatim, without quotation marks, in the entry "Société" in the *Encyclopédie* to show how God has provided for our natural sociability by the marvellous ease with which the passions communicate themselves from one brain to another.

The rise of rhetorical expressivism and its fellow concepts was concurrent with new efforts to understand the nature of language and its place in the entire spectrum of human communication, as if to create a media theory for the times. The seventeenth century could believe that our speech somehow had its origin in better times before the Fall when Adam named the animals, but with that faith gone, what would take its place? How could we become self-starters? Obviously, we could not have begun by inventing language by some discursive plotting even in a small way, for doing that would require that we already had a discourse to work with – this was one of the aporias made popular by Rousseau. But with natural sociability, spontaneous emotive expression, and sympathy we could have a proto-language which met the condition that the background of language was certainty, as ensured by action without forethought, and not acts of error-prone reasoning. Discursivity is bought at the cost of potential error, doubt, deceit, and simulation.

Condillac and signs

What Condillac says can be summarized as follows: Nature begins everything, and we are so made that from the first instant of sensation we actively engage with the world in which we live and survive. We owe so much to the passions that without them "the understanding is virtually at a standstill" (I, 2, §106). There is nothing at all passive or mechanical in this philosophy.[14] Though we do not know how, we are

---

[13] *Crit. Refl.* I.39–40. *Crit. Refl.* was first published in two volumes in 1719, and later, first in 1733, in three volumes and was often reissued. The term *sympathie* is rarely used in French at the time, but *sensibilité* either alone or suitably qualified, as in "the natural sensibility of the heart," serves just as well. The *Encyclopédie* has an entry "Sympathie (*Physiolog.*)" which opens with a glowing statement that could have come from Hume or Adam Smith. It is curious that Alan Bewell in his fine book *Wordsworth and the Enlightenment* (Princeton, NJ, Princeton University Press, 1989), p. 77, writes that "*Sympathy* . . . is the pivotal term in Condillac's account of the origin of language," for Condillac never uses the word in *Origin*, but Bewell's perception that he might have is right.

[14] Nicolas Rousseau, *Connaissance et langage chez Condillac* (Geneva, Droz, 1986), p. 194.

made to become speaking creatures, unlike other animals, though with them we share consciousness, attention, reminiscence, and a limited form of imagination. Knowledge and discursivity cannot occur without the power of recall, recall not without memory, and neither without signs. These signs cannot be private but must be public. Since we are born with neither innate ideas nor signs, how do we get the signs?

Condillac distinguishes three kinds of signs (1, 2, §35). The first are "accidental signs," which have the effect of producing in us the feeling of having previously experienced a present situation, like a déjà vu without illusion. One does not need to have read Proust to know what that is. Condillac calls this feeling reminiscence, and it carries the great lesson that a past experience can flash vividly on the mind with conviction both that it is not illusory and that it is not produced by intentional recall. What was accidentally encountered triggered the recall. Obviously, with signs having that power, it would be wonderful to have control over them.[15]

Secondly, there are the sounds that spontaneously give expression to affective states of mind such as joy, fear, pain – or what is sometimes called "groans and grunts" or avowals. When thus uttered, these sounds are not signs, but they become so if a hearer or spectator owing to sympathy recognizes them as expressions of familiar states of mind and then in turn acts deliberately by projecting a particular sound as a sign with the intent of communication. Though the sound or gesture is the

---

[15] It is worth noting that in the *Encyclopédie* the entries "Mémoire (*Métaphysiq.*)" (10 [1765], 326a–328b) and "Réflexion (*Logique*)" (13 [1765], 885a–886a) refer to *Origin* and that both quote extensively from it. The *Encyclopédie* has a brief entry entitled "Signe (*Métaphysiq.*)" (15 [1765], 188a) which quotes, without indication of source, Condillac's entire I, 2, §35 on the three kinds of signs, with this telling addition at the end: "These last [instituted] signs are necessary for human beings in order for them to have the power of being in control of their imagination." Presumably Condillac supplied this entry. The attentive reader will understand that one thing Condillac has in mind here is that animals do not have control over their imagination; they are therefore not free, in contrast to humans, who are. Condillac's brief addition about being in control of the imagination is a reminder that his entire project relates to current issues in cognitive science. At a recent meeting the distinguished neurobiologist Eric R. Kandel spoke about long-term memory. After the paper a colleague asked if Kandel would comment on "the general phenomenon of recall." As printed in the official volume, the answer took this form: "Recall is an extremely interesting problem because cognitive psychological studies suggest that it is not simply a question of turning a flash light on a memory process; it's a creative event." See Alexander G. Bearn (ed.), *Useful Knowledge: The American Philosophical Society Millennium Meeting* (Philadelphia, APS, 1999), p. 128. The lesson is this: both Condillac and Kandel (1) make the crucial distinction between storage and recall; and (2) both argue that recall is creative. Readers may know that in the fall of 2000 Kandel received the Nobel Prize for his work on memory.

same, at that point it ceases to be natural. It joins Condillac's third category of signs, the instituted signs we have ourselves chosen. In this act the hearer or spectator exercises the control over attention that is called reflection, which, once awakened, interacts with signs in a process of reciprocal progress of both. Without natural cries and gestures we could not become self-starting communicators, and Condillac stresses again and again that nascent speech for a long while needs the support of action. All modes of expression, everything that later becomes the separate arts, initially exist together until, ages later, prose emerges from poetry as a language that is ready to serve the needs of analysis and cognition. For Condillac language continues to have many forms and uses; he dismissed the rationalist claim that only the fixed subject–predicate order exhibited the true nature of language.

It is important to understand that the sign function is not the creation of the utterer, but that of the hearer. This is one of the radical differences that separate our two centuries. In the seventeenth century the dominant mode was vision, which by the light of nature reveals truth to the silent and isolated individual. For the eighteenth century the informing agency was hearing, which encompasses both the natural and social worlds. This is why Wordsworth sought to escape from what he called "the tyranny of vision." Speech is created in dialogue, and it becomes the source of self-knowledge. Above it all hovers imagination, which seeks synthesis of all the things that attention has connected for reflection to work on. In a later work Condillac wrote that a person of imagination is a "creative mind" by virtue of being able to join "diverse parts into a single whole that exists only in the mind" (CO 1.413b), which amplifies the remark he has already made in *Origin* that "genius adds to talent the idea of the intellect as being somehow creative" (I, 2, §104).

Condillac was of course well aware of the problem of getting from action to speech and thought – what can perhaps be called the boot-strapping problem. In the crucial chapter "Reflection" he admitted that he faced an impasse, for if "the exercise of reflection can only be acquired by the use of signs," how do we acquire the instituted signs unless some degree of reflection was already possible at an earlier stage (I, 2, §49)? When in the opening chapter of Part II he gives the solution (II, 1, §3), he refers back to the earlier mention of the problem. By repeatedly hearing the spontaneous avowals, the new speakers came to do by reflection what they had so far done by instinct. Nature begins everything. The proto-language is part of our natural history. From that opening chapter on the language of action, Condillac continues with close focus on the forms of action until, in the opening of chapter 9, he stops to say that he could not interrupt what he "wished to say about the art of gestures, dance, declamation, music, and poetry" because they are all so "closely interrelated as a whole and to the language of action which is their principle." These eight exciting chapters constitute the heart of *Origin*.

Did Condillac give too much to signs?

Condillac occasionally exchanged ideas about language with Maupertuis, a distinguished French scientist who was then president of the Prussian Academy in Berlin. In response to an essay on language he had received from Maupertuis, he wrote that he wished Maupertuis had shown how the progress of the mind depends on language. He then continued with these words: "I tried to do that in my *Origin*, but I was mistaken and gave too much to signs" (CO 2.536a). This has been read as an admission that Condillac was wrong about signs and thus, astonishingly, about the entire argument of *Origin*. But the evidence does not support that reading. Condillac wrote much on language the rest of his life, in *Course of Study for the Prince of Parma*, in *Logic*, and in *The Language of the Calculus* without retreating from the argument of *Origin*. By his own admission, *The Art of Thinking* for the most part repeated, usually verbatim, the text of *Origin*. When he came to the chapter on how we give signs to ideas in Part I, Section 4 of *Origin*, he changed the title in *The Art of Thinking* to "The Necessity of Signs," and to this new title he further added a note in which he said that since the printing of *Origin*, "I have completed the task of showing the necessity of signs in my *Grammar* and in my *Logic*" (CO 1.731a), both of which have searching chapters on the language of action. Obviously, Condillac's remark about having given too much to signs cannot be read as an admission of fatal error on an issue that lies at the center of his philosophy.[16] So what did he mean?

---

[16] See N. Rousseau, *Connaissance et langage chez Condillac*, pp. 22–3 and references given there.

He meant that he had failed to give sufficient emphasis to the equal necessity of social intercourse. This is already implied in what he next says in the letter to Maupertuis, whom he criticizes for assuming that a single isolated person could hit upon the notion of giving signs to ideas. In *Origin* the chapter on how we give signs to ideas was followed by a chapter with "Facts that confirm what was proved in the previous chapter," as also in *The Art of Thinking* after the chapter with the new title. The facts were the accounts of the two boys who for lack of participation in social life could not rise above the state of animals. About the first, the boy from Chartres, Condillac concluded that since he was deprived of hearing and speech, he could not connect ideas with instituted signs, and thus would have no memory, no command of imagination, and no capacity for reflection (I, 4, §20). This is also the chapter that ends with a severe critique of Locke for not having fully grasped the necessity of signs. In the letter to Maupertuis, Condillac did not, perhaps tactfully, refer to this chapter about the two deprived boys. But he did a few years earlier in letters to the Swiss mathematician Gabriel Cramer.[17]

We cannot go into detail about these rich letters. It is sufficient to note that Condillac forcefully insists on the need for social life with frequent references to his chapter on the two boys, that he does not retreat from his view of the necessity of signs, and that he does admit that his exposition was not clear enough. To Cramer's question whether natural signs count for nothing, Condillac answers:

> I answer that before social life, natural signs are properly speaking not signs, but only cries that accompany sentiments of pain, joy, etc., which people utter by instinct and by the mere form of their organs. They must live together to have occasion to attach ideas to these cries and to employ them as signs. Then these cries blend with the arbitrary signs. That is what I am supposing in several

---

[17] Georges le Roy (ed.), *Condillac, lettres inédites à Gabriel Cramer* (Paris, PUF, 1953). With these letters belongs an illuminating "Mémoire," here printed pp. 89–109. Le Roy's datings were revised by Piero Peccato in "Note sul carteggio Condillac–Cramer," *Belfagor*, 26 (1971), 83–95; I follow the Peccato datings, citing from a letter of the early part of 1747. This volume will be referred to as "Cramer." Maupertuis's essay was entitled "Réflexions critiques sur l'origine des langues et la signification des mots." In 1750 the young Turgot also remarked on the very same passage Condillac criticized; he called it a ridiculous supposition that a lone person would begin to use signs; "a single person . . . would never be tempted to find marks to designate his perceptions; it is only in company (*vis-à-vis des autres*) that we seek to do that." Gustav Schelle (ed.), *Œuvres de Turgot* (Paris, 1913–23), vol. I (1913), 162.

places [with his own references to I, 4, §§23–4 and II. I. §§2–3].
But I appeared to suppose the contrary, and thus to make too great
a difference between natural and arbitrary signs; and in that I was
wrong. (Cramer, pp. 85–6)

That is, he had seemed to give the impression that he thought natural
cries could be signs before or without social intercourse. This reading is
borne out by what comes next: "That's what my entire system comes
down to in this matter. Social intercourse gives occasion (1) to change
the natural cries into signs; (2) to invent other signs that we call
arbitrary; and these signs (the natural as well as the arbitrary) are the
first principles of the development and progress of the operations of the
mind. I admit that on all this my work is not clear enough. I hope I'll do
better another time" (Cramer, pp. 84–5). We again note how thoroughly
anti-Cartesian the argument is, against solipsism, and against the still
prevailing notion that any acceptable explanation of mental life must
begin with speculation about what goes on or might go on in the mind
of the silent, isolated individual.

Condillac's unbroken commitment to the argument of *Origin* with its
doctrine of signs that are generated within a form of life raises a radical
question not only about the reading of Condillac, but also about the
conventional view of eighteenth-century thought. The question is this:
how is it possible to reconcile his argument about communication and
signs with the widely credited dogma that his philosophy is most fully
represented by the famous statue in his *Treatise on the Sensations* (1754)?
This dogma holds that as the statue is in turn endowed with each of the
five senses, it becomes a full-fledged human being, ready to acquire and
exercise the entire range of intellectual abilities. Seen in this perspective,
Condillac is said to wish "to eliminate all autonomous activity from the
mind" by making reflection "depend upon the mechanical association
of ideas." These words proclaim the familiar knee-jerk belief that "the
informal metaphysics of the Enlightenment tended toward a mechanical
philosophy which saw nothing artificial in likening man to an animated
statue, even as the universe was likened to a watch." Obviously, if that
reading is credited, *Origin* and *Sensations* cannot be reconciled. But the
resolution is simple, for in spite of its prestige, that reading is false,
chiefly because it grasps neither the pivotal role of the necessity of signs
and communication in Condillac's argument nor his persistent affirmation of the creativity and action of the mind. The decisive fact is that,

like the two deprived boys, the statue is radically speechless because its existence is wholly private and unsocial; its mental life is that of an animal.[18]

This bizarre misreading is a measure of the stubborn failure to recognize the centrality of language in eighteenth-century French thought where this conception was born – to use the appropriate organismic metaphor – before it spread over the intellectual landscape of Europe.

Inversions or the problem of word order

Condillac's discussion of inversions brings out the deep implications of his argument that all languages ultimately stem from and still to some degree bear the mark of the emotion-based, expressive language of action. Treating the subject briefly in the chapter "Music," he observed that compared with French-speakers, the Greeks had a much livelier imagination because their language was closer to the language of action, which itself is a product of the imagination; by contrast, French is so proselike and analytical "that it hardly requires more than the exercise of memory" (II, 1, §51). In the later chapter "Inversions" he challenged the rationalist term-by-term position by declaring that it did not make sense to claim one could tell what the natural order was. The notion that the bound subject–predicate order was natural might merely be a French prejudice, since the French language leaves little choice in the matter. In *Letter on Deaf-Mutes*, Diderot suggested that the rationalists' faith in their natural order could be an effect of the long tradition of respect for Aristotelian logic. By contrast, Condillac argued, Latin grammar puts hardly any constraint on word order, thus leaving expression free to create the order that best suits the emotions and the intended emphasis.

In support of his thesis, Condillac cited and analyzed two passages of Latin poetry, which brought him to the conclusion that the free Latin order has two great and related benefits. It makes it possible to give expression a form that comes close to the language of action, and also to

---

[18] The quoted passages are from Isabel F. Knight, *The Geometric Spirit* (New Haven, CT, Yale University Press, 1969), pp. 29, 37, 85. It is telling that "reason" has a long entry in the index to this book, but "imagination" has none at all. See also Aarsleff, "Condillac's Speechless Statue" in FLS, pp. 210–24.

create a picture (*tableau*) which "in a single word unite[s] the circumstances of an action, much as a painter unites them on the canvas" (II, I, §122). Coming close to the language of action is a virtue, because early language, like poetry, is more spontaneous and true than the analytical prose that later developed. And creating a picture brings the expression close to the instantaneousness of thought, thus escaping from the time-bound, linear order of French, which can only produce "a plain narrative."

This last point is weighty, for it implies that the sentence is the unit of meaning, as Condillac made clear when he said that people who are familiar with the language of action know that "a single gesture is often equivalent to a long sentence" (II, I, §51). This is an important conception throughout the eighteenth century, and it corresponds to what is nowadays called semantic holism. Here again we note the contrast to rationalism, for which individual words are the prime carriers of meaning. Condillac was pointedly criticized in two long articles in the *Encyclopédie*, "Inversion" (8 [1765], 852–62a) and "Langue" (9 [1765], 249a–266a), by the great universal grammarian Nicolas Beauzée, who argued that at the beginning there was only one language, divine and Adamic, which followed the analytical order of ideas; a language of inversions was artificial ("Langue," 258a–259b). In favor of this stance he invoked both Descartes and the Bible.

For Condillac the quality of the language of action that was recaptured by inversions gave the expression vivacity and force; he did not use the word "energy," but Diderot did with much emphasis in his *Letter on Deaf-Mutes*, which is about the aesthetics of inversion and is much indebted to *Origin*.[19] The concept of expressive energy became so well known that it gained an entry in EMGL: "Energy is the quality that in a single word or in a small number of words causes us to perceive or feel a large number of ideas; or which by means of a small number of ideas expressed by words excites in the mind sentiments of admiration, respect, horror, love, hate, etc., which words alone do not signify" (EMGL 1 [1784], 713a). This of course could have come right out of *Origin*, and indeed for illustration the entry immediately cited the Horatian lines Condillac had quoted and analyzed to make this point (II, I, §121).

---

[19] See Jacques Chouillet, *Diderot poète de l'énergie* (Paris, PUF Ecrivains, 1984), esp. pp. 27–43.

This entry was written by the splendid Nicolas Beauzée, and he opened with these thought-provoking words: "Energy is a Greek word *energeia* [printed in Greek], *actio, efficacia*; in this sense its roots are in *en* (*in*, dans, en) and *ergon* (*opus*, ouvrage, oeuvre)." What the entry is saying is that the energy created by inversions and their model, the language of action, constitutes the true nature of language; its nature is action, not ready-to-hand finished work, and this quality of creativity can be attained only in languages which, like Latin, have a grammar that places few or no constraints on word order. In words that are widely taken to express the heart of his linguistic thought, Wilhelm von Humboldt declared that language "in itself is no product (*Ergon*) but an activity (*Energeia*) . . . It is the ever-repeated *mental* labor of making the *articulated* sound capable of expressing *thought*."[20] Humboldt's distinction between what he in German called *Werk* (work) and *Thätigkeit* (activity) corresponds wholly to the one Beauzée made between the two Greek words and the Latin and French equivalents he gave. Humboldt found the best embodiment of this true nature of language in the heavily inflected Sanskrit and Greek. It is not plausible to believe that Humboldt cooked up his distinction, its formulation, and its terms without knowledge of what was already in print about inversion and energy.

Condillac's sources

Origin is so generous with references that there is little problem about the sources. Locke clearly is prominent for the important but limited reasons I stated earlier in this introduction. The resurgence of rhetorical expressivism since the beginning of the eighteenth century evidently favored and advanced Condillac's project. In addition there are three figures who claim attention.

For the account of the two deprived boys Condillac refers to a work by the German philosopher Christian Wolff, who began the section in which they appear with these words: "The use of speech promotes and

---

[20] Wilhelm von Humboldt, *On Language: The Diversity of Human Language Structure and its Influence on the Mental Development of Mankind*, tr. Peter Heath, with an introduction by Hans Aarsleff (Cambridge, Cambridge University Press, 1988), p. 49. The Condillac–Beauzée context in which Humboldt's statement occurs clearly lends strong support to my argument in the introduction to the Humboldt volume, where see esp. pp. liv–lvii.

enlarges the use of reason; without the use of speech the use of reason is quickly lost." This opens up perspectives that are too wide to explore here. Let me summarily mention a few points. Like Condillac, Wolff is very strong on the enchainment of all things and the connection of ideas; he makes pain and pleasure grounds of action; he says that reflection cannot occur without words and that reason is manifested only by virtue of speech; he stresses that signs and words are indispensable for thinking; and he presents the architecture of the soul and the process of getting to know in ways that are closely similar to what Condillac offers in Part I of *Origin*, including the terminology. But they also differ in salient ways. Wolff used references to God as grounds of explanation and understanding, and he often likened the workings of nature to clockwork, in contrast to Condillac's preference for organic terms and metaphors. In Wolff there is also no trace of Condillac's evolutionary conception of the origin and progress of language. This last feature may explain why he found that Wolff "did not know the absolute necessity of signs any more than the manner in which they contribute to the progress of the operations of the mind" (1, 4, §27).

Warburton is much more prominent than Wolff, with extensive quotation and comment in the chapter "Writing" and in the crucial chapter on the language of action with which Part II opens. Here the quotations all come from a few pages devoted to what Warburton indicated was "Language" (*Hiérogl.*, pp. 118–23; *Div. Leg.* 2.81–7). In these pages Warburton's argument is that in the times of early religion speech was so rude and simple that the Old Testament prophets instructed the people by "actions . . . and conversed with them in signs," to which he added that such "speaking by action" was also common in pagan antiquity, as, for instance, by the Delphic oracle. The English bishop argued that this early speech would in the course of time be improved "by use and custom," thus implying that development could occur even in this sacred territory. It is this notion of development that interests Condillac in the first long quotation that occurs in a note at the very beginning of Part II. Warburton spoke openly about development, where more orthodox belief surely would not have allowed it. One suspects that Condillac was eager to cite the English divine in order to bolster the legitimacy of an enterprise that without precaution might easily have run afoul of religious authority. There is additional reason to think this was his primary concern, for the actions

Warburton chiefly talks about are divine and deliberate and not at all like the involuntary expressions, the "groans and grunts," that form the basis of the language of action.

Still, it is a curious fact that Condillac certainly must have found the term "language of action" (*langage d'action*) in Léonard des Malpeines's translation, in which it occurs twice in the text (pp. 127, 134) and three times in the prominent marginal summaries which the translator added for the convenience of the reader (pp. 120, 123, 127). In his text Warburton never used the phrase "language of action," and he did not even consistently use the same phrase for what he was talking about. Also puzzling is the fact that nothing is known about Léonard des Malpeines except that he made this translation and that he was a printer. But he surely deserves credit for having had the inspiration to coin a term that calls to mind the nature and role of action in oratory. I have not come upon the term in any earlier text, and it has only recently gained an entry in the French dictionary, *Le Grand Robert*, with a citation from Condillac, of course.[21]

We have already met Jean-Baptiste Du Bos in the congenial company of Hume and Adam Smith, sharing their views of sympathy and sociability. In *Origin* Condillac cites *Critical Reflections* more than any other text, no fewer than seven times at great length. These citations all occur in the chapters on prosody, gesture, and music, that is in chapters on the language of action, which was Du Bos's subject in his third volume. The chief source of this volume was Lucian of Samosata's dialogue "On the Dance," which for Lucian is a term that covers all

---

[21] It has been argued that Condillac is much indebted to Mandeville's *Fable of the Bees* (1729), and that this debt rests chiefly on the language of action. This argument was first advanced in the 1920s by the editor of *Fable*, F. B. Kaye, and was later repeated at much greater length by Rüdiger Schreyer in "Condillac, Mandeville, and the Origin of Language," *Historiographia Linguistica*, 5 (1978), 15–43. Among the common features cited are emphasis on sociability and communication by rude gestures that later develop into human speech; but these and other details do not go beyond the sort of familiar account presented by Diodorus Siculus and other classical writers. Mandeville entirely lacks Condillac's argument about the necessity of signs, about the three kinds of signs, about reminiscence and memory, and about the overlap from action to meaning that occurs when the hearer or spectator reacts to expressions of sentiment. Mandeville freely talks about the invention of speech and presumes the first speaking was motivated by eagerness to persuade. Mandeville has no concept of sympathy but instead points to pity, which for him is not instinctual but intentional on the basis of reflex thinking about oneself. Mandeville makes no reference to Cicero or Quintilian. There is the additional and rather disturbing detail that Schreyer has not seen either the English or French text of Warburton. So it is hard to see what can be left of the claim that Condillac was inspired by Mandeville.

forms of expression on the stage. Against a sceptical critic he argued that dance creates both pleasure and harmony by its combined uses of music, song, rhythm, ballet, pantomime, declamation, and other forms of expression, including eloquence. Thus dance corresponds to what Condillac in the opening pages of *Origin* calls the language of action; the list he there gives of its forms seems almost to have been lifted from Lucian. There cannot be any doubt that Jacques Chouillet is right when he says that Condillac "owes the theory of the language of action and of music to Du Bos."[22]

But Condillac's debt to Du Bos goes far beyond what he cites. His citations from Cicero and Quintilian show that he understood well that rhetorical doctrine was the conceptual source of the language of action; most of these citations were borrowed from *Reflections*. Du Bos also had a chapter on the writing of poetry in French and Latin which presents an argument that closely prefigures Condillac's argument in the chapter on inversions. The tenor of *Reflections* is that discursivity lacks the energy and immediacy of wordless communication. Du Bos believed that we judge a poem or a painting as we do a ragout, by sentiment, which he says is the way the heart works, "by a movement that precedes all deliberation."[23]

Wittgenstein

Something that I think is important may already have crossed the reader's mind – the similarity of conceptions and arguments in Condillac and the later Wittgenstein. This is not surprising. Both take aim at the same target, the Cartesian dualism of body and mind, and their arguments follow similar paths through a non-Cartesian proto-language to the conclusion that language could not have emerged from the privacy of the individual mind, but is a function of social life and communication. For both men the proto-language provided a firm, doubt-free beginning, and for both that beginning was action. The language of action initiates a language game that occurs within a form of life, and like a game the language of action carries no implication that it

---

[22] Jacques Chouillet, *La Formation des idées esthétiques de Diderot* (Paris, Colin, 1973), p. 239.

[23] *Crit. Refl.* 2.238–9. For Lucian's dialogue, see *Lucian*, tr. A. M. Harmon (8 vols.), vol. 5 (1936), 209–89 (Loeb Classical Library). The original Greek title of the dialogue is PERI ORCHESEOS, in Latin *De saltatione*. Du Bos's treatment of inversion in poetry occurs in *Crit. Refl.* 1.246–77.

is guided by reason. Brief attention to some passages in Wittgenstein will show what I mean.

In 1937 Wittgenstein wrote: "Language – I want to say – is a refinement, 'In the beginning was the deed (*Im Anfang war die Tat*).'"[24] Spoken early in Goethe's *Faust*, the quoted words are Faust's defiant reaction to the words his eyes had first fallen upon when he idly opened a book, "In the beginning was the word," which is of course the opening phrase of the famous first verse of the Gospel according to John. Faust's commitment to the deed and Wittgenstein's quotation of his words must obviously be understood with the echo of that verse in mind. I take it that Wittgenstein wished to say that logos, reason, and discursivity cannot be radically original and natural with human beings, an anti-Cartesian reading that is borne out by the statement that immediately precedes the sentence with the Faust quotation: "The origin and the primitive form of the language game is a reaction; only from this can more complicated forms develop." It is the hearer or spectator who opens up the game.

On the next page of "Cause and Effect" follow several passages that agree so well with Condillac that they can be cited with little comment. "The primitive form of the language game is certainty, not uncertainty," wrote Wittgenstein. "For uncertainty could never lead to action (*zur Tat*). I want to say: it is characteristic of our language that it grows on the foundation of stable forms of life, regular ways of acting. Its function is determined *above all* [emphasis in text] by action (*durch die Handlung*), which it accompanies." These words are immediately followed by commitment to development: "We have an idea of what sort of forms of life are primitive, and of those that could have developed from them. We believe that the simplest plough was there before the complicated one." This implies the conception of the natural history of human beings, which Wittgenstein writes about elsewhere (e.g., PI §415).

As in Condillac, this history includes what humans share with animals. *On Certainty* §471 says that "it is so difficult to begin at the

---

[24] "Cause and Effect: Intuitive Awareness" in *Philosophical Occasions 1912–1951*, ed. James C. Klagge and Alfred Nordmann (Indianapolis, IN, Hackett, 1993), p. 395. The passage appears the same year in a nearly identical verbal context (see *Culture and Value*, ed. G. H. von Wright in collaboration with Heikki Nyman, tr. Peter Winch [Chicago, University of Chicago Press, 1984], p. 31); and toward the end of Wittgenstein's life in *On Certainty*, ed. G. E. M. Anscombe and G. H. von Wright, tr. Denis Paul and G. E. M. Anscombe (New York, Harper Torchbook, 1972), §402. *Philosophical Occasions* is abbreviated "PO." "PI" stands for Wittgenstein, *Philosophical Investigations*, tr. G. E. M. Anscombe (Oxford, Blackwell, 1958).

beginning. And not try to go further back." Soon after in §475 we read: "I want to regard man here as an animal; as a primitive being to which one grants instinct but not ratiocination (*Raisonnement*). As a creature in a primitive state. Any logic that is good enough for a primitive means of communication needs no apology from us. Language did not emerge from some kind of ratiocination." As we know, Condillac also began with the instinct we share with animals. But he also addressed the question of deeper origin, which Wittgenstein never treated overtly, though he sometimes came close.

We have met the paradigmatic example of the reaction to someone else's pain in Hume, Adam Smith, and Condillac, and in a quotation from Du Bos (at n. 13 above). It was if anything more frequent in Wittgenstein, and the lesson was the same. In two late entries in *Zettel*, so presumably dating from his last years, Wittgenstein wrote:

> It is a help to remember that it is a primitive reaction to tend, to treat, the part that hurts when someone else is in pain; and not merely when oneself is – and so to pay attention to other people's pain-behaviour, as one does *not* [emphasis in text] pay attention to one's own pain-behaviour. But what does the word "primitive" mean here? Presumably that this sort of behaviour is prelinguistic (*vorsprachlich*), that a language-game is based *on it* [emphasis in text], that it is the prototype of a way of thinking and not the result of thought.[25]

In 1937 "Cause and Effect" already contained a passage that made much the same point about the birth of the game: "The game doesn't begin with doubting whether someone has a toothache, because that doesn't – as it were – fit the game's biological function in our life; in its most primitive form it is a reaction to somebody's cries and gestures, a reaction of sympathy or something of the sort (*eine Reaktion des Mitleids, oder dergleichen*). We comfort him, try to help him" (PO, p. 381).

In these passages the instinctual, non-deliberative nature of the reaction is stressed, and the magic word "sympathy" appears as the translation of the German *Mitleid*, which we have already traced back through *compassio* to the Greek "sympathy." In *Zettel* (§545) Wittgenstein has a passage about how a child learns the use of the word pain. This is how it ends:

[25] *Zettel*, ed. G. E. M. Anscombe and G. H. von Wright, tr. G. E. M. Anscombe (Oxford, Blackwell, 1967), §§540–1.

> Being sure that someone is in pain, doubting whether he is, and so
> on, are so many natural, instinctive, kinds of behaviour towards
> other human beings, and our language is merely an auxiliary to,
> and further extension of, this reaction. Our language-game is an
> extension of primitive behaviour. (For our *language-game* [empha-
> sis in text] is behaviour.) (Instinct).

This remark about language as being auxiliary to action recalls
Condillac's notion of the long and never entirely relinquished coex-
istence of action and articulated speech before the latter can take care of
itself.

David Pears has written that Wittgenstein's private-language argument "puts language back in its place in human life." He then continues
with this statement, which can also be applied to the Du Bos–Condillac
conception of the nature and role of the language of action in human
life. Pears writes that Wittgenstein

> insists on the need for criteria of correct application which are
> based on links between sensations and the physical world, and this
> need is met by connections which are part of the natural history of
> our species before the advent of language. For example, among us,
> as among other social animals, pain is connected with a character-
> istic cry, and when we use the word "pain" instead of that cry, we
> are relying on a natural connection which does most of the work of
> ensuring that we are using it correctly. So the acquisition of this
> skill is not a purely intellectual achievement. Similarly, the convic-
> tion that someone else is in pain is not founded on an argument
> from analogy with one's own case, but on a natural sympathy
> which antedates language.[26]

If Condillac pulled oars with Adam Smith and Hume "without any
promise," it looks as if Wittgenstein, also without promises, joined in
the rowing.

There is no likelihood that Wittgenstein had looked at Condillac, Du
Bos, Fénelon, and Adam Smith, or that he had come upon the rhetorical
expressivism that for a while at least prevailed over Cartesian dualism.
But attention to Wittgenstein evokes a good sense of Condillac's
achievement. In his own time and for some decades after his death,
Condillac's influence was wide and deep. Diderot must surely be

---

[26] Anthony Kenny and David Pears (eds.), *The Oxford History of Western Philosophy* (Oxford, Oxford University Press, 1994), pp. 267–8.

counted one of the most interesting minds of the eighteenth century, yet without Condillac his *Letter on Deaf-Mutes* would not have been the same. It is a serious question why these things remain largely unperceived; how has history become so weird that this could happen? It is a knee-jerk claim that the *Encyclopédie* was "a monument to reason." But that is nonsense. It was something more refreshing and innovative. It was a monument to communication.

Chronology

1768	Is elected member of the Académie Française; regularly attends its sessions, spending part of the year in Paris and part of the year in the country
1773	From now on he spends most of the year on an estate he had bought for his niece near Beaugency in the region of Orléans
1775	Publication in sixteen volumes of the *Course of Study* he had prepared for the Prince of Parma. It is often reprinted and becomes vastly influential. It contains *Grammar, The Art of Writing, The Art of Reasoning, The Art of Thinking, Ancient History*, and *Modern History*. In his later years Condillac revises most of his writings for future publication
1776	*Le Commerce et le gouvernement considérés relativement l'un à l'autre*
1777	Writes *Logic* at the request of the education authorities in Poland. It was published in 1780
1778	During his last years, writes *La Langue des calculs*, which remains unfinished
1780	Dies on 3 August
1798	First collected and still the most complete edition of Condillac published in Paris in 23 volumes. Here *La Langue des calculs* appears in print for the first time
1947–51	Publication of *Oeuvres philosophiques*, which in volume three (1951) contains the first publication of Condillac's *Dictionnaire des synonymes*
1980	First publication of a treatise on the Leibnizian philosophy of monads, written for a prize-essay contest set by the Berlin Academy in 1746. Favorable to Leibniz, it did not gain the prize, but Condillac later used part of it in his *Treatise on Animals*

Further reading

In addition to the text of *Origin* in CO, there is a separate issue: *Essai sur l'origine des connaissances humaines*, ed. Charles Porset (Paris, Galilée, 1973), with an important introduction by Jacques Derrida. This introduction was published separately as *The Archeology of the Frivolous*, tr. John P. Leavey, Jr. (Lincoln, University of Nebraska Press, 1987). *Corpus Condillac (1714–1780)*, ed. Jean Sgard et al. (Geneva, Slatkine, 1981), has biography, catalog of correspondence, bibliographies of manuscripts and of printed works, and general bibliography. For a concise and respected presentation of the tenor of Condillac's thought, see G. Madinier, "Les Orientations psychologiques et réflexives de la pensée de Condillac" in Madinier, *Conscience et mouvement* (Paris, Alcan, 1938), pp. 1–38.

On Condillac's linguistic thought, two volumes stand out. *Condillac et les problèmes du langage*, ed. Jean Sgard (Geneva, Slatkine, 1982), contains papers that were given at a colloquium held at Grenoble in October 1980. Among the many good essays, the reader would want to pay attention to T. Takesada on imagination and the language of action in *Origin*; Jean-Louis Labarrière on the conception of genius and language; and Serge Baudiffier on Condillac's influence on Diderot at the crucial moment in his career when he wrote *Letter on Deaf-Mutes* (1751), in which Diderot first related the primal nature of language to creativity and art. The other important volume is Nicolas Rousseau, *Connaissance et langage chez Condillac* (Geneva, Droz, 1986). This admirable book offers a comprehensive treatment of all aspects of Condillac's philosophy of language and knowledge; the author strongly emphasizes Condillac's stature as a true innovator. This book has a rich bibliography of both primary and secondary literature.

For a general introduction to Condillac in English, there is a fine essay by Catherine Hobbs Peaden, "Condillac and the History of Rhetoric," in *Rhetorica*, 11 (1993), 136–56. For a good understanding of Condillac's place in the linguistic thought of his century, see Ulrich Ricken, *Linguistics, Anthropology and Philosophy in the French Enlightenment: Language Theory and Ideology*, tr. Robert E. Norton (London, Routledge, 1994). This book repeats the essence of Ricken's earlier *Grammaire et philosophie au siècle des lumières: Controverses sur l'ordre naturel et la clarté du français* (Publications de l'Université de Lille, 1978), which must be counted among the half-dozen basic books on the philosophy of language in the eighteenth century. There is a powerful essay by François Dagognet, "L'Animal selon Condillac," in Condillac, *Traité des animaux* (Paris, Vrin, 1987), pp. 9–131. This essay is chiefly on Condillac's relation to Cartesianism, but it also discusses the interrelations among *Origin*, *Treatise on the Sensations*, and *Treatise on Animals*. At the outset Dagognet states the view, now widely accepted, that the charge of materialism often raised against Condillac is too silly to need an answer. On Condillac's place in the history of aesthetics, see Annie Becq, *Genèse de l'esthétique française moderne 1680–1814* (Paris, Albin Michel, 1994), pp. 444–64.

On Condillac and Christian Wolff, see Gianni Paganini, "Signes, imagination et mémoire: De la psychologie de Wolff à l'*Essai* de Condillac," *Revue des Sciences Philosophiques et Théologiques*, 72 (1988), 287–300. On the presence of Condillac in French linguistics in the decades before Saussure's *Cours* (1916), see Simon Bouquet, *Introduction à la lecture de Saussure* (Paris, Payot, 1997), pp. 214–45. On the much-debated issue of Condillac's relation to Herder, see Rudolf Schottlaender, "Die verkannte Lehre Condillacs vom Sprachursprung," *Beiträge zur Romanische Philologie*, 8 (1969), 158–65; Hans Aarsleff, "The Tradition of Condillac: The Problem of the Origin of Language in the Eighteenth Century and the Debate in the Berlin Academy before Herder" (1974) in FLS, pp. 146–209; Aarsleff, "Condillac's Speechless Statue" (1975) in FLS, pp. 210–24; Jörn Stückrath, "Der junge Herder als Sprach- und Literaturtheoretiker – ein Erbe des französischen Aufklärers Condillac?" in Walter Hinck (ed.), *Sturm and Drang: Ein literaturwissenschaftliches Studienbuch* (Athenäum Verlag, 1978), pp. 81–96; and Aarsleff, "Herder's Cartesian *Ursprung* vs. Condillac's Expressivist *Essai*" in *Language Philosophies and the Language Sciences: A Historical Perspective in Honour of Lia Formigari*, ed. Daniele Gambarara, Stefano Gensini, and Antonino Pennisi (Münster, Nodus, 1996), pp. 165–79.

A handbook that can be strongly recommended for reliable orientation in the aesthetics of the eighteenth century is Rémy G. Saisselin, *The Rule of Reason and the Ruses of the Heart: A Philosophical Dictionary of Classical French Criticism, Critics, and Aesthetic Issues* (Cleveland, OH, Press of Case Western Reserve University, 1970). It has essays on major figures (e.g., Condillac, Descartes, Diderot, Du Bos) and on terms (e.g., imagination, imitation, opera, pantomime).

Note on the text and translation

The French text is that printed in Le Roy's edition of Condillac's *Œuvres philosophiques*, which follows the text printed in vol. 1 of the *Œuvres complètes* published in 1798. The separate publication of *Essai sur l'origine des connaissances humaines*, ed. Charles Porset (Paris, Galilée, 1973), has some important textual and bibliographical information on pp. 291–4. Condillac cites extensively from texts first published in English, but, not reading English, he cites from French translations, from Pierre Coste's translation of Locke's *Essay* and from Léonard des Malpeines's translation of some 150 pages from Warburton's *Divine Legation of Moses*. I have in all cases translated the cited passages directly from Condillac's text. It would have been misleading to substitute the original English, first because that was not what Condillac read and had in mind, and secondly because the translations, especially Malpeines's, differ somewhat from the originals and because Condillac himself on several occasions made changes and omissions in his quotations. Similarly, I have not substituted Thomas Nugent's English version of Du Bos's *Critical Reflections* (1748) for the original French. For the convenience of the reader, however, I make references to Nugent's English text. I refer to *Origin* by part, section, and paragraph; thus I, 4, §27 refers to Part I, Section 4, paragraph 27. Since the paragraph numbers run consecutively through each section, the chapter numbers are not used in my reference system.

Condillac's many notes are of two kinds: some are very long quotations from Warburton and Du Bos, others are brief references which are in all cases too sparse to satisfy current practice. The former have of course been left in place. For the latter I have followed two procedures.

References that, even when they were made adequate, were still short, I have moved into the text in square brackets; thus for Locke's *Essay*, "[E 3.5.15]" refers to Book III, Chapter 5, section 15. In some cases I have supplied information or references that are not in Condillac's text; these are in all cases put in square brackets and preceded by an asterisk (*); thus "[*Crit. Refl. 3.184]" is my addition. Longer references have been put in the editorial notes. It goes without saying that I have not tried to identify every conceivable reference, which is a task that only a major edition can undertake.

Condillac sometimes quotes at great length without always clearly indicating that he is quoting. In these cases the quotation is indicated by being indented and set in small type. I have normalized quotation from Locke's *Essay* to current usage in regard to spelling, capitalization, use of italics, and grammar (as, e.g., "has" for "hath"). References to Cicero and Quintilian are to the usual numbering of those texts, not to pages. Condillac occasionally marks omissions in quotation; they are indicated thus: (. . .).

In a good number of cases I have made my own translations from texts I cite, or have modified an existing English translation.

Essay on the Origin of Human Knowledge

Introduction

Since metaphysics more than any other science ensures the clarity, precision, and scope of the mind, it is also the best preparation for the study of all the other sciences. It is today so little regarded in France that many readers will no doubt find my claim paradoxical. I confess that there was a time when I would have shared that opinion. Of all the philosophers, the metaphysicians seemed the least wise: their words did not tell me anything, hardly ever did I find anything but airy speculations, and I charged metaphysics with gross errors that were in fact the aberrations of its practitioners. Wishing to overcome this illusion and to find the source of so many errors, I found those who were farthest from the truth to be the most useful. I had scarcely recognized the uncertain paths they had followed before I thought I saw the way that I should follow. It appeared to me that one could reason in metaphysics and in the moral sciences with as much precision as in geometry, that we could form accurate ideas as well as the geometricians, like them determine the sense of expressions in a precise and invariable manner, and perhaps better than they have done prescribe a simple and easy procedure to attain certain knowledge.

We must distinguish two sorts of metaphysics. One has the ambition of solving all mysteries; nature, the essence of all beings, the most hidden causes, those are the things that embellish it and that it promises to open up. The other is more modest and adjusts its inquiries to the weakness of the human mind, and being as unconcerned about what must lie beyond its grasp as it is avid to seize what lies within it, this sort of metaphysics is content to stay within the bounds that are marked out for it. The first turns all nature into a kind of enchantment that

3

vanishes with it; the second, seeking to see things only as they really are, is as simple as truth itself. With the former, errors multiply endlessly and the mind is satisfied with vague notions and words without meaning; with the latter, we gain little knowledge, but avoid error, as the mind gains accuracy and always forms clear ideas.

Philosophers have chiefly practiced the former and have looked upon the latter as a mere addition that barely merits the name of metaphysics. Only Locke, I believe, is the exception: he has limited himself to the study of the human mind and has completed his task with success. Descartes knew neither the origin nor the generation of our ideas.[1] To that failure we must attribute the inadequacy of this method; for we will not find a safe way of conducting our thoughts as long as we do not know how they are formed. Malebranche, who of all the Cartesians has best understood the causes of our errors, sometimes draws comparisons from matter to explain the faculties of the soul,[2] sometimes loses himself in a "world of pure intellect" where he imagines that he has found the source of our ideas.[3] Others create and annihilate beings, joining them to our soul or taking them away from it as they please and believe that such fantasizing will account for the different operations of the mind and of the manner in which it acquires or loses its knowledge.[4] The Leibnizians finally make a more perfect being of this substance: according to them it is a little world, a living mirror of the universe, and by the power they give it to represent everything that exists, they flatter themselves that they explain its essence, nature, and all its properties. Thus everyone allows himself to be seduced by his own system. Seeing only what surrounds us, we believe we see everything that exists; we are like children who think that they can touch the sky at the far side of a plain.

Is it then useless to read the philosophers? Who could claim to succeed better than so many geniuses who have been the wonder of their century, unless he at least studies them to profit from their errors? For

---

[1] I refer to the Third Meditation. I find what he says on this subject entirely unphilosophical.

[2] *The Search after Truth*, Bk. I, Ch. 1.

[3] Ibid., Bk. III. See also his dialogues and metaphysical meditations, with his answers to Antoine Arnauld.[a]

[4] The author of the action of God on the creatures. [*L. F. Boursier, *De l'action de Dieu sur les créatures: Traité dans lequel on prouve la prémotion physique*, 2 vols. (Paris, 1713).]

[a] Condillac is referring to Nicolas Malebranche, *Entretiens sur la métaphysique et la religion* (Paris, 1687), *Méditations chrétiennes et métaphysiques* (Paris, 1683), and *Réponse du P. Malebranche à M. Arnauld 1684–1703* (Paris, 1709).

anyone who wishes to make progress in the search for truth, it is essential to know the mistakes of those who first sought to open the way. The experience of the philosopher, like that of the pilot, is the knowledge of the rocks on which others have foundered; and without this knowledge no compass can guide him.

It would not be sufficient to uncover philosophical errors unless we get at their causes; we should even rise from one cause to the next till we reach the first; for there is one that must be the same for everyone who goes astray, and that is like the unique point that is the beginning of all the paths that lead to error. Here then, perhaps, at this point we will find another where the unique road to truth begins.

We must never forget that our first aim is the study of the human mind, not to discover its nature, but to know its operations, to observe how artfully they interact, and how we ought to conduct them in order to acquire all the knowledge of which we are capable. We must ascend to the origin of our ideas, reveal how they are generated, trace them to the limits that nature has set for them, and thereby determine the extent and limits of our knowledge and invest human understanding with new life.

The success of these inquiries depends entirely on the results of observation, and our only aim should be the discovery of a fundamental fact of experience that no one can cast doubt on and that is sufficient to explain all the rest. It ought to point clearly to the source of our understanding, to the materials from which it is formed, to the principle that activates the materials, the means we use in that process, and the manner in which we should employ them. I believe I have found the solution to all these problems in the connection of ideas, either with signs or among themselves. The reader may decide whether I am correct in the course of his reading of this work.

It is evident that my design is to reduce everything that pertains to the human mind to a single principle, and that this principle shall be neither a vague proposition, nor an abstract maxim, nor a gratuitous supposition, but a firm fact of experience whose consequences will all be confirmed by new acts of experience.

Ideas connect with signs, and it is, as I will show, only by this means that they connect among themselves. Thus after a word on the materials of our knowledge, on the distinction of soul and body, and on the sensations, I have been obliged, in order to reveal my principle, not only to trace the operations of the soul in all their advances, but in addition to explore how we have acquired the habit of using signs of all kinds, and the use to which we should put that habit.

In order to fulfill this double task, I have traced things as far as I could. On the one hand I have taken a new look at perception, because it is the first operation of the soul that we notice, and I have shown how and in what order it produces all the operations we gain the power to exercise. On the other hand I have begun with the language of action. It will be shown how it has produced all the arts that pertain to the expression of our thoughts: the art of gesture, dance, speech, declamation, the art of recording it, the art of pantomime, of music, of poetry, eloquence, writing, and the different characters of languages. This history of language will show the circumstances in which signs are imagined; will reveal their true meaning and show how to prevent their abuse; and it will not, I believe, leave any doubt about the origin of our ideas.

Finally, having expounded the progress of the operations of the soul and of language, I try to indicate the means by which error can be avoided and to show the order we should follow, either to make new discoveries or to instruct others in those we have made. Such is the general plan of this essay.

A philosopher often declares himself in favor of a truth he does not know. He finds an opinion that has hitherto been unregarded and adopts it, not because he finds it superior, but in the hope of becoming the founder of a sect. In fact, the novelty of a system has nearly always been sufficient to ensure its success.

Perhaps this was the motive that made the Peripatetics adopt the principle that all our knowledge comes from the senses. They were so far from really knowing this truth that none of them has been able to explain it, so that after many centuries it was a discovery still in need of being made.

Bacon is perhaps the first to have seen it. This truth is the foundation of a work in which he gives excellent guidelines for the advancement of learning.[5] The Cartesians rejected this principle with contempt because they judged it only from the writings of the Peripatetics. Finally, Locke

---

[5] *Nov. org. scient.* [*The New Organon*, ed. Lisa Jardine and Michael Silverthorne (Cambridge, Cambridge University Press, 2000)].

addressed it, and he has the distinction of being the first to demonstrate it.

It does not seem, however, that this philosopher ever made the treatise he has given us on the human understanding his principal occupation. He undertook it by chance, and continued it in the same spirit; and though he was aware that a work so composed would not fail to face blame, he did not, as he said, have either the courage or the leisure to do it over.[6] To this we may charge the longueurs, the repetitions, and the lack of order that prevails in it. Locke was very capable of correcting these defects, and that perhaps makes him less excusable. He saw, for example, that words and the manner in which we use them can cast light on the primitive origin of our ideas [E 3.7.1], but having made that discovery too late,[7] it is only in the Third Book that he treated a matter that should have been treated in the Second. If he had been able to start afresh on his work, there is reason to believe that he would have given a much better account of the springs of human understanding. But since he did not do it, he passed lightly over the origin of our knowledge, and that is the part that is the most superficial. He assumes, for example, that as soon as the soul receives ideas by sense, it can at will repeat, compose, and unite them together with infinite variety and make all sorts of complex notions of them. But it is well established that in infancy we had sensations long before knowing how to turn them into ideas. Thus, as the soul does not from the first instant control the exercise of all its operations, it was necessary, in order to give a better explanation of the origin of our knowledge, to show how it acquires that exercise, and what progress it makes in it. It does not appear that Locke addressed that question, or that anyone has ever blamed him for the omission or has tried to remedy this part of his work. Perhaps even the design of explaining the operations of the soul, by deriving them from a simple perception, is so novel that the reader may find it hard to understand how I will proceed.

In the first book of his *Essay* Locke examines the doctrine of innate ideas. I am not sure that he has not spent too much time on opposing that error; the present work will destroy it indirectly. In some places in the Second Book, he treats, though superficially, the operations of the

---

[6] *Essay*, "Epistle to the Reader."

[7] "I admit" (he says, E 3.9.21), "that, when I began this work and long after, it did not at all occur to my mind that it would be necessary to devote any reflection to words."

soul. Words are the subject of the Third Book, and he seems to me the first who has written on this matter as a true philosopher. I have found, however, that it must occupy a large part of my work, both because it can still be viewed in a new and more extended manner, and because I am convinced that the use of signs is the principle that develops the seed of all our ideas. For the rest, among the excellent things that Locke says in his Second Book on the generation of several sorts of ideas, such as space, duration, etc., and in the Fourth, with the title "On Knowledge," there are many I am far from approving. But as they belong more narrowly to the extent of our knowledge, they do not enter into my plan, so there is no point in being detained by them.

Part I
The materials of our knowledge and especially the operations of the soul

Section 1

1 The materials of our knowledge and the distinction of soul and body

§1 Whether we raise ourselves, to speak metaphorically, into the heavens or descend into the abyss, we do not go beyond ourselves; and we never perceive anything but our own thought. Whatever the knowledge we have, if we wish to trace it to its origin, we will in the end arrive at a first simple thought, which has been the object of the second, which has been the object of the third, and so on. It is this order of thoughts we must explore if we wish to know the ideas we have of things.

§2 It would be useless to inquire into the nature of our thoughts. The first reflection on oneself is enough to convince us that we have no means of conducting that inquiry. We are conscious of our thought; we distinguish it perfectly from all that it is not; we even distinguish among all our thoughts, each from every other, and that is sufficient. If we stray from that, we stray from something that we know so clearly that it cannot lead us into any error.

§3 Let us consider a man at the first moment of his existence. His soul first has different sensations, such as light, colors, pain, pleasure, motion, rest – those are his first thoughts.

§4 Let us follow him in the moments when he begins to reflect on what these sensations occasion in him, and we shall find that he forms ideas of the different operations of his soul, such as perceiving and imagining – those are his second thoughts.

Thus, according to the manner in which external objects affect us, we receive different ideas via the senses, and, further, as we reflect on the operations which the sensations occasion in our soul, we acquire all the ideas which we would not have been able to receive from external objects.

§5 Thus the sensations and operations of the soul are the materials of all our knowledge, materials that are employed by reflection as it explores the relations they contain by making combinations of them. But the whole success depends on the circumstances we pass through. The most favorable are those that provide us with the greatest number of objects that may exercise our reflection. The great circumstances in which those who are destined to govern mankind find themselves constitute, for example, an occasion to form very extensive views; and those which continually repeat themselves in the world at large produce the sort of disposition we call natural because, since they are not the fruit of study, we cannot identify the causes that produce them. Let us conclude that there are no ideas that have not been acquired: the first come directly from the senses, the others from experience and increase in proportion to the capacity for reflection.

§6 Original sin has made the soul so dependent on the body that many philosophers have confused these two substances. They have believed that the former is merely the finest and most subtle part of the body and thus the more capable of movement; but that opinion results from their failure to base their reasoning on exact ideas. I ask them what they understand by body. If they seek to give a precise answer, they will not say that it is a single substance, but they will regard it as an assemblage, a collection of substances. Thus if thought pertains to body, it must be either because it is an assemblage or collection, or because it is a property of each substance in this collection. But these words "assemblage" and "collection" merely signify an external relation between several things, thus existing by virtue of their interdependence. By this union we regard them as forming a single whole, though in reality they are no more "one" than if they were separated. It follows that they are mere abstract terms which from without do not suppose a single substance, but a multitude of substances. Thus, when seen as an assemblage or collection, the body cannot be the subject of thought.

Shall we divide thought among all the substances of which the body is composed? In the first place, that is impossible if it is only a single and indivisible perception. In the second place, this supposition must also be rejected if thought is formed of a certain number of perceptions. Let *A*,

B, and *C*, which are three substances that enter into the composition of the body, be divided among three different perceptions; I ask from where is the comparison among them to be made. It cannot be in *A*, for it could not compare a perception it has with those it does not have. For the same reason it cannot be in *B*, nor in *C*. Thus we must admit a point of reunion, a substance that is at the same time a simple and indivisible subject of these three divisions, and consequently distinct from the body, or, in a word, a soul.

§7 I do not know how Locke [E 4.3.6] could propose that it would forever be impossible for us to know whether God had not given the power of thinking to a mass of matter fitly disposed. We must not imagine that for the resolution of this question it would be necessary to know the essence and nature of matter. The arguments founded on this ignorance are entirely frivolous. It is enough to observe that the subject of thought must be "one." But a mass of matter is not one; it is a multitude.[8]

§8 The soul being distinct and different from body, the latter can only be the occasional cause of what it seems to produce in the former. From this we must conclude that our senses are only the occasional cause of our knowledge. But whatever is occasioned by something can occur without it, for an effect does not depend on its occasional cause except according to a certain hypothesis. Thus the soul can absolutely acquire knowledge without the help of sense. Before the Fall an altogether different system prevailed from the one in which the soul exists today. Exempt from ignorance and concupiscence, it ruled the senses, and suspended and modified their action as it pleased. Thus it had ideas prior to the use of the senses. But things have greatly changed owing to its disobedience. God has deprived it of all its power; it has become as dependent on the senses as if they were the physical cause of what they merely occasion, and now it has only the knowledge that the senses provide. Hence follow ignorance and concupiscence. It is this

---

[8] It has been argued against me that the property of time is indivisible. It cannot be said that it is divided among the wheels of a watch: it is in the whole. Why then could the property of thinking not be an organized whole? I answer that the property of marking time can, by its nature, belong to a composite object; for since time is nothing but succession, anything that has motion can measure it. Another objection to my argument is that unity is applicable to a mass of matter fitly disposed, though it cannot be so applied when the confusion is so great that the possibility of considering it as a whole is ruled out. I agree, but I add that then unity is not understood in the rigorous sense. It is taken for a unit composed of other units so that it is consequently properly a collection, a multitude. But that is not the kind of unity I propose to deal with.

state of the soul that I propose to study, the only one that can be the object of philosophy, because it is the only one we can know by experience. Thus, when I say "that we do not have any ideas that do not come from the senses," it must be remembered that I speak only of the state we are now in after the Fall. This proposition would be altogether false if applied to the soul in the state of innocence or after its separation from the body. I do not treat the knowledge of the soul in these two states, because I cannot reason except on the basis of experience. Furthermore, if, as cannot be doubted, it is important for us to know the faculties of which God has granted us the use despite the Fall, it is pointless to wish to speculate on those He has taken away and will give back to us in the next life.

To say it again, I deal only with the present state. Thus our business is not to view the soul as independent of the body, for its dependence is only too well established, nor as united with a body in a system that differs from the one in which we find ourselves. Our only aim must be to consult experience, and to reason from those facts alone that no one can call in doubt.

2 Sensations

§9 It is evident that the ideas we call sensations are such that we would never have been able to acquire them if we had been deprived of the senses. Therefore no philosopher has claimed that they were innate, for that would too obviously have been a contradiction of experience. But they have claimed that they are not ideas, as if they were not, by themselves, as representative as any other thought of the soul. In other words, they have looked upon sensations as something that occurs only after the ideas and that modifies them, an error that has made them imagine systems that are as bizarre as they are unintelligible.

It takes little attention to know that when we perceive light, colors, solidity, these sensations and others like them are more than sufficient to give us the ideas of bodies that we generally have. Is there in fact any idea that is not contained within those first sensations? Do we not in them find the ideas of extension, figure, place, motion, rest, and all those that derive from them?

Let us therefore reject the hypothesis of innate ideas and instead assume that God gives us, for example, just the perceptions of light and color. Do these perceptions not trace before our eyes extension, lines, and figures? But it will be objected that our senses cannot give assurance that these things are really such as they appear: then the senses give no ideas of them at all. Imagine the consequence! Do innate ideas give us greater assurance? What does it matter whether the senses give us certain knowledge of the shape of a body? The question is to know whether the senses do not give us the idea of a shape even when they deceive us. I see one that I judge to be a pentagon, though on one of its sides it forms an imperceptible angle. But for all that, does it not give me the idea of a pentagon?

§10 Nevertheless, the Cartesians and the Malebranchists make such a loud cry against the senses, they repeat so often they are nothing but errors and illusions that we end up considering them an obstacle to the acquisition of any knowledge; and in our zeal for truth we would, if it were possible, be glad to be rid of them. Not that the complaints of those philosophers are entirely without foundation. On this subject they have discovered so many errors that we cannot justly disavow the obligations we owe them. But is there not a middle way? Can we not in our senses detect a source of truths as well as of errors, and distinguish one from the other well enough always to draw on the former? This is what we need to inquire into.

§11 First of all, it is very certain that nothing is clearer and more distinct than our perception when we have particular sensations. Can anything be clearer than the perceptions of sound and color! Has it ever occurred to us to confuse these two things? But if we wish to study their nature and find out how they are produced in us, it is no use saying that our senses deceive us or that they give us obscure and confused ideas; the least reflection tells us that they do nothing of the sort.

At the same time, whatever the nature of these perceptions and the manner in which they come about, if we look for the idea of extension, of a line, an angle, it is manifest that we find them there with great clarity and distinctness. If we further ask to what we attribute this extension and these shapes, we will find with equal clarity and distinctness that we do not attribute them to ourselves or to what is the subject of our thought, but to something outside us.

But if we ask about the idea of the absolute magnitude of certain bodies, or even their relative magnitude and about their true shape, we will have reason to doubt our judgments. Depending on whether an object is near or distant, the appearances of size and shape in which they present themselves will be altogether different.

It follows that we must distinguish three things in our sensations: (1) The perception we have. (2) The reference we give it to something outside ourselves. (3) The judgment that what we refer to things really belongs to them.

There is neither error, nor obscurity, nor confusion in what occurs within us any more than in the reference we make to something outside us. If we consider, for instance, that we have the ideas of a certain size and of a certain shape and that we assign them to some body, there is nothing that is not true, clear, and distinct; from that all truths draw their force. If error occurs, it merely lies in the fact that we judge that a particular size and shape really belong to a particular body. If for instance I see a square building from the distance, it will appear round. In that case, is there any obscurity or confusion in the idea of roundness or in the reference I give it? No, but I judge this building to be round, and that is where the error lies.

When I say that all our knowledge comes from the senses, we must not forget it holds only insofar as we draw that knowledge from the clear and distinct ideas contained in the senses. As for the judgments of sense, they can be of no use to us until their errors have been corrected by experience and reflection.

§12 What we have said about extension and shapes also applies perfectly to other ideas of sensations and can serve to resolve the Cartesian question: to know whether colors, scents, etc., are in the objects themselves.

There is no doubt that we must allow bodies to have the qualities that occasion the impressions they make on our senses. The difficult question that is raised is to know whether these qualities are similar to what we experience. No doubt what confounds us is that since, when having the idea of extension, we do not hesitate to refer it to something similar in the body, we also imagine that colors, scents, etc., have something that resembles our sensations. But that is a hasty judgment based merely on this analogy and about which we in fact have no idea.

When the notion of extension is stripped of all its difficulties and seen in the clearest light, it is nothing but the idea of several beings that appear to us as being outside one another.[9] That explains why, when we assume that something external conforms to this idea, we always represent it for ourselves in a manner that gives it the same clarity it would have if we contemplated the idea itself. With colors, scents, etc., it is an altogether different story. So long as we reflect on these sensations, we regard them as ours, as if they belong to us, and we have very clear ideas of them. But if we wish, so to speak, to detach them from us and invest the objects with them, then we have no idea what we are doing. We find ourselves attributing them to objects only because, on the one hand, we must suppose they are caused by something, and because, on the other, this cause is altogether hidden from us.

§13 It is no use having recourse to obscure and confused ideas and sensations. Such language ought not to be admitted by philosophers, who can never be too exact in their expressions. If you come upon a portrait that has an obscure and confused resemblance, examine that thought, and you will find that the portrait conforms to the original in some respects and not in others. It is the same with each of our perceptions: what they really contain is clear and distinct; and what we

---

[9] And united, say the Leibnizians. But that is pointless when we speak of extension in the abstract. We cannot represent separate beings to ourselves without supposing others which separate them, and the totality implies the idea of union.

consider obscure and confused does not belong to them at all. One cannot say, as with the portrait, that they have only a partial resemblance. Each is so simple that whatever would bear a relation of equality with them, would do so in all respects. That is why I warn that, in my language, to have clear and distinct ideas is, in brief, to have ideas; and to have obscure and confused ideas is to have no ideas at all.

§14 What makes us think that ideas are susceptible to obscurity is that we do not distinguish them from the expressions commonly used. We say, for example, that "snow is white"; and we make a thousand other propositions without thinking of removing the ambiguity of the words. Therefore, since our judgments are expressed obscurely, we imagine that this obscurity redounds on the judgments themselves and on the ideas that compose them. A definition would correct everything. The snow is white if by "whiteness" we have in mind the physical cause of our perception; but it is not white if by "whiteness" we understand something similar to the perception itself. Thus these judgments are not obscure; but they are true or false according to the sense in which we take the terms.

There is another reason for letting obscure and confused ideas into our minds, namely our zeal to know a great deal. It seems that it is a consolation for our curiosity to know at the least obscurely and confusedly. That is why we sometimes find it difficult to realize that we lack ideas.[10]

Others have proved that colors, scents, etc., are not in the objects. But it has often seemed to me that their reasonings are not sufficient to enlighten the mind. I have taken a different tack, and in this matter as in many others, I have come to believe that to settle on the opinion we should prefer, it is sufficient to examine our ideas.

---

[10] Locke admits clear and obscure ideas, distinct and confused, true and false, but the explanations he gives make it clear that we differ only in the manner of expressing ourselves. Mine has the advantage of being neater and simpler, and should therefore be preferred. For only the simplification of language can prevent its abuse. This entire work will be a proof of that.

Section 2

Analysis and generation of the operations of the soul

The operations of the soul can be divided in two sorts, depending on whether they are referred more specifically to the understanding or to the will. The object of this essay makes it clear that I propose to consider them only by the relation they have to the understanding.

I shall not limit myself to giving definitions. I intend to try and envisage them in a clearer light than has hitherto been the case. The point is to examine their progress and to see how they are all generated from a single starting point which is nothing but a simple perception. This examination is by itself more useful than all the rules of the logicians. Indeed, could we be ignorant of the right way of conducting the operations of the soul if we knew well how they are generated? But this entire part of metaphysics has so far been in such a state of chaos that I have been obliged somehow to make a new language for myself. I did not find it possible to combine precision with signs that are as ill determined as they are in common usage. All the same, it will be easier to understand me for those who will read me with attention.

1 Perception, consciousness, attention, and reminiscence

§1 The perception or the impression occasioned in the mind by the action of the senses is the first operation of the understanding. The idea of it cannot be caused by any form of discourse. It can be supplied only by reflection on what we experience when we are affected by some sensation.

§2 Objects would have no effect on the senses and the mind would not notice any such action unless accompanied by perception. Thus the first and least degree of knowledge is perception.

§3 But since perception necessarily follows impressions that are made on the senses, it is obvious that the first degree of knowledge ought to be more or less extensive depending on whether one is so organized as to receive a greater or lesser variety of sensations. Take creatures that lack vision, others that lack vision and hearing, and so on successively; you will soon have creatures that gain no knowledge at all since they lack all the senses. Imagine the contrary, if that is possible: new senses in animals that are more perfect than man. What a wealth of new perceptions! And further, think of the wealth of knowledge within their reach that we would never be able to attain and of which we could not even form any conjecture!

§4 Our inquiries are often made more difficult when their object becomes simpler. Perceptions are a case in point. What is apparently simpler than deciding whether the mind takes notice of all the perceptions it has? Is anything else necessary apart from reflection on oneself? No doubt the philosophers have done just that. But caught in their basic commitments, some have been obliged to admit that the mind has perceptions of which it never takes notice;[11] and others have found this opinion altogether unintelligible.[12] In the next paragraphs I shall try to resolve this question. For the moment it is enough to observe that everyone agrees that the mind has perceptions that are not there without its knowledge. The sentiment that produces this knowledge and that tells us at least partially what goes on in it I call "consciousness." If, as Locke says, the mind has no perception of which it does not take notice, seeing that it would be a contradiction for a perception not to be noticed, then perception and consciousness must be taken for the same single operation. But if on the contrary the opposite sentiment was the true one, they would be two distinct operations; and it would be with consciousness and not perception, as I have supposed, that our knowledge properly begins.

§5 When we are conscious of several perceptions at the same time, we often have greater consciousness of some than of others or make a more lively response to their existence. More than that, as the consciousness of some increases, that of others will diminish. Imagine someone at a

---

[11] The Cartesians, the Malebranchists, and the Leibnizians.
[12] Locke and his followers.

theater performance where a multitude of objects seem to fight for his attention – his soul will be attacked by a large number of perceptions of which he certainly takes notice. But little by little some will please and interest him more than others, and he will more willingly surrender to them. From then on he will begin to be less affected by the others; his consciousness of them will insensibly diminish to the point where, when he comes to himself again, he will not remember having had any consciousness of them. This is proved by the illusion that is created in the theater. There are moments when consciousness does not seem to be divided between both the stage action and the rest of the theater experience. It would seem right off that the illusion should be livelier if there were fewer distracting objects. It is, however, within everyone's experience that we never so strongly feel ourselves to be the only audience of a captivating scene as when the house is full. Perhaps that is because the number, variety, and magnificence of the objects move the senses, and fire and elevate the imagination, thus making us more attuned to the impressions the poet seeks to engender in us. Perhaps the spectators even offer mutual support to fix our eyes on the stage by the example they give to one another.[b] However that may be, this operation by which the consciousness in response to certain perceptions becomes so lively that they seem to be the only ones of which we take notice, I call "attention." Thus being attentive to something is being more conscious of the perceptions it engenders than of those that others produce when acting in the same way on our senses; and attention has been the greater in proportion to the slight memory one has of the latter.

§6 Thus I distinguish two sorts of perceptions among those we are conscious of: the ones that we remember at least the next moment, and those that we forget as soon as we have had them. This distinction is based on the evidence I have just given. A person who has been entirely absorbed in the illusion will readily remember his impression of a lively

[b] Condillac's sense of heightened absorption in the stage action when the theater is full was also noted by David Hume. Anyone entering a theater, he wrote, "is immediately struck with the view of so great a multitude, participating of one common amusement; and experiences, from their very aspect, a superior sensibility or disposition of being affected with every sentiment, which he shares with his fellow-creatures." For Hume this was an example of the "sympathetic movement of pleasure or uneasiness" which we naturally share with others. See *Enquiries Concerning Human Understanding and Concerning the Principles of Morals*, ed. L. A. Selby-Bigge, 3rd ed., rev. P. H. Nidditch (Oxford, Clarendon Press, 1975), p. 221.

and moving stage action, but he will not always recall his impression of what else went on during the performance.

§7 One could here form two opinions that differ from mine. The first would be to say that the mind has not, as I assume, had the perceptions that I make it forget so quickly, which my opponents would try to account for in terms of physical events. It is evident, they would say, that the mind has perceptions only insofar as the action of objects on the senses is communicated to the brain.[13] So one could suppose that the fibers of the brain have suffered such a strain from the impression they receive from the action that causes the illusion, that they would turn back any other impression. From which one would conclude that the mind has not had any other perceptions than those it remembers.

But when giving attention to an object, it is not likely that all the fibers of the brain are agitated to the same degree without a great many others remaining that are capable of receiving a different impression. We can therefore presume that perceptions occur in us which we do not remember the moment after we have had them. What is so far only a presumption will soon be shown to be true even of most of them.

§8 The second opinion would be to say that no impression is made on the senses that is not communicated to the brain and does not produce, consequently, a perception in the mind. But this opinion further holds that the impression occurs without consciousness and that the mind takes no notice of it. Here I agree with Locke, for I cannot form an idea of any such perception; I might just as well say that I perceive without perceiving.

§9 I therefore believe that we are always conscious of the impressions made on the mind, but sometimes so faintly that we do not remember them the next moment. Some examples will cast light on what I am saying.

I admit that there was a time when I thought that we have perceptions of which we are not conscious. I thought so on the basis of the seemingly simple experience that we shut our eyes a thousand times without having any consciousness of being in the dark; but further experience made me discover my error. Certain perceptions which I had not forgotten, but which necessarily presupposed that I had had others I did

---

[13] Or, if you wish, the part of the brain that is called *sensorium commune*.

not remember the next moment, made me change my opinion. Among the several experiments one can try, here is one that is telling.

If we reflect on what we have been doing the moment we stop reading, it will seem as if we have only been conscious of the ideas it has generated. It will not seem that we have also perceived each letter as well as the darkness every time we closed our eyelids. But we will not be deceived by this appearance if we consider that, without consciousness of the perceptions of the letters, we would not have had the perception of the words and thus the ideas.

§10 This example naturally leads us to account for something that everyone has experienced, namely the astonishing speed with which time on some occasions seems to have passed. This appearance has its source in the fact that we have forgotten the greater part of the perceptions that have succeeded each other in the mind. Locke has shown that we form an idea of the passage of time only by the succession of our thoughts. But the moment they are forgotten, all perceptions are as if they had never existed. It follows that their succession must constitute a corresponding abridgment of time. Consequently, a considerable passage of time, hours for instance, will seem to have passed with the swiftness of a few moments.

§11 This explanation alleviates the need for other examples: it will provide enough more for those who wish to reflect further. Everyone can observe that among the perceptions he has had during a time that seemed very short, there are a great number of which his conduct shows he was conscious, though he has entirely forgotten them. Still, the examples are not all equally appropriate. That is what fooled me when I imagined that I involuntarily closed my eyelids without being conscious that I was in the dark. But nothing is more reasonable than explaining one example by another. My mistake was that the perception of darkness was so ready, so sudden, and the consciousness so feeble that no memory remained behind. However, when I turn my attention to the movement of my eyes, this same perception becomes so lively that I can no longer doubt having had it.

§12 Not only do we regularly forget some of our perceptions, but sometimes we forget all of them. When we do not apply our attention, but receive the perceptions produced within us without taking more notice of some than of others, the consciousness of them is so faint that, when we cease to be in that state, we do not remember that we have had any perception at all. Suppose that I am placed before a very detailed painting of which upon first sight no parts strike me with greater liveliness than others, and that it is taken away before I have had time to consider its details. It is certain that each one of its sensible parts has produced perceptions in me; but I have been so little conscious of them that I cannot remember any of them. This forgetting does not stem from their short duration. If one were to suppose that I had my eyes fixed on this painting for a long time and that I had not in succession enlivened my consciousness of the perceptions of each part, I would be no more able after several hours to render an account of it than after the first instant.

What is true of the perceptions that this painting occasions ought for the same reason to be true of those that the objects around me produce. If, acting on the senses with almost equal force, they produce perceptions in me of pretty much the same vivacity, and if my mind submits to the impression without seeking to be more conscious of one perception than of another, I will have no memory of what went on in me. It will seem to me that my mind during this time was in a sort of slumber unoccupied by any thought. Whether this state lasts several hours or merely some seconds, I will not afterwards be able to differentiate my perceptions, because they are just as forgotten in one case as in the other. Even if one lets it last days, months, or years, when one emerges from it as a result of some lively sensation, it would turn out that several years were recalled as being a single moment.

§13 Let us conclude that we cannot grasp the greater part of our perceptions, not because they were without consciousness, but because they are forgotten an instant later. There is none of which the mind is not conscious. Thus perception and consciousness are different names for the same operation. When it is looked upon as the impression made in the mind, we can keep the name "perception." When it makes its presence known to the mind, we can call it "consciousness." From now on, it is in this sense that I will use these two words.

§14 Things attract our attention by the aspect that is most relevant to our disposition, our passions, and our condition of life. It is these relations that cause things to affect us with greater force and to make us have a more active consciousness of them. Hence it follows that when they change, we see objects altogether differently and bring quite contrary judgments to bear on them. We are usually so strongly duped by judgments of this sort that a person who at one time sees and judges one way and at another sees and judges otherwise, always believes that his observations and judgments are good. This bias becomes so natural that, by making us always consider objects by the relations they have to us, we do not fail to blame the conduct of others as much as we approve our own. Add to this that our love of self easily persuades us that things are praiseworthy when they have attracted our attention with some satisfaction on our part, and you will understand why even those who have discernment enough to evaluate things generally apply their estimation so poorly that they sometimes unjustly withhold it and at other times grant it with abandon.

§15 When objects attract our attention, the perceptions they occasion in us become linked with our sentiment of our being and to everything that can bear some relation to it. It follows that consciousness not only gives us knowledge of our perceptions, but furthermore, if those perceptions are repeated, it often makes us aware that we have had them before and makes us recognize them as belonging to us or as affecting a being that is constantly the same "self," despite their variety and succession. Seen in relation to these new effects, consciousness is a new operation which is at our service every instant and is the foundation of experience. Without it every moment of life would seem the first of our existence, and our knowledge would never advance beyond an initial perception. I shall call it "reminiscence."

It is evident that if the connection between the perceptions I have now, those that I had yesterday, and my sentiment of myself was broken, I could not know that what happened to me yesterday, happened to myself. If this connection was interrupted every night, I would, so to speak, each day begin a new life, and no one would be able to convince me that today's self was the self of the day before. Thus reminiscence is the product of the connection that preserves the sequence of our perceptions. In the next chapters, the effects of this connection will become more and more evident. But if I am asked how it can itself be formed by attention, I answer that the reason lies entirely in the nature of the soul and the body. That is why I regard this connection as a fundamental experience which has a right to be considered sufficient to explain all the others.

To make a closer analysis of reminiscence, we should give it two names: one insofar as it makes us know our being, the other insofar as it makes us aware of the perceptions that are repeated in it, for those are quite distinct ideas. But the language has no term that I can use, and it is not important enough to my project to make one up. It will be sufficient to have noted the simple ideas of which the complex notion of this operation is constituted.

§16 The progress of the operations whose analysis and explication I have given is obvious. At first there is in the mind only a simple perception which is merely the impression it receives from the presence of objects, while the other three operations arise in turn from it. This impression, considered as giving the mind notice of its presence, is what I call consciousness. If the cognizance we take of it is such that it seems to be the only perception of which we are conscious, it is attention. Again, when it makes itself known as already having affected the mind, it is reminiscence. Somehow consciousness says to the mind: there is a perception; attention says there is a perception that is the only one you have; reminiscence says there is a perception you have had before.

2 Imagination, contemplation, and memory

§17 Experience tells us that the first effect of attention is to make the mind retain its perceptions in the absence of the objects that occasioned them. Usually they even stay there in the same order in which they occurred when the objects were present. By this means a connection is formed between them to which several operations, like reminiscence, trace their origin. The first is imagination; it occurs when a perception, by the mere force of the connection that attention has established between it and an object, is recalled at the sight of the object. Sometimes, for instance, it is enough to hear the name of a thing to evoke a representation of it, as if it were before one's eyes.

§18 Still, we are not always able to revive the perceptions we have had. It can happen that we manage only to recall the name, some of the circumstances that accompanied the perceptions, and an abstract idea of perception, which is an idea that we can form at any moment, for we never think without being conscious of some perception which only we can make general. Let us think, for example, of a flower with a familiar scent; we recall the name, remember the circumstances in which we have seen it, and represent the fragrance as the general idea of a perception that affects the sense of smell; but we cannot reawaken the perception itself. The operation that produces this effect I call "memory."

§19 Still one more operation arises from the connection that attention establishes between our ideas, namely contemplation. It consists in preserving, without interruption, the perception, the name, or the circumstances of an object that is no longer there. By this means we can continue to think of something the moment it ceases to be present. This operation we may, as we please, attribute to the imagination or to memory; to imagination if it conserves the perception itself, to memory if it conserves only the name or the circumstances.

§20 It is important to distinguish clearly the point that separates imagination from memory. Everyone can judge for himself when he sees what light this distinction, which is perhaps too simple to appear essential, will cast on the entire generation of the operations of the mind. What philosophers have hitherto said on this matter is so confused that what they say about the imagination can often be applied to memory, and what they say about memory to the imagination. Locke himself makes memory consist in the mind's ability to revive the perceptions it has already had, accompanied at the same time by a sentiment that convinces the mind that it has had them before. That, however, is not clearly understood, for it is beyond doubt that we may very well remember a perception which we do not have the power to revive.

All philosophers have fallen into the same error as Locke. Those who believe that each perception leaves an image of itself in the mind, much as a seal leaves an imprint, do not form an exception, for what would the image of a perception be if not the perception itself? Here the mistake stems from the fact that, owing to failure to take a close look at the matter, they have substituted for a perception of the object itself various circumstances, or some general idea, which actually call it to mind. To avoid that sort of mistake, I will distinguish the different perceptions we can have, and I shall examine each of them in turn.

§21 The ideas of extension are those that we revive most easily, because the sensations from which we derive them are such that we cannot be without them so long as we are awake. The sense of taste and smell may be unaffected; we may not hear any sound or see any color; but only sleep can deprive us of the sense of touch. It is absolutely necessary that our body rest on something and that its parts must weigh on each other. This causes a perception that makes them appear distant and limited, thus implying the idea of some extension.

But we can generalize this idea by considering it as being indeterminate. Then we can modify it and derive the idea, for example, of a straight or curved line. But we would not be able to revive exactly the perception of the size of a body, because on that point we have no absolute idea that can serve as a given measure. On these occasions the mind can remember only the names "foot," "fathom," etc., along with an idea of size that becomes vaguer as the idea it wishes to represent to itself grows more comprehensive.

With the help of these first ideas, we can in the absence of objects represent exactly to ourselves the simplest figures such as triangles and squares. But if the number of sides increases a great deal, our efforts become useless. If I think of a figure with a thousand sides and one with nine hundred and ninety-nine, I distinguish them not by my perceptions but by the names that I have given them. The same holds for all complex notions. Everyone can observe that, when we want to use those notions, we call to mind only their names. As for the simple ideas they contain, we can revive them only one at a time, and this we must attribute to an operation that is different from memory.

§22 The imagination naturally makes use of everything that can be of any assistance to it. It is by comparison to our own stature that we represent to ourselves the stature of an absent friend; and we will imagine that he is large or small because we somehow measure his size by our own. But the chief aids of the imagination are order and symmetry, for here it finds different points as a standard to which it refers everything. If I think of a beautiful face, the eyes or other features which have struck me most will first come to mind; and it will be in relation to these first features that the others will take their place in my imagination. The more regular a figure is, the easier it is to imagine. We might even say that it is easier to see, for one can form an idea of it by the first glance. But if on the contrary the figure is very irregular, we will not get to the end until after we have spent a good deal of time thinking about the different parts.

§23 When the objects that cause the sensations of taste, of sound, smell, color, and light are absent, we have no perception left which we could modify to something that resembles the color, scent, and taste of an orange, for example. In addition there is no order or symmetry that could assist the imagination. These ideas cannot be revived unless they have become familiar to us. For this reason the ideas of light and colors ought to be revived most easily, and after them sounds. In regard to scents and tastes, we revive only those for which we have a particular preference. Thus there are many perceptions that we can remember, though we still recall only the names. Does this not often happen even with the most familiar perceptions, especially in conversation, in which we often make it a habit to talk of things without imagining them?

§24 We can observe different stages of progression in the imagination.

If we wish to revive a perception that is slightly familiar to us, such as the taste of a fruit we have had only once, our efforts will usually eventuate in a shock to the fibers of the brain and the mouth; and the perception we are going to have will not resemble the taste of the fruit. It will be the same for a melon, a peach, or even for a fruit we have never tasted. The same observation can be made in regard to the other senses.

When the perception is familiar, the fibers of the brain will more easily submit to our efforts, since they are accustomed to bend to the action of objects. Sometimes even, our ideas are revived without any efforts on our part and present themselves with such vivacity that we are fooled into believing that the objects are before our eyes. That is what happens to madmen and to all people when they are dreaming. These disorders are probably produced by the close relation of the movements that are the physical cause of the imagination with those that cause the perception of objects actually before us.[14]

§25 There is between imagination, memory, and reminiscence a progression by which they are alone distinguished. The first revives the perceptions themselves, the second recalls only the signs or the circumstances, and the last reports those we have already had. Here it must be observed that the same operation that I call "memory" in regard to the perceptions of which it evokes only the signs or the circumstances, is imagination in regard to the signs and circumstances that it revives, since these signs and circumstances are themselves perceptions. As for contemplation, it forms part of imagination or of memory, depending on whether it conserves the very perceptions of an absent object about which one continues to think, or whether it conserves only the name or the circumstances in which one has seen it. It does not differ from either except insofar as it supposes no interval between the presence of an object and the attention we still give it when it is absent. These differences will perhaps seem very minor, but they are absolutely incontrovertible. It is the same with numbers, where the neglect of a fraction, because it seems of little consequence, invariably creates an error in calculation. There is reason to fear that those who treat such precision as sophistry will never be able to provide the sciences with the exactness required to succeed in them.

§26 In observing, as I have just done, the difference between the perceptions that remain with us except when we are asleep, and those we have only by intervals even when awake, we right away see how far

---

[14] Here and elsewhere I suppose that the perceptions of the mind have their physical cause in the shock to the fibers of the brain, not because I take this hypothesis to be demonstrated, but because I find it best suited to support my thought. If the thing is not caused in this manner, it must be in some other not very different manner. The brain can work only by motion. Thus, whether one accepts that the perceptions are occasioned by shock to the fibers, by the circulation of animal spirits, or by some other cause, that is all the same in regard to the purpose I have in mind.

our power of reviving them extends. We see why the imagination at our command evokes certain figures of simple composition, while we can distinguish others only by the names that memory brings to mind. We see why the perceptions of color, taste, etc., are not at our command unless they are familiar to us, and how the vivacity with which ideas present themselves is the cause of dreams and madness. Finally, we see the evident differences between imagination and memory.

3 How the connection of ideas, formed by attention, brings forth imagination, contemplation, and memory

§27 In the light of what has been said in the preceding chapter, one could ask two questions: how do we have the power to revive some of our perceptions? The second: how is it that when we lack this power, we can often recall at least the names or the circumstances?

To answer the second question first, I say that we cannot recall the names or the circumstances unless they are familiar; in that case, they enter into the class of perceptions that are at our command; we shall say more about that in the answer to the first question, which requires more detailed discussion.

§28 The connection of several ideas can have no other cause than the attention we have paid to them when they occur together; thus things gain our attention by no other means than the relation they bear to our disposition, to our passions, to our general state, or in a word to our needs. It follows that the same attention all at once embraces our ideas of needs and of the things relevant to those needs, thus connecting them.

§29 All our needs are interdependent, and perceptions can be seen as a series of basic ideas to which we may refer everything that forms part of our knowledge. Above each of these, other series of ideas would rise, thus forming something like chains whose strength will lie entirely in the analogy of the signs, in the order of the perceptions, and in the connection that would have been formed by the circumstances which sometimes join the most disparate ideas. A need is connected to the idea of the thing that can relieve it; this idea is connected to the idea of the place where this thing is found; this in turn to the idea of the persons we have seen there; and this last idea with the ideas of pleasures and pains we have experienced, and with several others. We can even observe that as the chain becomes longer, it subdivides into new chains, so that the farther we get from the first link, the more the chains increase in number. An initial basic idea is connected to two or three others, each of these with an equal or even greater number, and so on.[c]

---

[c] Here and in the next paragraphs Condillac first broaches the subject of analogy. It plays a crucial role in his conception of language. It is a product of comparison and resemblance, and it shows in all aspects of language – in grammar, word-formation, phonology, etymology, and style – thus interacting with and mirroring the mind's corresponding effort to create order and coherence in the connection of ideas. It follows that "the poorer a language is in analogous expressions, the less

§30 The different chains or links, both large and small, that I assume to rise above each fundamental idea would in turn be connected by the sequence of fundamental ideas and by some links that would most likely be common to several. For the same objects and consequently the same ideas are often related to different needs. Thus all the knowledge we have would form one and the same chain, with the smaller chains coming together at certain links and separating at others.

§31 With these presuppositions, it would be sufficient, in order to recall familiar ideas, to direct attention to one of the fundamental ideas to which they are connected. But that is always possible, for so long as we are awake, our disposition, passions, and general state will at every moment cause us to have some of the perceptions that I call fundamental. Thus we will succeed with more or less ease in proportion as the ideas we wish to revive pertain more immediately to a greater number of needs.

§32 My presuppositions are not gratuitous; I refer to experience, and I am certain that everyone will acknowledge that he does not seek to remember something[15] except by the relation it bears to the circumstances in which he finds himself, and that he will succeed more easily when the circumstances are more numerous or have a more immediate connection to the thing. The attention that we give to a present perception recalls its sign, which in turn recalls others to which it bears some relation; these latter revive the ideas to which they are connected; these ideas revive other signs and other ideas, and so on. Two friends meet, for example, who have not seen each other for a long time. The attention they pay to the surprise and joy they feel will immediately produce the words they will suitably exchange. They will express regret at their long separation; talk about the pleasures they formerly enjoyed together and about everything that has happened to them in the mean-

---

assistance it gives to memory and imagination" (II, 1, §147). Since any particular and original language embodies a ruling analogy, a language that is a mixture of idioms gives less assistance to the mind (II, 1, §146; see also §§151−2). It is this role of analogy that lies behind the conception of language as organism. See also I, 4, §25 and II, 1, §35. Since there are always a variety of possible relations of resemblance, analogy does not act as a deterministic vise on the mind; quite the contrary, it opens scope for creativity. Quintilian IV, vi, 1−27 offers a useful discussion of analogy with many examples; it begins with the remark that "analogy" is a Greek word that was translated as "proportion" in Latin.

[15] I take the word "remember" in conformity with common usage; that is to say, as the power of reviving the ideas of an absent object or of recalling its signs. It thus applies equally to imagination and memory.

time. It is easy to see how all these things are connected together and with many others. Here is another example.

Let us suppose that someone raises a difficulty about this work to which I do not at the moment know how to answer. It is certain that, if the difficulty is not well founded, it ought of itself to indicate my response. I apply myself to considering all the parts, and I come upon some parts that, being connected with some ideas that pertain to the solution I seek, do not fail to revive them. Owing to the close connection they have with the others, these revive them in sequence, and at length I see how to answer.

Many other examples will occur to those who pay attention to what happens in the salons. No matter how rapidly the subject of the conversation changes, he who keeps a cool head and has some knowledge of the characters of the speakers always understands by what connection of ideas the conversation moves from one subject to the next. I therefore believe that I can rightly conclude that the power to revive our perceptions, their names or their circumstances, derives entirely from the connection which attention has established between these things and the needs to which they relate. Take away this connection, and you destroy imagination and memory.

§33 Not everyone can connect ideas with equal force and in equal number; that explains why imagination and memory do not serve all of us equally well. This incapacity comes from the different conformation of the organs and perhaps even from the nature of the mind. Thus the reasons one could give are entirely physical and lie outside the purview of this work. I shall only remark that the organs are sometimes not well suited for the connection of ideas merely for lack of exercise.

§34 The power to connect ideas has its inconveniences as well as advantages. To cast light on this matter I suppose two men, one who could never connect ideas and another in whom ideas connect so easily and forcefully that he is unable to separate them. The first would lack imagination and memory and consequently could not perform any of the operations that they are capable of producing. He would be absolutely incapable of reflection; he would be an idiot. The second would have too much memory and imagination, and this excess would produce much the same effect as a total deprivation of either. He would barely have the exercise of reflection; he would be a lunatic. Since the most disparate ideas would be strongly connected in his mind for the mere reason that they had presented themselves together, he would judge them to be naturally connected and would place one after the other in sequence, as if that would produce a well-founded series.

Between these extremes one can imagine a mean where the excess of imagination and memory would not harm the soundness of the mind and their weakness would not impair its amusements. Perhaps this mean is so difficult to attain that the greatest geniuses have only come near it. As different minds deviate from it and tend toward the opposite extremes, they have more or less incompatible qualities, because these qualities will more or less share in the extremities that absolutely exclude each other. Thus those who approach the extreme where imagination and memory rule, in proportion lose the qualities that make the understanding accurate, rational, and methodical. And those who move to the other extreme are in equal proportion deprived of the qualities that make for pleasure and agreeableness. The former write with more charm, the latter with more coherence and depth.

We have seen not only how the facility with which we connect ideas produces imagination, contemplation, and memory, but also how it is the true principle of the perfection of these operations as well as of their corruption.

4 The use of signs is the true cause of the progress of imagination, contemplation, and memory

To gain a full understanding of what activates imagination, contemplation, and memory, we must study what assistance these operations draw from the use of signs.

§35 I distinguish three kinds of signs. (1) Accidental signs, or the objects that some particular circumstances have connected with some of our ideas so that those ideas may be revived by them. (2) Natural signs, or the cries that nature has established for the sentiments of joy, fear, pain, etc. (3) Instituted signs, or those that we have ourselves chosen and that have only an arbitrary relation to our ideas.

§36 These signs are not necessary for the exercise of the operations that precede reminiscence; for perception and consciousness cannot fail to occur so long as we are awake; and since attention is nothing but the consciousness that tells us more particularly about the presence of a perception, all it takes to evoke it is that one object acts on the senses with greater vivacity than other objects. Up to that point the signs would serve only to provide more frequent opportunities for the exercise of attention.

§37 But let us suppose a man who has no use of any arbitrary sign. With the sole assistance of accidental signs, his imagination and reminiscence could already have gained some exercise; this is to say, that at the sight of an object, the perception with which it is connected may be revived and that he may recognize it as the one he had before. But we must note that this will not happen unless some unrelated cause puts the object before his eyes. When it is absent, the man I imagine does not by himself have any means of reviving it, since he is not in control of any of the things that could be connected with it. Thus it is not within his power to revive the idea to which it is attached. It follows that the exercise of the imagination is not yet at his command.

§38 With regard to natural cries, this man will make them as soon as he has the sentiments to which they belong. But the first time they will not be signs for him, for instead of reviving perceptions in him, they will be the very consequences of those perceptions.

When he has often had the same sentiment and also often uttered the cry that is its natural accompaniment, both will become so intimately connected in his imagination that he will not hear the cry without

36

somehow having the sentiment. That is when the cry becomes a sign, but the cry will not open the exercise of this man's imagination until he has heard it by chance. This exercise will therefore be no more in his power than in the case of accidental signs.

My argument cannot be countered by saying that the man may in time be able to use these cries to revive at will the sentiments that they express. I answer that they would then cease to be natural signs, for those signs have the quality that, by themselves, without any choice on our part, they proclaim the impression that we feel, thereby causing others to feel something similar.[d] They would be sounds that this man had chosen, just as we have chosen those of fear, joy, etc. Thus he would have made use of some instituted signs, which is contrary to the supposition of my argument at this stage.

§39 As we have seen, memory consists in the power we have to recall signs of our ideas or the circumstances that have accompanied them; but this power will not act except when, owing to the analogy of the signs we have chosen and the order we have established among our ideas, the objects we wish to revive pertain to some of our present needs. In short, we cannot recall a thing unless it is at some point connected with some of those things that we control. For a man who has only accidental signs and natural signs has none that is at his command. Thus his needs can cause only the exercise of his imagination, and by that token he will be without memory.

§40 On that basis we conclude that animals do not have memory and that they have only an imagination which they cannot direct. They represent something absent to themselves only to the extent that the image in the brain is closely connected with a present object. It is not memory that guides them to a place where they found food yesterday, but the feeling of hunger is so strongly connected with the ideas of this place and the path that leads to it, that these ideas are revived as soon as they have the feeling. It is not memory that makes them flee animals that are their enemies; but with some of their species having been devoured before their eyes, the cries which then pierced their ears

---

[d] Though Condillac in *Origin* never uses the term "sympathy," this passage, among many others, reveals how firmly his argument rests on the workings of this human faculty. It is sympathy that enables the spontaneous language of action to become the proto-language for the language of intentional signs. By its nature language is always interpersonal and social. Sympathy is embedded in rhetorical expressivism. Condillac shares Hume's and especially Adam Smith's notion of sympathy.

revived in their minds the sentiments of pain of which those cries are the natural signs, and they fled. When these enemies appear again, they revive the same sentiments in them because the connection was made when these sentiments were produced by them at the first encounter. They then take flight once more.

In regard to those who have never seen another animal perish in that manner, we can with good reason suppose that their mothers or some others have on the first occasion taken them along in flight by using cries to communicate to them the terror by which they are seized and which always occurs again at the sight of their enemy. If all these suppositions are rejected, I do not see what can make them take flight.

Perhaps someone will ask me: Who has taught them to recognize the cries that are the natural signs of pain? Experience. There is none of them that has not had an early experience of pain and who consequently has not had occasion to connect the cry with the sentiment. There is no need to imagine that they would not flee unless they had a precise idea of the peril that threatens them; it is sufficient that the cries of their own species should awaken the sentiment of some pain.

§41 We see that if, for lack of memory, animals cannot, like us, by themselves and at will, recall the perceptions that are connected in their brains, imagination perfectly makes up for that defect. For by reviving in them the very perceptions of absent objects, it enables them to behave as if they had these objects before their eyes and thereby to provide for their preservation with greater promptness and assurance than we sometimes do with the aid of reason. We can note something like it in ourselves on occasions when reflection is too slow to make us escape danger. At the sight, for example, of a body about to crush us, imagination evokes the idea of death in us or something like it, and this idea at once makes us avoid the blow that threatens us. In such moments we would infallibly perish if we relied only on memory and reflection.

§42 Often the imagination even produces effects in us that would seem to proceed from the most immediate reflection. Though we may be strongly preoccupied with an idea, the objects that surround us continue to act on our senses; the perceptions that they occasion revive others with which they are connected, and these bring about certain movements in our body. If all these things affect us less vividly than the idea that occupies us, they cannot distract us from it, and so it happens that without reflecting on what we are doing, we act as if we were guided by reason; there is no one who has not been in that situation. A man walking in Paris avoids all the things in his way with as much care as if he were thinking of nothing else; all the same, it is certain that he was thinking of something else altogether. Still more, it even happens often that we give an exact answer though our mind was busy about something else. That is because the words that express the question are connected with those that form the answer, and these latter determine the movements that pertain to their articulation. The connection of ideas is the principle of all these phenomena.

Thus we know by experience that the imagination, even when we are not able to govern the exercise of it, is sufficient to explain actions that appear rational even though they are not; that is why there are grounds for believing that there is no other operation in animals. Whatever the facts that are reported about them, we shall in human beings find others that are as extraordinary and which can be explained by the connection of ideas.

§43 By following the explications I have given, we can form a clear idea of what I call "instinct." It is an imagination which in the presence of an object revives the perceptions that are immediately connected with it and which by that means guides all kinds of animals without the assistance of reflection.

For lack of knowing the analyses I have just given and especially of what I have said about the connection of ideas, philosophers have been very much at a loss to explain instinct in animals. What has happened to them is what cannot fail to happen when people begin to reason without retracing their steps to the origin of things; that is, being unable to find a middle way, they have lost themselves in two extremes. Some have placed instinct next to or even above reason; others have rejected instinct by taking the animals for pure automatons. Both opinions are equally ridiculous, not to say more. The similarity between animals and us proves that they have a soul; and the difference between us proves that it is inferior to ours. The matter is made evident by my analyses, for the operations of the animal soul are limited to perception, consciousness, attention, reminiscence, and to an imagination which is not at their command, whereas ours possesses additional operations which I am going to explain.

§44 What I have said about imagination and memory must be applied to contemplation, depending on whether it is related to the one or the other. If we make it consist in the preservation of perceptions, its exercise does not pertain to us before the use of instituted signs; and if we make it consist in the preservation of the signs themselves, it does not act on its own at all.

§45 So long as imagination, contemplation, and memory have no exercise, or so long as the first two have none that we control, we cannot by ourselves govern our attention. In fact, how could we govern it when the mind does not as yet have the operation in its power? Thus it does not go from one object to another except as it is carried along by the impression that things make on it.

§46 But as soon as someone begins to attach ideas to signs he has himself chosen, memory is formed in him. Once memory has been acquired, he begins to gain mastery of his own imagination and to give it a new exercise. For by the assistance of signs he can recall at will, he revives, or at least is often able to revive, the ideas that are attached to them. In due course he will gain greater command of his imagination as he invents more signs, because he will increase the means of exercising it.

At this point we begin to perceive the superiority of our soul over that of the animals. For on the one hand, it is certain that they cannot attach their ideas to arbitrary signs; on the other, it would seem that this inability does not altogether stem from the nature of their organism. Is their body not as well suited as ours for the language of action? Is it not true that many of them have what is required for the articulation of sounds? So why, if they are capable of the same operations as ourselves, do they not give any evidence of that capability?

These details show how the use of different kinds of signs contributes to the progress of the imagination, contemplation, and memory. All this will be more fully set forth in the next chapter.

5 Reflection

§47 As soon as memory is formed and the exercise of the imagination is within our power, the mind begins to be set free from its former dependence on the objects that acted on it, owing to the signs that memory recalls and the ideas that imagination revives. With the full ability to recall things it has seen, it can direct its attention to them, away from those it has before the eyes at the moment. Afterwards it can turn to the latter again, or merely to some of them, and alternatively give it to either the former or the latter. Seeing a painting, for instance, we recall our knowledge of nature and the rules that teach us to imitate it; and we direct our attention successively from the painting to our knowledge, and from the knowledge to the painting, or in turn to its different parts. But in doing so, it is evident that our attention is governed by the activity of the imagination that is produced by a capacious memory. Without that we could not rule it ourselves, for it would obey only the action of objects.^c

§48 This manner of applying, on our own, attention to different objects in succession, and to different parts of a single object, is called "to reflect." Thus we clearly see how reflection is born from imagination and memory. But there is a progression that we must understand.

§49 The beginning of memory is sufficient to begin making us the masters of the exercise of our imagination. A single arbitrary sign is enough for a person to revive an idea by himself, and there we certainly have the first and the least degree of memory and of the power we can acquire over the imagination. The power it gives us to govern the attention is the least possible, but such as it is, it makes us begin to see the advantage of signs. And for that reason it will make us grasp at least some of the occasions in which it will be useful or necessary to invent new signs. By this means it will increase the exercise of memory and imagination; at the same time reflection may also be improved, and by reacting on the imagination and memory that first produced it, it will in

---

^c Condillac's word for painting is *tableau*, that is, a two-dimensional object in which all details exist together apart from the dimension of time imposed by speech. He returned to this conception in the chapter on inversions (II, 1, Ch. 12). Inversion has the capacity to lift language into this time-free state and thus closer to the presumed instantaneousness of thought. In his *Letter on Deaf-Mutes* (1751), Diderot brilliantly developed this notion as the core of an aesthetics of language and poetry. Only languages with a rich system of inflections, such as Greek and Latin, can produce inversions.

turn give them a new exercise. Thus by the mutual aid that these operations give each other, they reciprocally contribute to their progress.

If by reflecting on these feeble beginnings we do not clearly see their reciprocal influence, it will be sufficient to apply what I have said to these operations when considered in the state of perfection in which we possess them. Think for example of how much reflection it has taken to form languages, and the assistance that these languages give to reflection! But that is a matter to which I mean to devote several chapters.

It seems that one would not know how to make use of instituted signs if one was not already capable of sufficient reflection to choose them and attach ideas to them: how then, so goes the objection, is it that the exercise of reflection can only be acquired by the use of signs?

I answer that I shall meet that difficulty when I treat the history of language. Here it is enough for me to say that the difficulty has not escaped me.[f]

§50 From what has been said, it is obvious that the best way to increase the activity of the imagination and the scope of memory, and to facilitate the exercise of reflection, is to take an interest in the objects that, by their preeminent hold on the attention, connect the largest number of ideas and signs together; everything depends on that. This shows, as we may remark in passing, that making children study, during the early years of their education, only things they cannot understand or take any interest in, is inappropriate for the development of their talents. This practice does not form connections of ideas, or it forms them so feebly that they are not retained.

§51 It is reflection that makes us begin to discern the capability of the mind. So long as we cannot direct our own attention, the mind is, as we have seen, ruled by its environment and owes what it is to some extrinsic force. But if we are masters of our attention and direct it as we choose, then the mind is in control of itself, it draws ideas from it that it owes only to itself, and it gains enrichment from its own resources.

The effect of this operation is increased still more by putting us in command of our perceptions, almost as if we had the power to create and to annihilate them. If I choose one from among the perceptions I am now having, my consciousness of it is at once so lively and that of the others so feeble that it will seem to me to be the only one I am aware of.

---

[f] This forward reference to II, 1, §3 establishes the connection between the arguments of Part I and Part II.

Suppose that I decide the next moment to abandon it to occupy myself chiefly with one of those that affected me the least, then it will seem to vanish into nothingness, while another emerges from it. To speak less figuratively, the former will become faint and the latter so lively that it will seem to me that I have had them only in succession. We can put this to the test by considering a very complex object. There is no doubt that we do not simultaneously have consciousness of all the perceptions which are produced by the different parts that are disposed to act on our senses. But we could say that reflection freely suspends the impressions that occur in the mind in order to preserve only one of them.

§52 Geometry shows us that the best means of facilitating our reflection is to place before the senses the very objects of the ideas that are our concern, for then our consciousness of them is more lively, but this is an artifice that cannot be used in all sciences. One expedient that can always be used with success is to invest our meditations with clarity, precision, and order. Clarity because the clearer the signs are, the better our consciousness of the ideas they signify and the less chance that they will escape us; precision because undivided attention is firmer; order because a fundamental, better-known, and more familiar idea prepares our attention for what follows.

§53 The same person can never exercise his memory, imagination, and reflection with equal facility in all subjects. That is because these operations rely on attention as their cause, and attention treats an object in proportion to the relation it bears to our temperament and everything that touches us. That explains why those who aspire to omniscience run the risk of failing in many categories of knowledge. There are essentially only two kinds of talent; one is acquired by doing violence to our native faculties; the other is the result of a happy disposition and a great facility for their development. The latter is in greater conformity with nature, more lively, more active, and produces greatly superior effects. The former, on the contrary, smacks of effort and labor, and it never rises above mediocrity.

§54 I have tried to determine the causes of the imagination, of memory, and of reflection in the operations that precede them because it is the aim of this section to explain how the operations evolve one from the other. It would be the task of physics to seek other causes, if it were possible to know them.[16]

---

[16] This entire work rests on the five chapters the reader has now perused. It is therefore important to have a perfect understanding of them before continuing.

6 Operations that consist in distinguishing, abstracting, comparing, compounding, and decompounding our ideas

We have now set forth the most difficult part in our understanding of the progress of the operations of mind. What remains for us to treat are such evident effects of reflection that their generation almost explains itself.

§55 From reflection, or the power we have of directing our own attention, results the ability to consider our ideas separately, so that the same consciousness that informs us in detail of the presence of certain ideas (which is what characterizes attention) also tells us that they are distinct. Thus, so long as the mind was not the master of attention, it could not by itself distinguish among the different impressions it received from objects. This happens to us whenever we wish to apply ourselves to subjects for which we are not qualified. Then we confound the objects so severely that we even find it hard to discern those that differ most. The problem is that because we do not know how to conduct reflection or direct our attention to all the perceptions occasioned by the objects, those that distinguish them escape our notice. On that basis we can judge that if we were altogether without the use of reflection, we would not be able to distinguish different objects unless each made a very lively impression on us. All those that left a faint impression would be counted for nothing.

§56 It is easy to distinguish two ideas that are absolutely simple, but as they become more compounded, things become more difficult. Then, as our notions resemble each other in more ways, there is a risk that we would take several of them to constitute a single entity, or at the very least we would not distinguish them as well as they ought to be distinguished. That often happens in metaphysics and moral philosophy. Our present subject is an obvious example of the difficulties that must be overcome. On these occasions we cannot be too careful about the notice we take of the slightest difference, for that is what both determines the clarity and correctness of the mind and contributes the most to giving our ideas the order and precision that are requisite for gaining any form of knowledge. All the same, this truth is so little recognized that one runs the risk of making oneself ridiculous when engaging in analyses that are somewhat subtle.

§57 In distinguishing among our ideas, we sometimes take qualities that are absolutely essential to them as if they were entirely separated from their subject. That is what properly is called "to abstract." The ideas that result are called "general" because they represent qualities that belong to several different things. If, for instance, I pay no attention to what distinguishes men from brutes, but reflect only on what they have in common, I am making an abstraction that gives me the general idea of "animal."

This operation is indispensable for limited minds that can consider only a few ideas at the same time and who for that reason are obliged to refer several to the same class. But we must take care not to take things to be distinct that in fact are so only owing to our manner of conceiving them. That is a frequent mistake among philosophers; I intend to address that issue in the Fifth Section of this First Part.

§58 The reflection that gives us the power to distinguish our ideas also makes us capable of comparing them in order to know their relations. We do that by alternately directing our attention to one or the other, or by simultaneously fixing it on many. When notions that are only slightly compounded make an impression that attracts our attention without any effort on our part, the comparison is not difficult. But the difficulties increase as the ideas become more compounded and make a lighter impression. Comparisons are, for example, generally easier to make in geometry than in metaphysics.

With the aid of this operation we bring the least familiar ideas closer to those that are more so, and the relations we discover establish connections among them that strengthen the memory, imagination, and, by a sort of rebound, reflection.

§59 Sometimes, after first distinguishing several ideas, we consider them as making up a single notion; at other times we subtract from a notion some of the ideas that compose it. This is what is called "to compose" and "to decompose" our ideas. By means of these operations we can compare our notions in regard to all sorts of relations and make new combinations as often as we please.

§60 For the proper conduct of composition we must identify the simplest ideas of these notions, how and in what order they again unite themselves to those that come after them. This prepares us also for handling decomposition, for all we need to do is to undo what we have done. This shows that both have their source in reflection.

7 Digression on the origin of principles and of the operation that consists in analysis

§61 The faculty of abstracting and decomposing soon gave rise to the use of general propositions. Since they are the result of several particular forms of knowledge, it was soon understood that these propositions had the effect of relieving the memory and giving greater precision to discourse. But they soon degenerated into abuse and became the occasion for very imperfect ways of reasoning. I shall now show why.

§62 The first discoveries in the sciences were so simple and easy that they were made without the aid of any method. People could not even imagine rules until after they had made the sort of progress which, by making them see how they had gained some truths, showed them how they could attain others. Thus those who made the first discoveries could not show others what way to follow, since they did not themselves yet know what route they had taken. To demonstrate the certainty of their discoveries, all they could do was to show that they agreed with general propositions that no one would doubt. That caused the belief that these propositions were the true source of our knowledge. Consequently, they were given the name "principle," and it became a generally accepted prejudice, still honored, that one should reason only according to principles.[17] Those who discovered new truths believed that, to give a grander idea of their insight, they should make a mystery of the method they had followed. They were content to explain their discoveries by generally accepted principles. Once accepted and steadily gaining further credit, this prejudice gave birth to innumerable systems.

§63 The uselessness and abuse of principles showed especially in synthesis, a method in which it seems that truth is not allowed to appear unless it has been preceded by a host of axioms, definitions, and other propositions of pretended fertility. The evidence of mathematical demonstrations and the approbation which the learned world gives to this manner of reasoning might be sufficient to convince people that I am advancing a groundless paradox; but it is easy to show that mathematics does not owe its certainty to the method of synthesis.

---

[17] Here I do not take "principles" in the sense of observations confirmed by experience. I take this word in the sense common among philosophers, who use the word "principle" to name the general and abstract propositions on which they build their systems.

Indeed, if this science had been susceptible to as many errors, obscurities, and equivocations as metaphysics, the synthetic method would have been just the right one to maintain and multiply those errors. If the ideas of the mathematicians are exact, it is because they are the work of algebra and analysis. Being of little use for correcting a vague principle or a poorly defined notion, the method I condemn leaves all the defects of an argument uncorrected or hides them under the appearance of an impressive order that is in fact as superfluous as it is dry and tedious. To convince my readers, I refer them to works of metaphysics, moral philosophy, and theology in which the authors have chosen to use this method.[18]

§64 It is sufficient to see that a general proposition is only the result of our knowledge of particulars, in order to understand that we cannot draw conclusions beyond the knowledge on which the proposition is based or beyond those that might equally well have opened the way for us. Consequently, far from being the origin of the knowledge of particulars, it assumes that all the particulars are known by other means, or at least that they could have been so known. And indeed, to expound the truth with the scaffolding of the principles that the synthetic method demands, it is evident that we must already know it. Being at best appropriate for demonstrating things in a very abstract manner that one could prove by much simpler means, this method enlightens the mind so little that it conceals the way that leads to discoveries. There is even reason to fear that it deceives us by giving plausibility to deeply false paradoxes, for with isolated and often far-fetched propositions it is easy to prove whatever one wishes without making it easy to tell where an argument goes wrong. Metaphysics is full of examples. Finally, this method does not result in brevity, as is often believed, for no authors fall so often into frequent repetitions and the most useless details as those who employ it.

§65 It seems to me, for instance, that in order to have evidence that the whole is greater than the part, it is sufficient to reflect on how we

---

[18] Did Descartes, for example, cast greater light on his metaphysical meditations when he tried to demonstrate them by this method? Are there worse demonstrations than those of Spinoza? I could also cite Malebranche, who sometimes used synthesis; Arnauld, who uses it in a rather poor treatise on ideas, and elsewhere; the author of God's action on the creatures; and many others. One could say that the writers imagined that to demonstrate geometrically it is sufficient to put the different ideas of an argument in a certain order under the names "axioms," "definitions," "postulates," etc.

form the ideas of the whole and of the part. All the same, after blaming Euclid for failing to demonstrate these kinds of propositions, several modern geometricians have undertaken to provide the remedy. In fact, the synthetic method is too scrupulous to leave anything without proof. It allows us only a single proposition which it regards as being the origin of all the rest, and even this proposition must be a tautology. Here, consequently, is how a geometrician goes about proving that the whole is greater than the part.

He first establishes by definition "that a whole is greater whose part is equal to another whole"; and as an axiom "that the same is equal to itself." That is the only proposition he does not attempt to demonstrate. He then reasons as follows: "A whole whose part is equal to another whole is greater than this other whole (by the definition), but each part is equal to itself (by the axiom); consequently a whole is greater than its part."[19]

I admit that this argument would need a commentary for me to grasp it. However that may be, it seems to me that the definition is neither clearer nor more evident than the theorem, and that consequently it cannot be used to prove it. But this demonstration is still given as an example of a perfect analysis, because, it is said, "it is included" in a syllogism "of which one premise is a definition and the other an identical proposition, which is the mark of a perfect analysis."

§66 If that is what the geometricians understand by "analysis," I know nothing that is more useless than this method. They no doubt have a better one, and the progress they have made proves it. Perhaps their analysis would not even seem so far removed from the one that can be used in the other sciences, except for the fact that the signs are peculiar to geometry. All the same, as I see it, to analyze is nothing but an operation that results from the conjunction of the preceding operations. It merely consists in composing and decomposing our ideas to create new combinations and to discover, by this means, their mutual relations and the new ideas they can produce. This analysis is the true

---

[19] This demonstration is from the elements of mathematics by a famous man. Here it is in the words of the author: "§18. *Def.* Majus est cujus pars alteri toti aequalis est; minus vero quod parti alterius aequale. §73. *Axiom.* Idem est aequale sibimetipsi. *Theor.* Totum majus est sua parte. *Demonstr.* Cujus pars alteri toti aequalis est, id ipsum altero majus (§18). Sed quaelibet pars totius parti totius, hoc est, sibi ipse aequalis est (§73). Ergo totum quaelibet sua parte majus est." [*The source is Christian Wolff, *Elementa matheseos universae*, vol. 1 (Halle, 1742), ed. J. E. Hofmann (Hildesheim, Olms, 1968), pp. 24 and 33 in Ch. 1, "Elementa arithmeticae," §§20, 81, 84. Condillac's paragraph numbering shows he must have used another edition.]

secret of discoveries because it always makes us go back to the origin of things. It has the advantage of never presenting more than a few ideas at a time, and always in the simplest gradations. It is the enemy of vague principles and of everything that is contrary to exactness and precision. It is not with the help of general propositions that it seeks the truth, but always with a sort of calculus, that is to say, by composing and decomposing our notions in order to compare them in the manner that is most favorable for the discoveries we are looking for. Neither does it work by definitions, which usually only multiply disputes, but by explicating the generation of each idea. Hence we see that it is the only method we ought to follow in the search for truth. But it presupposes that those who use it have a solid knowledge of the operations of the mind.

§67 We can now conclude that principles are only the results that can show us the stages we have passed through; as useless as Ariadne's thread in the labyrinth when we wish to go forward, they merely make it easier for us to retrace our steps. If they can serve to relieve the memory and shorten disputes by indicating in few words the truths that both sides agree on, they usually become so vague that if they are not used with caution they multiply disputes and cause them to degenerate into mere verbal disputes. Consequently, the only means of acquiring knowledge is to return to the origin of our ideas, follow their generation, and compare them in terms of all their possible relations. That is what I call to "analyze."

§68 It is commonly said that we must have principles; I agree. But either I am much mistaken or most of those who repeat this maxim do not know what they are asking for. It even seems to me that we count as principles only those that we have ourselves adopted while we accuse others of lacking them when they refuse to accept ours. If by "principles" we understand general propositions which we can apply as needed to particular cases, who does not have them? But at the same time, what merit is there in having them? They are vague maxims, whose correct application cannot be taught. To say of someone that he has such principles amounts to saying that he is incapable of having clear ideas of what he is thinking about. If then we ought to have principles, it is not because we must begin there in order later to arrive at less general knowledge, but because we must first study particular truths and then ascend by one abstraction after the other to universal propositions.

Principles of this sort are naturally determined by the specific knowledge that leads to them; we see their full extent and can always use them with exactness. To say that a person has those qualities is to proclaim that he has perfect knowledge of the arts and sciences he studies and that he proceeds in every respect with clarity and precision.

8 Affirming. Denying. Judging. Reasoning. Conceiving. The understanding

§69 When we compare our ideas, the consciousness we have of them can tell us either that they are identical in regard to the aspects we consider, which we declare by connecting these ideas by the word "is," which is called "affirming"; or else consciousness tells us that they are not the same, which we declare in separating them by the words "is not," which is called "denying." This double operation is called "judging." It is evident that it is a consequence of the other two.

§70 The operation of judging gives birth to that of reasoning. Reasoning is nothing but a linking together of judgments that are interdependent. There is little need to dwell on these operations. What the logicians have said in many volumes appears to me to be entirely superfluous and of no use. I shall limit myself to explaining something we experience.

§71 The question is how we are able to develop long strings of reasoning in conversation, often without hesitating. Are all the parts present simultaneously? And if they are not (as is likely, since the mind is too limited to grasp a large number of ideas at the same time), by what good chance does it conduct itself in an orderly fashion? That is easy to explain from what has already been shown.

At the moment when someone proposes to present an argument, the attention he gives to the proposition he intends to prove makes him perceive the sequence of the principal propositions that are the results of the different parts of the argument he is about to make. If they are firmly connected, he runs through them so rapidly that he can imagine seeing them all together. Having grasped these propositions, he thinks about the one that should be explained first. By this means, the ideas that pertain to setting the argument in the proper light come to life in him in the order of their connection. From there he goes to the second, repeating the same operations, and so forth until the end of his argument. Thus his mind does not at the same time embrace all the parts, but following their connection he runs through them with sufficient rapidity always to be ahead of his speech, almost as the eyes of someone reading aloud are ahead of the pronunciation.

Perhaps it will be asked how we can perceive the outcome of an argument without having grasped its different parts in detail. I answer that this happens only when we speak of subjects that are familiar to us, or are not far from being so in regard to the relation they have to those we know better. That is the only case in which we can observe the phenomenon I am talking about. In all other situations we speak with hesitation, which has its source in the fact that when the connection of ideas is weaker they come to mind slowly; or we speak incoherently, which is the result of ignorance.

§72 The operation we call "conceiving" occurs when we are conscious that we have framed exact ideas along with knowledge of their relations by the exercise of the preceding operations, or at least of some of them. Consequently, an essential condition for conceiving well is always to represent things under their own ideas.

§73 These analyses prepare us to form a more exact idea of the understanding than is generally the case. We view it as a faculty that is separate from our knowledge and as the place where all our knowledge comes together. I believe, however, that to speak with greater clarity we must say that the understanding is nothing but the collection or combination of the operations of the mind. Here is what characterizes the understanding: to perceive or to be conscious, to pay attention, to recognize, to imagine, to remember, to reflect, to distinguish ideas, to abstract them, compare them, compose them, decompose them, to analyze, affirm, deny, judge, reason, and to conceive.

§74 In these analyses I have made an effort to show the interdependence of the operations of the mind and how they are all engendered by the first. We begin by having perceptions of which we have consciousness. We then form a livelier consciousness of some perceptions, and this consciousness becomes attention. From that time on, the ideas interconnect so that we come to recognize the perceptions we have had and recognize ourselves to be the same being who has had them, all of which constitutes reminiscence. If the mind revives its perceptions, conserves them, or recalls only the signs, then we have imagination, contemplation, and memory. If the mind itself controls its attention, we have reflection. Finally, reflection gives birth to all the others. It is properly reflection that distinguishes, compares, composes, decomposes, and analyzes, for those are merely different ways of conducting the attention. From that, judgment, reasoning, and conception are naturally formed in sequence, and the result is understanding. But I thought that I ought to consider the different ways in which reflection is exercised as so many distinct operations, because there are gradations in the results. Thus, for example, it does more when it compares ideas than when it merely distinguishes them; in composing and decomposing than when it confines itself to comparing them such as they are; and so forth. There is no doubt that we could increase the operations of the mind more or less according to the manner in which we choose to conceive of things. We could even reduce them to just one, namely consciousness. But there is a middle way between dividing too much and dividing too little. In order to complete the task of setting this matter in its proper light, we must proceed to new analyses.

9 Defects and advantages of the imagination

§75 The ability we have to revive our perceptions in the absence of objects gives us the power to reunite and connect together the most disparate ideas. There is nothing that cannot take a new form in our imagination. By the readiness with which it transfers the qualities of one subject to another, it puts together in a single subject what would naturally suffice to embellish many subjects. At first nothing seems more contrary to truth than the way in which the imagination manages our ideas. In fact, if we do not become masters of this operation, it will invariably lead us astray, but if we know how to control it, imagination becomes one of our chief sources of knowledge.[20]

§76 Connections of ideas are formed in the imagination in two different ways: sometimes voluntarily, and at other times as the effect of an unexpected impression. Connections of the former kind are usually not very strong, which means that we can easily break them: of those we agree that they are instituted. Those of the latter kind are often so solidly embedded that it is impossible for us to destroy them: we easily agree that they are natural. They all have their advantages and disadvantages, but the latter are the more useful or dangerous, as they act on our minds with greater vivacity.

§77 Language is the most obvious example of the connections we form voluntarily. It alone is enough to show what advantages this operation gives us, just as the care we must take to speak with precision shows how difficult it is to master. But proposing soon to treat the indispensability, use, origin, and progress of language, I will not take

---

[20] Hitherto I have taken the imagination only for the operation that revives perceptions in the absence of objects; but now that I am considering the effects of this operation, I see no reason not to follow accepted usage, even finding myself obliged to do so. That is why, in this chapter, I take the imagination for an operation that, in the act of reviving ideas, constantly makes new combinations subject to our will. Thus from now on I am using the word "imagination" in two different senses, but this will not cause equivocation, for the contexts in which I use it will on each occasion define the particular sense I have in mind.[g]

[g] This distinction between the two kinds of imagination is a reminder of the creative role that Condillac assigns to the imagination. In a later work he wrote that a person with imagination is "a creative mind" (*un esprit créateur*) because, "of the several qualities which the author of nature has scattered in the variety of things, he makes a single whole, thus creating something that exists only in his own mind" (CO 1.413a; cf. CO 2.385a). Imagination keeps company with synthesis. Voltaire wrote "Imagination" for the *Encyclopédie* (7 [1757], 560a–563a), in which he distinguished between the passive and the active imagination. In 1777, Marmontel published yet another entry in which he described what he called the creative imagination (*Encyclopédie. Supplément* 3.567a–568a). This entry was repeated in EMGL, 2 (1785), 297a–298a.

time here to expound the advantages and drawbacks of this aspect of the imagination. I turn instead to the connections of ideas that are the effect of some unexpected impression.

§78 I have said that these ideas are useful and necessary. It was necessary, for instance, that the sight of a precipice from which we are in danger of falling should evoke in us the idea of death. For attention cannot fail to form this connection on the first occasion, which must be so much the stronger as it is determined by the most urgent motive, the preservation of our own being.

Malebranche thought that this connection is natural or in us from the moment of birth. "The idea," he says, "of a great depth that we see below us into which we might fall or the idea of some great body which is poised to fall and crush us, is naturally connected with the idea of death and with a movement of the animal spirits that disposes us to flee or to desire to flee. This connection never changes, because it is necessary that it must always remain the same; and it consists in a disposition of the fibers of the brain that is with us from infancy" [*The Search after Truth*, Bk. II, Ch. 5].

It is evident that if experience had not taught us that we are mortal, so far from having an idea of death we would be very surprised at the first sight of death. This idea is therefore acquired, and Malebranche has made the mistake of confusing what is natural or with us from birth, with what is common to all mankind. This error is universal. People do not understand that the same senses, operations, and circumstances must everywhere produce the same effects.[21] They are determined to have recourse to something innate and natural that precedes the action of the senses and the exercise of the operations of the mind and of communally shared circumstances.

§79 If the connections of ideas that are formed in us by external impressions are useful, they are also often dangerous. Suppose that we are by education in the habit of connecting the idea of shame or infamy with that of surviving an affront, and the idea of generosity and courage with that of giving up one's life or risking it trying to kill one's offender: there we have two received opinions. One of them was the point of

---

[21] Suppose that a mature person is born on the edge of a precipice, and that I have been asked whether it is likely that he can avoid falling from it. For my part, I think so, not because he fears death, for one cannot fear what one does not know; but because it seems to me natural that he will direct his steps to the side where his feet have ground under them.

honor of the Romans; the other is known in parts of Europe. With age, these connections enforce themselves and become more or less importunate. The force of the temperament one grows into, the passions to which one is subject, and the state of life one adopts either make the ties stronger or break them.

Seeing that such prejudices are the first impressions we have, they do not fail to appear to be incontestable principles to us. In the example I have given, the mistake is obvious and the cause is known. But there is perhaps no one who has not on occasion fallen into bizarre arguments and in the end become aware of how ridiculous they are, without being able to understand how one could even for a moment become duped by them. They are often the effect of a single connection of ideas, a cause that is humiliating to our vanity and therefore the harder for us to detect. If its manner of acting is so secret, think of the arguments it produces in the common man.

§80 In general the impressions we have in different circumstances make us connect ideas we are no longer able to separate. In our dealings with other human beings, for instance, we imperceptibly connect ideas of certain turns of mind and character with the most notable outward aspects. That is why people with a marked physiognomy please or displease us more than others, for the physiognomy is merely a collection of features to which we have connected ideas that do not come to life unless they are accompanied by pleasure or dislike. Thus it is not surprising that we judge other people by their physiognomy and that we sometimes even at first sight find them off-putting or attractive.

Owing to these connections, we often feel excessive attraction to some people, while we are altogether unjust to others. That is because what strikes us in our friends as well as our enemies naturally connects with the agreeable or disagreeable sentiments they have raised in us; and furthermore, because the shortcomings of the former always borrow something agreeable from what we find most amiable in them, just as the better qualities of the latter seem infected by their defects. For these reasons these connections have an enormous influence on our conduct. They nourish our love or our hate, arouse our esteem or contempt, excite our approval or resentment, and produce the sympathies, antipathies, and all the bizarre inclinations we often find it so hard to account for. I believe I have read somewhere that Descartes always had a liking for the squint-eyed because the first woman he fell in love with had this defect.

§81 Locke showed the great danger of the connection of ideas when he remarked that they are the origin of madness: "A man," he says, "who is very sober and of right understanding in all things, may in one particular be as frantic, as any in Bedlam; if either by any sudden very strong impression, or long fixing his fancy upon one sort of thoughts, incoherent ideas have been cemented together so powerfully, as to remain united."[22]

§82 To comprehend the justness of this reflection it is sufficient to observe that in physical terms imagination and madness can differ only by degrees. Everything depends on the vivacity and the abundance with which the animal spirits are carried to the brain. That is why perceptions reemerge in dreams so easily that upon awakening we sometimes have trouble recognizing our error. This is certainly a moment of madness. To remain mad, it would be sufficient to suppose that the fibers of the brain had been shaken too violently to recover. The same effect can be produced more slowly.

§83 There is no one, I think, who has not in idle moments imagined himself the hero of a romance. Such fictions, which we call "castles in Spain," usually cause only faint impressions in the brain, because we pay little heed to them and they are soon dissipated by more real objects that demand our attention. But if some occasion for melancholy occurs that makes us avoid our best friends and dislike what used to make us happy, then, seized by our sadness, our favorite romance will be the only idea that can distract us from it. The animal spirits will little by little dig foundations for this castle so deep that nothing will change their course. We fall asleep building it, we inhabit it in our dream, and in the end when the impression made by the spirits has imperceptibly become identical with what we would in fact be if we were what we have fancied, we will take chimeras for realities when we wake up. Perhaps the madness of the Athenian who believed that all ships entering the port of Piraeus belonged to him had no other cause.

§84 This explanation shows how dangerous the reading of romances is for young women, whose brain is impressionable. Since their mind is often too little engaged in education, it eagerly seizes fictions that flatter the natural passions at their age. There they find the materials for the

---

[22] *Essay* 2.11.13; he repeats pretty much the same thing in 13.4 of the same book.[h]

[h] It is curious that, for Locke's association of ideas, Condillac cites E 2.11.13 rather than the famous chapter on that subject (E 2.33). For more detail, see FLS, pp. 221–2.

most beautiful castles in Spain, which they build with a pleasure that increases as their eagerness to please and the flattery they constantly receive feed their fancy. Then it can happen that a small disappointment is enough to turn the head of a young girl, to persuade her that she is Angelica or some other figure who has pleased her, and to take every man who approaches her for a Medoro.[i]

§85 There are works written with a different aim that can have the same effect. I am thinking of certain books of devotions which were written by strong and contagious imaginations. They can sometimes turn the head of a young girl to the point of making her believe that she has visions, that she discourses with angels, or even that she is already in heaven with them. It is much to be hoped that young people of both sexes would always be counselled in this sort of reading by teachers who knew the temper of their imagination.

§86 Everyone recognizes the kinds of folly I have been talking about. There are other aberrations which we do not think of calling by that name; nevertheless, all those which have their source in the imagination should be put in that same category. By defining madness only by its consequences in error, we fail to fix its point of origin. So we ought to make it consist in an imagination which, though it lies beyond our observation, associates ideas in a manner that is altogether chaotic and sometimes influences our judgments and our conduct. If that is the case, it is likely that no one is exempt. The wisest man would differ from the greatest madman only by virtue of having the good luck that the eccentricities of his imagination do not interfere with the ordinary course of life and place him less visibly in contrast to the rest of mankind. Indeed, is there anyone who does not fall into the same errors because some favorite passion constantly, on certain occasions, invites him to conduct himself entirely according to the strong impression that things make on him? Consider especially the plans a man makes for his conduct, for that is the rock on which most people's reason founders. What prejudice, what blindness in him who has the best understanding! He does not change for the better even when failure makes him recognize that he has been wrong. The same imagination that seduced him will do so again; and you will see him ready to commit a mistake like the first one, without your being able to convince him to the contrary.

---

[i] Angelica and Medoro are characters in Ariosto's *Orlando Furioso* (1532).

§87 The impressions that are made on a phlegmatic brain do not last long. Thus people whose outward demeanor is poised and thoughtful have no other advantage, if it is one, than always to maintain the same eccentricities. By that means their madness, which one did not suspect at first sight, becomes the easier to recognize for those who observe the eccentricities for some time. By contrast, in brains with much fire and vivacity the impressions vanish and pop up again in a succession of mad actions. At first it is easy enough to see that someone's mind has some eccentricities, but they change with such rapidity that it is almost beyond observation.

§88 The power of the imagination has no limits. It reduces or even dissipates our pains, and it alone can give our pleasures the flavor that makes them priceless. But sometimes it is our cruellest enemy: it increases our harms, it inflicts other harms we did not have before, and in the end makes us plunge the dagger into our breast.

To explain these effects, I say first that as the senses act on the organ of the imagination, this organ reacts on the senses. This cannot be doubted, for experience shows a similar reaction in the least-elastic bodies. In the second place, I say that this organ's reaction is more lively than the action of the senses, because this organ does not act on them with the mere force of the perception they produced, but with the united forces of all those that are closely linked to this perception and which for this reason have invariably been revived. That being the case, it is not difficult to understand the effects of the imagination. Let us look at some examples.

The perception of pain revives all the ideas with which it has a close connection in the imagination. I see the danger, I am overcome by fear, I am downcast, my body can barely hold on to itself, my pain becomes more piercing, my dejection increases, and it may happen that merely because of a jolt to the imagination I am brought to my grave by an illness that had a mild beginning.

In the same manner a pleasure I have pursued revives all the agreeable ideas to which it can be connected. The imagination returns several perceptions to the senses for every one that it receives. My spirits are moving with a force that dissipates all that could deprive me of the sentiments I am having. In this state, being entirely absorbed by the perceptions I receive from the senses and by those which the imagination reproduces, I enjoy the most lively pleasures. But arrest the action of the imagination, and it is all gone as if I had been bewitched; I have before my eyes the objects to which I attributed my happiness; I pursue them, but I no longer see them.

This explanation helps us understand that the pleasures of the imagination are entirely as real and as somatic as the others, in spite of what is commonly said to the contrary. I will give only one more example.

A man tormented by gout and unable to stand on his feet sees, at the moment when he least expected it, a son he believed lost: there is no more pain. Soon after, his house catches fire: his bodily weakness is gone. He is already out of danger when people think of rescuing him. Suddenly jolted and brought to life, his imagination reacts on all parts of the body, thus producing the violent change that saves him.

Those are, I believe, the most astonishing effects of the imagination. In the next chapter I shall say something about the charms it lends to truth.

10 The source of the charms that imagination gives to truth

§89 The imagination borrows its charms from the right it has to appropriate whatever is most pleasant and amiable from nature in order to embellish its own subject. Nothing is beyond its range, everything belongs to it so long as those things can give it a more striking appearance. It is like a bee that makes its treasury from all the most beautiful flowers that a garden can produce. Always obliging, it accommodates itself to our taste, our passions, our weaknesses. It attracts and persuades one person by its lively and winning air, surprises and amazes another by its grandeur and nobility. One moment it amuses us by its gaiety, the next moment by the boldness of its flashes of wit. There, it affects softness to engage us; here, languor and tears to move us; and if necessary, it will assume a mask to make us laugh. But assured of its command, it exercises its capriciousness everywhere. Sometimes it likes to invest quite common and trivial things with grandeur, and at other times to transform low and ridiculous subjects into the most serious and sublime. Though it alters everything it touches, it often succeeds when it seeks only to please; but beyond that it must fail. Its dominion ends where analysis begins.

§90 It draws not only on nature, but on the most absurd and ridiculous things, provided that they are accepted by conventional opinion. It does not matter that they are false if we are made to believe they are true. Imagination seeks pleasure first of all, but it is not opposed to truth. All fictions are good as long as they conform to nature, our knowledge, and our prejudices; but when it deviates from these, it creates nothing but monstrous and extravagant ideas. This, I think, is what renders this thought of Boileau-Despréaux so fitting:

> Nothing is beautiful but the true; only the true is pleasing.
> It ought to reign throughout, even in fiction. [*Epistle* IX, 43–4]

In fact, truth belongs to fiction, not because things are absolutely as they are made to appear, but because it presents them to us in clear and familiar images which for that reason please us without leading us into error.

§91 Nothing is beautiful but the true, and yet every truth is not beautiful. To fill that void, imagination invests it with such ideas as are most proper to embellish it, in order by this reunion to create a whole in which we find both solidity and amusement. Poetry gives an infinite number of examples. Here we see fiction, which would always be silly without truth, decorate the true that would often be cold without fiction. This mixture is always pleasing, provided that the embellishments are chosen with discernment and judiciously applied. Indeed, imagination is to truth what finery is to a beautiful person: it must lend that person every aid to appear at the best possible advantage.

I shall not dwell further on the imagination, which would require a separate work. It is sufficient for my purpose that I have not forgotten to treat it.

11 On reason and on intellect and its different aspects

§92 All the operations we have described produce a single operation which, so to speak, crowns the understanding, namely reason. However we conceive it, everyone agrees that only reason enables us to conduct civic affairs wisely and to make progress in the search for truth. We can conclude that it is nothing other than our knowledge of the manner in which we must govern the operations of the soul.

§93 Putting it in those terms, I do not believe I go beyond common usage; I am merely defining a notion which I have nowhere found sufficiently exact. I even forestall all the invectives directed at reason for having been too vaguely understood. How could one say that nature made us a gift worthy of a stepmother when she has given us the means of wisely directing the operations of the mind? Could such a notion ever enter our heads? Shall it be said that if the soul were not endowed with all the operations we have mentioned, it would be happier, because they are the source of all the sorrows that result from reason's abuse of those operations? Why then do we not reproach nature for having given us a mouth, arms, and other organs that are often the instruments of our misfortune? Perhaps we might wish to have no more life than suffices to feel we exist, thus gladly giving up all the operations that place us so far above the animals merely to be left with their instinct.

§94 But what, someone will ask, is the use we ought to make of the operations of the soul? Has this task not been pursued with enormous effort and very little success? Are we in a better position to succeed today? I answer that it would seem then that our complaint is that reason is not our lot. But let us not exaggerate. Let us study the operations of the soul and know their scope without concealing their weaknesses; let us distinguish them precisely, get a clear view of their resources, reveal both their advantages and abuses, and find out what assistance they mutually lend each other; and finally, let us apply them only to things that are within our reach – then I promise we shall learn the use we should make of them. We will acknowledge that as much reason has become our lot as our condition required, and that if the one from whom we have everything we are is frugal with his favors, he knows how to dispense them wisely.

§95 There are three operations that we ought to compare in order to gain a better sense of how they differ. They are instinct, madness, and reason. Instinct is merely a form of imagination over which we have no control at all, but which by its vivacity contributes perfectly to our preservation. It excludes memory, reflection, and the other operations of the mind. Madness by contrast admits the exercise of all the operations, but it is directed by a chaotic imagination. Finally, reason results from the proper conduct of all our mental operations. If Pope had known how to get clear ideas of these things, he would not have inveighed so strongly against reason, let alone concluded:

> In vain you praise the excellence of Reason.
> Should it have preference over Instinct?
> How can those two faculties compare!
> God directs Instinct, Man the Reason.[j]

§96 Furthermore, it is easy to explain the distinction made here between "being above reason," "according to reason," and "contrary to reason." A truth is above reason when it contains some ideas that cannot be the object of mental operations because they cannot have entered by the senses or be derived from sensations. A truth that contains nothing but ideas on which the intellect can operate is according to reason. Finally, any proposition that contradicts another that results from rightly conducted mental operations is against reason.

§97 It is easy to see that in my notion of reason and in the new details I have given about the imagination, there are no other ideas than those that have been the subject of the first eight chapters of this section. And yet it was proper to consider these things separately, either to respect convention or to observe more precisely the different objects of the operations of the understanding. I believe I must also follow the conventional distinction among good sense, intellect, intelligence, penetration, profoundness, discernment, judgment, sagacity, taste, invention, talent, genius, and enthusiasm. It will be sufficient to say just a few words about each of these.

§98 Good sense and intelligence consist in conceiving and imagining, and they differ only in regard to their objects. For example, to understand that two and two make four or to understand an entire course of mathematics is equally to conceive, but with the difference that one is

---

[j] Condillac's passage is a conflation of several lines in Pope's *Essay on Man*, ending with the famous couplet "And Reason raise o'er Instinct as you can, / In this 'tis God directs, in that 'tis Man" (Epistle 3, lines 97–8).

called good sense and the other intelligence. Likewise, to imagine common things that are daily before our eyes requires only good sense; but we need intelligence to imagine new things, especially if they are somewhat extensive. Thus it seems that the object of good sense is found in what is easy and ordinary, while it pertains to intelligence to conceive or imagine things that are more composite or new.

§99 For lack of a good method to analyze our ideas, we are often content to understand each other approximately. A good example is the word "intellect," to which we usually attach a quite vague idea, though the word is spoken by everyone. Whatever its signification, it cannot extend beyond the operations I have analyzed; but according to whether we view these operations separately, join several of them together, or consider all of them at the same time, we form different notions to which we commonly give the name "intellect." It is a condition, however, that we conduct those operations in a superior manner that shows the activity of the understanding. Those in which the soul barely acts of its own accord do not deserve that name. Thus memory and the operations that precede it do not constitute intellect. Even if the activity of the soul has only common things for its object, it is still merely good sense, as I have already said. Coming immediately after, the highest degree of intellect is found in the man who on every occasion would know how perfectly to conduct the operations of his understanding, using every possible means. We will never actually find an instance of that notion, but we must suppose it exists in order to have a fixed point from which we can distance ourselves more or less, in different perspectives, in order to form an idea of the lesser degrees. I shall limit myself to those that have names.

§100 Penetration supposes a sufficient capacity for attention, reflection, and analysis to pierce into the interior of things; and profoundness, the ability to open them up to reveal all their inward springs as well as knowing their source, what they are, and what they will become.

§101 Discernment and judgment compare things, determine the difference, and weigh exactly the value of some vis-à-vis other things. But the former is especially said of those that pertain to speculation, the latter of what concerns practice. Discernment is the requisite of philosophy, judgment of the conduct of life.

§102 Sagacity is the agility with which we turn around to seize the object of attention with greater ease or make it better known to others, which can only be done by the collaboration of imagination with reflection and analysis.

§103 Taste is a manner of feeling that is so favored that we perceive the value of things without the aid of reflection, without any rule of judgment. It is the effect of an imagination which, having early on been busy about objects of its choice, keeps them present before the mind and naturally uses them as models for comparison. That is why good taste is usually the lot of people who know the world.

§104 We do not actually create ideas; what we do is to combine, by compounding and decompounding them, those that we have received from the senses. Invention consists in knowing how to form new combinations. There are two kinds: talent and genius.

Talent combines ideas of an art or science already known in the right manner to produce effects one would naturally expect. Sometimes it requires more imagination, sometimes more analysis. Genius adds to talent the idea of the intellect as being somehow creative. It invents new arts, or within the same art new forms that are as good as and sometimes even superior to those already known. It envisages things from points of view which are entirely its own; it gives birth to a new science or, in those already known, opens the way to truths that were thought beyond our reach. Over those that were known before, it spreads clarity and perspicuity formerly thought unattainable. The quality of a man of talent can be shared by others who may be his equal or even surpass him. The quality of a man of genius is original; it is inimitable. This is the reason why great writers after him rarely venture to write in the genre in which he has succeeded. Corneille, Molière, and Quinault[k] have not had imitators. And we have modern writers who probably will not either.

Genius is sometimes called extensive, sometimes immense; extensive when it makes great progress in one genre, immense when it unites so many genres to such a degree that we find it hard to imagine any limits.

§105 We cannot analyze enthusiasm when we feel it, for in that state we are not masters of our reflection. But how can we analyze it unless we feel it? We do that by considering the effects it has produced. In this case the knowledge of effects ought to lead us to knowledge of their

---

[k] Philippe Quinault (1635–88), French dramatist and in his later career librettist of Lully's operas.

cause, and this cause must be one of the operations which we have already analyzed.

When the passions jolt us so violently that we lose the exercise of reflection, we feel a thousand different sentiments. That happens because the imagination, when aroused in proportion to the degrees of strength exercised by the passions, with more or less force revives the sentiments that have some relation to and consequently connection with the state in which we find ourselves.

Let us imagine two men in the same circumstances and feeling the same passions, but with an unequal degree of force. Let us for the first example take the old Horace as he is portrayed by Corneille, with the Roman soul that prompts him to sacrifice his own children to save the republic. The impression he receives when he learns of his son's flight is a confused collection of all the sentiments that can be produced by love of one's country and of glory carried to their highest pitch, even to such a degree as not to regret the loss of two of his sons and to wish that the third had also perished. Those are the sentiments that perturb him, but will he express them in all their detail? No, it is not the language of the grand passions. Neither will he give expression to one of the more subdued passions. He will naturally prefer the one that perturbs him with the greatest violence and let it go at that, because it includes all the other passions well enough, owing to the connection it has with them. But what is this sentiment? It is to wish that his son were dead, for such a desire either does not enter a father's soul or, when it does, will take possession of the entire soul. Hence, when he is asked what his son could have done when facing three opponents, he is bound to answer: "He should have died" [*qu'il mourût*].[1]

On the other hand, let us suppose a Roman who, though sensitive to the glory of his family and the welfare of the republic, nevertheless would have felt much weaker passions than the old Horace; it seems to me that he would have retained nearly all his composure. The senti-ments that honor and love of country produced in him would have

---

[1] These words, "qu'il mourût," from Pierre Corneille's tragedy *Horace* (Act 3, sc. 6), are spoken by the old Horace when he learns that his son Horace, as the only survivor of three brothers, has fled single combat against the still surviving three opponents – though it soon turns out that his flight was a successful ruse. This phrase was cited often during the eighteenth century as proof that the sublime effect of speech can surpass the mere meaning of words. It was first so cited by Boileau in a late addition to the preface to his translation of Longinus, *On the Sublime*, in which "God said, Let there be light" had already been cited for the same purpose. It is characteristic that Condillac discusses the sublime in the context of enthusiasm.

affected him less, and each to an equal degree. This man would not have been inclined to give expression to one sentiment rather than the other; consequently, he would have proclaimed both in all their detail. He would have said how much he suffered at seeing the ruin of the republic as well as the shame which the son had brought upon himself. He would have forbidden him ever to come before his eyes again; and instead of wishing his death, he would merely have judged it better for him to have shared the fate of his brothers.

Whatever one understands by "enthusiasm," it is enough to know that it is opposed to composure in order for us to observe that without enthusiasm we cannot put ourselves in the place of the old Horace in Corneille, but the same is not true of putting ourselves in the place of the other man I have imagined. Let us look at another example.

If Moses, speaking of the creation of light, had been less suffused with the grandeur of God, he would have put more effort into demonstrating the power of this Supreme Being. On the one hand, he would not have failed to exalt the excellence of light; and on the other, he would have represented the darkness as a chaos in which all of nature was enshrouded. But to enter into details of that sort, he was too full of the sentiments that are produced by the sight of the Supreme Being and of the dependency of His creatures. Thus, since the ideas of command and obedience are connected with those of superiority and dependence, they must have come to life in his mind, and those he found sufficient to express all the other ideas. Therefore, all he said was, "God said, Let there be light: and there was light." By the number and beauty of the ideas that these expressions simultaneously evoke in the mind, they have the advantage of striking the soul in the most wonderful manner, and for that reason they are what we call "sublime."

In consequence of these analyses, here is my notion of enthusiasm: it is the condition of a person who, as he intently contemplates the circumstances in which he finds himself, is powerfully moved by all the sentiments they will produce in him and who, to express what he feels naturally, chooses from among these sentiments the one that is most lively and that by itself is equal to all the rest by virtue of the close connection it has with them. If this condition is only passing, it causes a single brilliant phrase; if it lasts a while, it can produce an entire work. By retaining our composure, we might be able to imitate enthusiasm if it were our habit to analyze the beautiful works which the poets owe to it. But would the copy always be the equal of the original?

§106 The intellect is properly our means of acquiring ideas that lie out of the ordinary, and it is for this reason that the nature of ideas differs in proportion to the kind of operations that more particularly constitute each person's intellect. The effects cannot be the same in a person to whom we would attribute a greater measure of analysis than of imagination, as in the person with more imagination than analysis. The imagination alone can vary greatly, enough to create very different intellects. We find models of each of these in our writers, but they do not all have names. Furthermore, to consider all the workings of the intellect, it is not sufficient to have analyzed the operations of the understanding, for it would still be necessary to do the same for the passions and to observe how all these things combine and blend in one single cause. The influence of the passions is so great that without it the understanding is virtually at a standstill, so much so that for lack of passions there is barely any intellect left. For certain talents they are even absolutely necessary. But an analysis of the passions would rather belong to a work that treated the progress of our knowledge than to one that is only concerned with its origin.

§107 The principal benefit of the way in which I have envisaged the operations of the soul is that we clearly see how good sense, intellect, reason, and their contraries are all equally the product of a single principle, namely the connection of ideas with one another; and that we see how, on a higher level, this connection is produced by the use of signs.[23] That is the principle. I proceed to finish with a recapitulation of what I have said.

[23] [*The Le Roy edition has an important note here, giving a different conclusion to this paragraph, taken, as Le Roy says, from the edition of 1746 (while his own text is the standard text of the 1798 edition). But in fact Thomas Nugent's English translation of 1756 has the same text as the 1798 edition. How so? Because there were two printings in 1746, and it was in the second of these that Condillac made the change. (I owe this information to Charles Porset; and I am not aware that it has been stated in print anywhere.) The wording of the first printing is revealing both by itself and when compared with its replacement.]

"the use of signs; and that consequently the progress of the human mind depends entirely on the skill we bring to the use of language. This principle is simple, and it casts great light on the matter; so far as I know, no one has recognized it hitherto.

"§108 I have said [in Sect. 1] without qualification that the operations of the soul together were, with the sensations, the materials of all our knowledge. I can now express myself with greater precision, for that proposition would be false if it were taken to cover all the operations. Its meaning must be limited to

We are capable of more reflection in proportion as we have more reason. Thus this latter faculty produces reflection. On the one hand, reflection gives us mastery of our attention; so it engenders attention. On the other hand, it makes us connect our ideas; so it is the occasion for memory. Thence we have analysis, and from it reminiscence is formed, which gives rise to imagination (I take this word here in the sense I have given it).

It is by means of reflection that we gain control of imagination, and the exercise of memory is not within our power until a long time after we have gained mastery of our imagination; and these two operations produce the act of conceiving.

The understanding differs from the imagination as the operation that consists in conceiving differs from analysis. As for the operations that consist in distinguishing, comparing, compounding, decompounding, judging, reasoning, they are born one from the other, and they are the immediate effects of imagination and memory. That is the generation of the operations of the soul.

It is important to have a good grasp of all these things, and especially to observe the operations that form the understanding (it is plain that I do not take this word in the same sense as other people do), and to distinguish it from those it produces. All the rest of this work is based on that distinction: it is the foundation of it. For those who do not grasp it, everything will be confused.

> perception, consciousness, reminiscence, attention, and imagination, and we must even suppose that we are not at all masters of the exercise of the last two. Up to that point we do not yet have knowledge, but we have all the materials from which it can be formed and of which the operations that follow later cannot form a part, for it is those latter operations that make use of those materials.
>
> "It is appropriate to interrupt our preoccupation with the operations of the soul in order to say a word about the division of ideas into simple and complex. Perhaps some will feel that this is where I should have begun, but they will change their mind when they see that I needed the second section to have the requisite examples for the third section."

Section 3
Simple and complex ideas

§1 A complex idea is the union or the collection of several perceptions; a simple idea is a perception considered distinct by itself.

> Though the qualities that affect our senses (says Locke [E 2.2.1])
> are so firmly united and so well blended together in the things
> themselves that there is no separation or distance between them, it
> is nonetheless certain that the ideas which these different qualities
> produce in the mind enter it by the senses in a manner that is
> simple and without any blending. For though sight and touch do
> often at the same time excite different ideas from the same object,
> as when someone sees motion and color simultaneously or when
> the hand feels the softness and warmth in a piece of wax, the
> simple ideas which are thus united in the same subject are as
> perfectly distinct as those that enter the mind by different senses.
> The coldness and hardness that we feel in a piece of ice are ideas
> that are just as distinct in the mind as the smell and whiteness of a
> lily or as the taste of sugar and the smell of a rose; nothing can be
> more evident to any man than the clear and distinct perception he
> has of those simple ideas, of which each taken separately is
> altogether uncompounded, consequently producing nothing in the
> mind but an entirely uniform conception that is not distinguish-
> able into different ideas.

Though our perceptions may have more or less vivacity, it would be a mistake to imagine that each is composed of several others. If you were to mix colors together that differed only by their degree of brightness, they would still produce only a single perception.

It is true that we regard perceptions that are closely interrelated as

71

different degrees of the same perception. But that is because we have been obliged, for lack of having as many names as perceptions, to assign the latter to certain categories. Taken separately they are all simple. How can we, for example, decompose the perception caused by the whiteness of snow? Should we distinguish several other whitenesses of which it is formed?

§2 From the point of view of their origin, all the operations of the mind are equally simple, for each is then a mere perception. But afterwards they combine in order to act together, thus forming compound operations. That becomes evident in what we call "penetration," "discernment," "sagacity," etc.

§3 In addition to the ideas that are really simple, a collection of several perceptions is often considered to be simple when it is related to a larger collection of which it forms a part. In fact, there is no notion, however compound it may be, that cannot be considered simple by attaching the idea of unity to it.

§4 Among complex ideas, some are compounded of different perceptions, such as that of body. Others are compounded of uniform perceptions, or rather they are merely the same perception repeated several times. Sometimes the number is indeterminate, such as the abstract idea of extension; sometimes it is determinate, as a foot is the perception of an inch repeated twelve times.

§5 With regard to the notions that are formed from different perceptions, there are two kinds: those of substances and those that are compounded of simple ideas that relate to different human actions. For the first to be useful, they must be based on the model of substances so as to represent only the properties that they have. We treat the others very differently. It is often important to form them before we have seen any examples, and in addition these examples would generally be too vague to serve as a model. Formed in that manner, a notion of virtue or justice would vary according as particular cases admitted or rejected certain circumstances; and the confusion could go so far that we could no longer distinguish justice from injustice, a familiar error with philosophers. All we can do is to choose to collect several simple ideas and, once formed, to take these collections as the model for our judgment of things. Such are the ideas attached to the words "glory," "honor," "courage." I call them "archetypal ideas," a term modern metaphysicians have made current.

§6 Since simple ideas are only our own perceptions, there is no other means of knowing them than reflecting on what we experience at the sight of objects.

§7 The same is true of those complex ideas that are only an indeterminate repetition of the same perception. To form the abstract idea of extension, for example, it is enough to consider the perception of extension, without considering any part as being repeated a certain number of times.

§8 Since I am looking at ideas only in regard to the manner in which we come to know them, I will make a single class of these two kinds. Thus when I speak of complex ideas, I am speaking of those that are formed from different perceptions or from repeating the same perception in a determinate manner.

§9 Taken in the limited sense I have just outlined, complex ideas cannot be known well without analyzing them: that is, we must reduce them to the simple ideas they are made from and follow their generation. This is how we have formed the notion of the understanding. Hitherto no philosopher has realized that this method could be practiced in metaphysics. The means they have used to make up for this lack have only increased the confusion and multiplied the disputes.

§10 From this we can infer the uselessness of definitions in which the intention is to explain the properties of something by genus and species. In the first place, this practice is impossible in regard to simple ideas, as Locke has shown [E 3.4], and it is astonishing that he is the first to have made that observation. It is easy to imagine the confusion that reigned before his time in the writings of philosophers who did not distinguish ideas that required definition from those that did not. The Cartesians were well aware that some ideas are much clearer than any definitions we can give them, but they did not know why that was the case, obvious as it would seem to be. Thus they spend much effort on defining simple ideas, while they consider it pointless to define some that are very complex. This shows how difficult it is to take even the smallest step in philosophy.

In the second place, definitions are ill suited to give an exact notion of things that are somewhat complex. The best of them are not even as good as an imperfect analysis. That is because something gratuitous enters into the process, or at least we have no rule to prevent it. In analysis we are obliged to follow the very generation of the thing. Thus when analysis is well done, it will invariably reconcile opinions and put an end to disputes.

§11 Though the geometricians have known this method, they are not beyond blame. They have sometimes failed to find the true generation of things, even on occasions when it was not difficult to do so. Of this we have proof at the very beginning of geometry.

After saying that a point is "that which terminates itself on all sides," "that which has no other bounds than itself," or "that which has neither length, breadth, nor depth," they make it move in order to generate the line. Next they move the line in order to generate the surface, and the surface to make a solid.

I observe first that here they fall into the same mistake as the philosophers by trying to define what is very simple, a mistake which follows from the method of synthesis to which they are so strongly wedded, with its demand that everything must be defined.

Secondly, the word "bounds" so obviously proclaims a relation to something extended that it is impossible to imagine something that terminates itself on all sides, or that has no other bounds than itself. Furthermore, the privation of all length, breadth, and depth is a notion that is too difficult to begin with.

Thirdly, we cannot represent to ourselves the movement of a point without extension, and even less the trace it is supposed to leave behind in producing the line. As for the line, we can conceive its movement according to the determination of its length, but not according to the determination that is said to produce the surface, for then it is in the same situation as the point. The same can be said about the surface being moved to create the solid.

§12 It is easy to see that the geometricians wished to accommodate themselves to the generation of things and of ideas, but they did not succeed.

We cannot have the use of our senses without immediately having the idea of extension with all its dimensions. The idea of the solid is therefore one of the first they give us. Now, take a solid and consider one extremity of it without thinking of its depth, and you will have the idea of a surface or of extension in length and breadth without depth. For your reflection is only the idea of the thing it is occupied with.

Then take this surface and think of its length without thinking of its breadth, and you will have the idea of a line, or of extension in length without breadth or depth.

If you follow this example, you will find it easy to form the ideas of point, line, and surface. It is evident that it all depends on the study of experience in order to explain the generation of ideas in the same order in which they are formed. This method is especially indispensable when we are dealing with abstract ideas; it is the only way they can be explained with perspicuity.

§13 We can note two essential differences between simple ideas and complex ideas. (1) The mind is entirely passive in the production of the former; it cannot form the idea of a color it has never seen. With the latter, on the contrary, it is active. It is the mind that unites simple ideas from some pattern or by its own choice: in a word, they are wholly the product of experience and reflection combined. More precisely, I call them "notions." (2) We have no measure to determine the quantitative difference of one simple idea compared with another, the reason being that we cannot divide them. The same is not true of complex ideas; we know, with minute precision, the difference between two numbers, because their common measure, the unit, is always the same. We can even count the simple ideas of complex notions, which, since they have been formed from different perceptions, cannot be measured by anything as precise as the unit. If there are any relations that cannot be rated, it will be true only of those between simple ideas. For example, we know exactly how many more ideas we attach to the word "gold" than to the word "tombac," but we cannot measure the color difference of these two metals, because the perception of color is simple and indivisible.

§14 Simple and complex ideas agree in this, that they can equally be considered absolute or relative. They are absolute when we fix our attention on them by making them the object of reflection, without relating them to other ideas; but when we consider some to be subordinate to others, we call them relative.

§15 Mixed modes have two advantages: the first is that they are adequate; they are fixed patterns of which the mind can acquire such perfect knowledge that nothing remains to be discovered. That is obvious because these notions cannot contain any other simple ideas than those the mind itself has put together. The second advantage follows from the first; it consists in this, that all the relations between them can be perceived, for, knowing all the simple ideas from which they are formed, we can make every possible analysis of them.

But the notions of substances do not have the same advantage. They are unavoidably inadequate, because we relate them to patterns in which we can always discover new properties. Consequently, we cannot know all the relations that exist between two substances. If it is praiseworthy to try to increase our knowledge in this regard little by little by experience, it is ridiculous to flatter ourselves that we can one day make it perfect.

And yet we must not forget that this knowledge is not obscure or confused, as some people imagine; it is only limited. It is our job to speak of substances with the utmost precision, provided that we do not include in our ideas and expressions anything except what we learn by steady observation.

§16 The synonymous words "thought," "operation," "perception," "sensation," "consciousness," "idea," "notion" are so widely used in metaphysics that it is essential to distinguish among them. I call "thought" everything the mind experiences, whether it be outward impressions or its reflection on itself; "operation," thought insofar as it can cause a change in the mind and by this means enlighten and guide it; "perception," the impression produced in us in the presence of objects; "sensation," this same impression insofar as it comes by sense; "consciousness," the notice we take of it; "idea," the notice we take of it as an image; "notion," any idea that is of our own making – these are the senses in which I use those words. They cannot be taken indiscriminately one for the other, except when we need only the principal idea they signify. We can indiscriminately call simple ideas perceptions or ideas; but we must not call them notions, for they are not made by the mind. We must not say the "notion of white," but the "perception of white." Notions in turn can be considered as images, and they can consequently be called "ideas," but never "perceptions." That would be saying that they are not made by us. We can say the "notion of boldness," but not the "perception of boldness," or if we wish to use this term we should say the "perceptions that compose the notion of boldness." In a word, since we are not conscious of the impressions that occur in the mind except as something simple and indivisible, the name "perception" ought to be reserved for simple ideas, or at least those we regard as such in relation to more complex notions.

I have one more remark to make on the words "idea" and "notion." It is that, as the former signifies a perception considered as image and the latter an idea the mind itself has made, ideas and notions can belong only to beings capable of reflection. As for other beings, such as animals, they have only sensations and perceptions. What for them is merely perception becomes for us an idea by the reflection we make that this perception represents something.

Section 4

1 The operation by which we give signs to our ideas

This operation is the result of the imagination, which presents signs to the mind as yet ignorant of their use, and of the attention which links them to ideas. This operation is one of the most essential in the search for truth, though it is among the least known. I have already shown the use and necessity of signs for the exercise of the operations of the mind. I shall now demonstrate the same thing with regard to the different kinds of ideas; this is a truth that cannot be presented from too many different points of view.

§1 Arithmetic is the most evident example of the necessity of signs. It would be impossible to make any progress in the knowledge of numbers if, after giving a name to the concept of unity, we did not successively keep unity in mind for all the ideas we form by the multiplication of this first one. We discern different collections only because we have digits that are themselves very distinct. Take away these digits, abolish the use of signs, and we will discover that it is impossible to preserve the ideas. Can we even have a notion of the smallest number without considering several objects each of which is, as it were, the sign to which we attach the unit? As for myself, I do not perceive the numbers "two" and "three" unless I represent for myself two or three different objects. When I go to the number "four," I am obliged for the sake of greater perspicuity to image two objects on one side and two on the other; for the number "six" I cannot get around distributing them two by two, or three by three. And if I wish to proceed, I will soon have to consider several unities as a single one and to unite them to this end in a single object.

§2 Locke [E 2.16.6][24] tells us of some American Indians who had no ideas of the number one thousand because they had imagined names only for counting to twenty. I may add that they would have had some difficulty forming an idea of the number twenty-one, for the following reason.

By the nature of the way in which we calculate, it would be sufficient to have ideas of the first numbers to be in a position to form any one of all those that can be determined. The reason is that once we have the first signs, we have rules for inventing others. Those who might be ignorant of this method, to the point of being obliged to attach each collection to signs that bore no analogy to one another, would have no means of guidance in the invention of signs. Therefore they would not have the same skill in making new ideas that we have. That was probably the situation of those American Indians. Thus, not only did they not have any ideas of the number one thousand, but they would even find it difficult to form any number above twenty with any readiness.[25]

§3 We see, then, that our progress in the knowledge of numbers relies entirely on the precision with which we add unity to itself by giving each forward step a name that distinguishes it from the one before and after. I know that one hundred is superior by one unit to ninety-nine, and inferior to one hundred and one, because I remember that those are the three signs I have chosen to designate three consecutive numbers.

§4 It would be an illusion to imagine that the ideas of numbers separated from their signs can be clear and determinate.[26] Only the name to which they are attached can combine several units in the mind. If someone asks me what the number one thousand is, what can I say if not that this word fixes a certain collection of units in my mind? If he questions me further on this collection, it is evident that it is impossible for me to make him understand what it is in all its parts. All I can do is to present to him successively all the names that have been invented to

---

[24] He says that he spoke with them.

[25] There can be no doubt about what I am arguing here after La Condamine's account. He speaks (p. 67) of a tribe that has no other sign for the expression of the number three but this one, "poellarrarorincourac." Having begun in this highly inconvenient manner, it was not easy for them to count further. We should not find it difficult to understand that those were, as we are assured, the limits of their arithmetic. [Charles-Marie de La Condamine, *Relation abrégée d'un voyage fait dans l'intérieur de l'Amérique méridionale* (Paris, 1745).]

[26] Malebranche believed that the numbers that are perceived by the "pure understanding" are something very superior to those that fall under the senses. St. Augustine (in his *Confessions*, Bk. 10, Ch. 12), the Platonists, and all the partisans of innate ideas have shared this prejudice.

signify the steps that lead up to it. I must teach him to join one unit to another, and to join them by the name "two"; then a third to the preceding and to attach the sign "three" to the combination, and so on. By this procedure, which is the only way, I will lead him from number to number up to one thousand.

If we next ask what will be clear in his mind, we find three things: the idea of unity, the idea of the operation by which he has several times added the unit to itself, and finally the memory of having imagined the sign "thousand" after the signs "nine hundred ninety-nine" and "nine hundred ninety-eight," etc. It is surely not by the idea of unity or by the operation of multiplying it that this number has been determined; for these things are equally found in all the other collections. But since the sign "thousand" belongs exclusively to this collection, it alone determines and distinguishes it.

§5 Thus there can be no doubt that if someone wanted to calculate privately in his own mind, he would be obliged to invent signs as if he intended to communicate his calculations. But why would what is true in arithmetic not be equally true in the other sciences? Would we ever be able to reflect in metaphysics and moral philosophy if we had not invented signs to fix our ideas all along as we formed new collections? Should not words in all the sciences be to ideas what numerals are to ideas in arithmetic? It is likely that ignorance of this truth is one of the causes of the confusion that reigns in works on metaphysics and moral philosophy. To treat this subject in an orderly fashion, we must briefly take a look at all the ideas that can be the object of our reflection.

§6 It seems to me that nothing needs to be added to what I have said about simple ideas. It is certain that we often reflect on our perceptions without recalling anything but their names or the circumstances in which we have had those perceptions. It is only by the connection with these signs that the imagination can revive them at will.

The mind is so limited that it cannot recall a large quantity of ideas so as to make them the object of reflection all at the same time. Nevertheless the mind must often consider several of them together. It does that with the help of signs which, by uniting them, makes it possible for it to regard them as if they were a single idea.

§7 There are two situations in which we collect simple ideas under a single sign: we collect them according to patterns or without patterns.

Coming upon a body, I see that it is extended, has a shape, is divisible, solid, hard, capable of motion and rest, yellow, fusible, ductile, malleable, very heavy, non-volatile, and is soluble in "aqua regia," etc. It is certain that if I cannot all at once communicate an idea of all these qualities to someone else, I cannot recall them myself except by letting them pass in review before my mind. But if, not being able to embrace all of them simultaneously, I wanted to think of just one of the qualities, say its color, the idea would be so inadequate as to be useless and would often make me confuse this body with those that resemble it in this regard. To overcome this difficulty, I invent the word "gold," and I accustom myself to connect it with all the ideas I enumerated. When I afterwards think of the notion of gold, I perceive only this sound "gold" and the memory of having it with a certain quantity of simple ideas, which I would not be able to recall all at once, but which I have found to coexist in the same object and which I can recall one after the other when I wish to do so.

We cannot therefore reflect on substances unless we have signs that determine the number and variety of properties we have observed in them and which we choose to unite in complex ideas, as they are outside us in the objects. If, for a moment forgetting all these signs, we try to recall the ideas, we will find that words, or other signs like them, are so necessary that in the mind they take the place, as it were, which the objects occupy outside us. As the qualities of things do not coexist outside us without the objects in which they are united, their ideas would not coexist in the mind without the signs in which they are likewise united.

§8 The necessity of signs is even more obvious in the complex ideas we form without patterns. When we have assembled ideas which we nowhere see united, as is commonly the case with mixed modes, what is it that can hold the collections together if we do not connect them with words, which are, so to speak, like bonds that prevent them from coming apart? If you think you do not need words, pull them out of your memory and try to reflect on civil and moral laws, on virtues and vices, in short on all human actions, and you will see how mistaken you were. You will admit that you cannot take a single step without finding yourself in a state of chaos, if you do not have signs to determine the number of simple ideas you have collected together. You would face the same difficulty as someone who would try to calculate by several times repeating one, one, one without imagining signs for each collection.

This man would never be able to form the idea of twenty, because nothing could give him assurance that he had exactly repeated all the units.

§9 Let us conclude that in order to have ideas on which we may be able to reflect, we need to imagine signs that function as bonds for the different collections of simple ideas, and that our notions are not exact except insofar as we have, in an orderly fashion, invented signs that can fix them.

§10 This truth will make all those who are willing to reflect on themselves recognize how much the number of words we have in our memory exceeds that of our ideas. That will naturally be so, in part because, with reflection coming after memory, it has not always reviewed with sufficient care the ideas to which signs have been given, and in part because we find that there is a great interval between the time we begin to cultivate the memory of a child by engraving on it many words which the child is as yet unable to take in, and the time when the child begins to be capable of analyzing his notions in order to give some account of them. When this operation ensues, it finds itself too slow to follow memory, which long exercise has made quick and agile. Just think how laborious it would be if it were necessary for this operation to examine all its signs! We therefore use them as they present themselves, and we are generally satisfied by pretty much getting their meaning. It follows that, of all the operations, analysis is the one whose usage we know the least about. Lots of people never have any idea of it! Experience alone shows that its exercise is the less in proportion as that of memory and imagination is the greater. Let us therefore repeat: anyone who looks into himself will find a large number of signs which he has only connected with very imperfect ideas, and even some to which he has connected none at all. That is the source of the chaos that prevails in the abstract sciences, a chaos the philosophers have never been able to clear up because none of them has known the first cause. Locke is the only one for whom one can make some exception.

§11 This truth also shows the simplicity and wonder of the springs of knowledge. Given a human mind with sensations and operations, how will it gain control of these materials? By gestures, sounds, numerals, letters – it is with instruments so foreign to our ideas that we put them to work to raise ourselves to the most sublime knowledge. The materials are the same in all human beings, but their agility in the use of signs varies, which causes the inequality we find among them.[m]

If you deprive a superior mind of the use of written signs, he will be blocked from access to much knowledge that a mediocre mind would attain with ease. Deprive him, furthermore, of speech, and the fate of those who are mute will show you the narrow bounds in which he has been enclosed. Finally, deprive him of the use of any sort of signs so that he will not even be able to use the smallest gesture to express the most common thoughts – then all you will have left is an imbecile.

§12 It is desirable that those who have charge of the education of children should not be ignorant of the first springs of the human mind. If a teacher who perfectly knew the origin and progress of our ideas talked to his pupil only about things that are closely related to the pupil's needs and to his age; if he had the skill to place him in the circumstances that will best teach him to make his ideas precise and to give them the stability of lasting signs; if even in playful talk he never in his discourse used words other than those whose sense is precisely determined – just think of the clarity and scope he would give to the mind of his pupil! But how few are the parents who can produce such teachers for their children, and how rarer still the teachers who would be qualified to meet those expectations! Still, it is useful to know everything that can contribute to a good education. If we cannot always put it into practice, we might at least avoid what is directly contrary to it. One should never, for example, entangle children in paralogisms, sophisms, or other forms of bad reasoning. If we allow such chatter, we run the risk of making the mind confused or even untrue to its nature. It is only after their understanding has acquired a large measure of clarity and accuracy that we might entertain them with specious discourse in order to train their good judgment. I would even suggest that we should take great care to prevent bad consequences. But reflections on this subject would lead me too far away from my subject. In the following chapter I will give facts that confirm what I believe I have demonstrated in this chapter. It will give me the opportunity to develop my thoughts more fully.

---

[m] Could this remark about inequality having its source in the more or less effective use of signs have been the occasion for the prize topic set by the Dijon Academy in November 1753, "What is the origin of inequality among men, and is it authorized by natural law?" This was of course the subject of Rousseau's Second Discourse, which in the discussion of the early stages of speech refers to Condillac.

2 Facts that confirm what was proved in the previous chapter

§13 At Chartres a young man of twenty-three or twenty-four, the son of an artisan and deaf-mute from birth, suddenly began to talk, to the astonishment of the entire town. It was known that three or four months earlier he had heard the sound of bells and been extremely surprised by this new and unknown experience. Afterwards something like water issued from his left ear, and he then heard perfectly with both ears. During the next three or four months he was listening without saying a word, making it a habit to repeat very softly all the words he heard and strengthening his command of pronunciation and of the ideas connected with words. At long last he was prepared to break the silence, and he made known that he spoke, though as yet only imperfectly. Good theologians immediately began to interrogate him on his past state, with questions chiefly about God, the soul, and on the moral good and evil of human actions. He did not seem to have carried his thoughts that far. Though his parents were Catholic, though he attended mass, was instructed in making the sign of the cross, and in kneeling in the posture of a person at prayer, he had never joined any intention to all those actions nor understood what others connected with them. He barely knew what death was, and he never thought about it. He led a mere animal life, wholly occupied with sensible and present objects and the few ideas he received by the eyes. From these ideas he did not even draw what he would have seemed able to draw from them. It is not that he did not naturally have a mind, but the mind of a person who is deprived of human intercourse is so little exercised and cultivated that he does not think except when he is absolutely forced to do so by external objects. The principal fund of the ideas of mankind is their mutual converse.

§14 These facts are reported in the memoirs of the academy [for the year 1703].[n] It would have been desirable to interrogate this young man on the few ideas he had when he was without the use of speech, on the first ideas he acquired after he became able to hear; on what assistance he received either from external objects, from what he heard people say, or from his own reflection, toward the formation of new ideas: in a word, on everything that might offer the mind the opportunity to form

[n] Condillac is reproducing verbatim the text printed in *Histoire de l'Académie des Sciences, avec les mémoires de mathématique et de physique* (Paris, 1705), pp. 18–19.

itself. Experience acts on us so early that it is not surprising we often mistake it for nature itself. By contrast, here it acted so late that it would have been easy not to make that mistake. But the theologians were eager to know what was given by nature, with the result that, in spite of their cleverness, they gained no knowledge either of experience or of nature. We have no remedy for that except conjectures.

§15 I imagine that for twenty-three years this young man was pretty much in the same condition in which I have described the soul, which, before it has command of its attention, gives it to objects not by choice but as it is impelled by the force with which they act on it. It is true that, growing up in society, he received some assistance that made him connect some of his ideas to signs. He no doubt knew how to use gestures to communicate his principal needs and the things that could satisfy them. But since he lacked words to indicate the things that were not so urgent for him, had little inducement to supply them by other means, and received no external assistance, he never thought about them except when he had an actual perception. Since his attention was entirely absorbed by the sensations of the moment, it ceased with those sensations. So he did not have the exercise of contemplation and even less that of memory.

§16 Sometimes our consciousness, when divided among a large number of perceptions that act on it with nearly equal force, is so feeble that we have no memory of what we have felt. In such moments we barely feel that we exist; days run by like moments, leaving no difference between them behind, and we may feel the same perception a thousand times without noting that we have already had it. A man who by the use of signs has acquired many ideas and made himself familiar with them, cannot for long remain in such a state of lethargy. The greater his fund of ideas, the more likely it is that one of them will have occasion to come alive, to exercise his attention, and to draw him out of this sleepy state. Consequently, the fewer the ideas, the more common the lethargy. You can judge for yourself whether this young man could often use his attention, reminiscence, and reflection during the twenty-three years he was deaf and mute.

§17 If the exercise of these first operations were so limited, that of the others would have been even more limited. Incapable of fixing and determining with any precision the ideas he received by the senses, he could not make notions of his own by composition and decomposition.

Having no ideas that were sufficiently suitable for the comparison of his most familiar ideas, he rarely formed any judgment. It is even likely that during the course of the first twenty-three years of his life he did not make a single judgment. Reasoning consists in making judgments and connecting them by noticing their interdependence. But this young man would not be able to do that so long as he did not have the use of conjunctions and particles that express the relations of different parts of the discourse. It was natural, therefore, *that he did not draw all the use it seems he might have from the comparison of his ideas*. Having for its object only lively or fresh sensations, his reflection had no influence on the greater part of his actions and very little on the rest. His conduct was entirely determined by habit and imitation, especially in regard to things that bore little relation to his needs. Thus, while doing what the piety of his parents required of him, he had never thought they might have a motive and was ignorant that it should be accompanied by intention. It is even possible that the imitation was the more precise because it was unaccompanied by any reflection, for distractions would be less frequent in a person who has little capacity for reflection.

§18 It would seem that to know what life is, it is sufficient to exist and to feel. Still, at the risk of advancing a paradox, I would say that this young man hardly had any idea what life is. For beings who reflect like ourselves, it is true that in moments when we merely vegetate though we are awake, our sensations are mere sensations and become ideas only when reflection causes us to consider them as images of something. It is true that they guided the young man in his search for what was useful for his preservation and kept him away from what might harm him; but he followed their impression without reflecting on what might preserve or harm him. One test of the truth of what I am advancing is that he did not know very distinctly what death is. If he had known what life is, would he not have seen as clearly as we do that death is merely the privation of life?[27]

§19 In this young man we see a few feeble traces of the operations of the mind, but if we except perception, consciousness, attention, remi-

---

[27] Death can also be understood as the passage from this life into another. But that is not the sense in which it must be understood here. With Fontenelle having said that this young man had no idea either of God or the soul, it is evident that he did not have any idea of death either, understood as the passage from this life into another.

niscence, and imagination before any one of them is at our command, we would not find any vestige of operations beyond that in someone who has been deprived of all social intercourse and who, with sound and well-constituted organs, had, for instance, grown up among bears. Virtually without reminiscence, he would often be in the same state without knowing he had been in it. Without memory, he would not have any sign to remedy the absence of things. Having only an imagination he had no control over, his perceptions would not come alive except if by chance he was confronted by an object with which some circumstances had connected them; in a word, without reflection he would receive the impressions which the objects make on the senses, but would obey them only by instinct. He would imitate the bears in all respects, would make a cry similar to theirs, and crawl on feet and hands. We are so strongly prompted to imitate that perhaps even a Descartes in the same situation would not try to walk only on his feet.

§20 But wait, someone will say, would the necessity of providing for his needs and satisfying his passions not be sufficient to develop all the operations of his mind?

I answer no; for so long as he lived without any social intercourse, he would not have occasion to connect his ideas with arbitrary signs. He would be without memory; consequently he would have no command of his imagination, with the result that he would be entirely incapable of reflection.

§21 His imagination would, however, have one advantage over ours; it would revive things in a much livelier manner. For us it is so convenient to revive our ideas with the help of memory that our imagination is rarely exercised. In him, by contrast, with this operation taking the place of all the others, the exercise of the imagination will be as frequent as his needs, and it will revive the perceptions with greater force. That is confirmed, by example, by the blind, who usually have a more acute sense of touch than we do; the same reason can be applied in both cases.

§22 But this young man cannot himself make use of the operations of his mind. To understand why, let us consider in what circumstances they could undergo some exercise.

Let us imagine that a monster, which he has seen devouring other animals or been taught to flee by his companions, approaches him: the sight would capture his attention, revive sentiments of fright, and induce him to flee. He escapes from this enemy, but the trembling that agitates his entire body preserves for a while the present idea in him; so there he has contemplation; a moment later chance brings him back to the same place, the idea of the place revives that of the monster with which it has been connected, and that is imagination; finally, since he recognizes himself to be the same being who had already been in that place, he also has reminiscence. This example tells us that the exercise of the operations of the mind depends on a certain concurrence of circumstances that affect it in a particular manner and that the exercise will consequently cease as soon as the circumstances are no longer there. When this man's fright is over, if we suppose that he does not return to the same place at all or does so only after the idea will no longer be connected with the monster, nothing could have the effect of making him remember what he has seen. We can revive our ideas only insofar as they are connected with some signs: but his are connected only to the circumstances that have given birth to them. On this depends the exercise of the operations of his mind. Let me repeat, he does not have the power to conduct them by himself. He can only obey the impression that objects make on him, and we should not expect that he can show any sign of reason.

§23 I am not advancing mere conjectures. In the forests between Russia and Lithuania a boy of about ten, who lived among the bears, was found in 1694. He gave no sign of reason, walked on hands and feet, had no language, and formed sounds that had nothing in common with human sounds. It took a long time before he could utter a few words, which he still did in a very barbarous manner. As soon as he could speak, he was asked about his former state. But he could not remember any more than we can recall what happened to us in the cradle.[28]

§24 This fact perfectly proves what I have said about the progress of the operations of the mind. It was easy to predict that this child would not remember his former state. He would have some memory of it in the moment he was found; but this memory, being uniquely produced by a rare act of attention and never strengthened by reflection, was so feeble that its traces vanished during the interval between the moment he began to make ideas for himself and the moment the questioning began.

---

[28] Connor in *Evang. Med.*, art. 15, pp. 133 et seq. [Bernard Connor, *Evangelium medici: seu medicina mystica de suspensis naturae legibus sive de miraculis* (Amsterdam, 1699; also London, 1697)].

In order to exhaust all the hypotheses, if we suppose that he would still have remembered the time he lived in the forests, he would never be able to represent that time to himself except by the perceptions he could call to mind. These perceptions would be very few in number. Not remembering those that had preceded, followed, and interrupted them, he would not be able to recollect the succession of the parts of time. From this it follows that he would never have suspected that the succession would have had a beginning; and that he would, all the same, have considered it only as an instant. In a word, his confused memory of his former state would have reduced him to the absurdity of imagining himself to have always existed and to be unable to conceive of his pretended eternity except as a moment. Therefore I have no doubt that he would have been very surprised if he were told that his existence had a beginning and even more surprised if it were added that he had passed through several stages of growth. Since he was incapable of reflection up to that time, he would never have taken note of such insensible changes, and he would naturally have become inclined to believe that he had always existed in the state in which he found himself the moment he was first induced to reflect on himself.

§25 The illustrious secretary of the academy of sciences [*Fontenelle] has very aptly remarked that the principal stock of the ideas of mankind is derived from their mutual dealings with one another. The further discussion of this truth will complete the confirmation of all I have been saying.

I have distinguished three kinds of signs: accidental signs, natural signs, and instituted signs. A child raised among bears has only the use of the first. It is true we cannot deprive him of the cries that are natural to each passion; but how would he suspect that they are suited to become signs of the sentiments he feels? If he lived among other people he would so often hear them utter cries similar to his own that sooner or later he would connect these cries with the sentiments they are intended to express. The bears cannot offer him the same occasions; their roar does not have sufficient analogy with the human voice. In their own intercourse, the animals probably connect their cries with the perceptions of which they are the signs, but this is what this child did not know how to do. Thus, to conduct themselves by the impression of natural cries, the animals have resources which he cannot have; and it would seem that attention, reminiscence, and imagination gain more exercise in them than in him, but that is the limit of all the operations of the soul of animals.[29]

Since human beings cannot make signs for themselves except when living together, it follows that the fund of their ideas, when their mind begins to be formed, consists entirely in their mutual intercourse. I say "when their mind begins to be formed" because it is evident that when it has made some progress, it knows the art of making signs and can acquire ideas without any external help.

It is pointless to object that before this social converse, the mind already had ideas because it has perceptions, for perceptions that have never been the object of reflection are not properly speaking ideas. They are merely impressions that have been made on the mind which cannot become ideas until they have been considered as images.

§26 It seems to me that it is unnecessary to add anything either to these examples or to the explications I have given of them; they confirm very clearly that the operations of the mind develop more or less in proportion to the use of signs.

There is a difficulty, however: if our mind fixes its ideas only by signs, our reasonings run the risk of turning often merely on words, a fact that would draw us into many errors.

I answer that the certainty of mathematics removes this difficulty. Provided that we determine the simple ideas connected with each sign so precisely that we can analyze them when required, we need not be afraid of fooling ourselves any more than the mathematicians when they make use of their numerals. Indeed, this objection shows that we must conduct ourselves with much caution not to get entangled, like the philosophers, in disputes over words and in empty and puerile questions. But in saying that, the objection merely confirms what I have been saying.

§27 We see here how slowly the mind rises to knowledge of the truth. Locke has provided a curious example of that.

Though the necessity of signs for the ideas of numbers has not escaped him, he still does not talk about it as a person who is confident

---

[29] Locke (E 2.11.10–11) rightly remarks that animals do not form abstractions. Consequently, he denies that they are capable of reasoning about general ideas; but he takes it to be evident that on certain occasions they reason about particular ideas. If this philosopher had seen that we cannot reflect unless we have the use of instituted signs, he would have recognized that animals are absolutely incapable of reasoning, and that consequently their actions, when they appear rational, are merely the effect of an imagination that is not at their command.

of what he says. He says that without the signs by which we distinguish each collection of units, we can hardly make use of numbers, especially where the combinations are made up of many units [E 2.16.5].

He has understood that names are necessary for mixed modes, but he does not grasp the true reason. "The mind," he says, "having made the connection between the loose parts of those complex ideas, this union, which has no particular foundation in nature, would cease again, were there not something that did, as it were, hold it together" [E 3.5.10]. This reasoning would, as it did, prevent him from seeing the necessity of signs for the notions of substances; for since these notions do have a foundation in nature, it followed that the collection of their simple ideas would be preserved in the mind without the assistance of words.

It takes very little to stop the greatest geniuses in their progress. As we see here, all it takes is a small stumble at the very moment when they are defending the truth. That is what prevented Locke from discovering the great importance of signs for the exercise of the operations of mind. He imagines that the mind makes mental propositions in which it joins or separates ideas without the intervention of words [E 4.5.3–5]. He even claims that the best way to knowledge is to consider ideas in themselves, but he notes that we rarely do that, because the habit of using sounds for ideas has come to prevail among us [E 4.6.1]. After what I have said, I do not need to take the time to show how inaccurate all that is.

Wolff has observed that it is very difficult for reason to have any exercise in a person who does not have the use of instituted signs. As evidence he gives the two cases that I have cited [*Psychol. Ration.*, §461],° but he does not explain them. Furthermore, he did not know the absolute necessity of signs any more than the manner in which they contribute to the progress of the operations of the mind.

With regard to the followers of Descartes and Malebranche, they were as far removed as one can possibly be from making this discovery. How can anyone suspect the necessity of signs if with Descartes he believes that ideas are innate or with Malebranche that we see all things in God?

° Christian Wolff, *Psychologia rationalis methodo scientifico pertractata* (Frankfurt and Leipzig, 1740), ed. Jean École (Hildesheim, Olms, 1972). In §461 (pp. 376–81) the cases of both boys are cited to show "the dependence of the use of reason on the use of speech."

Section 5
Abstractions

§1 We have seen that abstract notions are formed by ceasing to think of the properties by which things are distinguished in favor of thinking only of the qualities in which they agree. Once we stop considering what makes something extended to be such, or a whole to be such, we will have the abstract ideas of extension and of a whole.[30]

Thus ideas of this kind are merely denominations that we give to things when we consider them in light of their resemblance; that is why they are called "general ideas." But it is not sufficient to know their origin; there are also important considerations that bear on their indispensability and on the disadvantages that surround them.

§2 General ideas are without doubt absolutely indispensable. Since people are obliged to talk about things as being either different or alike, it became necessary to refer things to classes that were distinguished by signs. By this means they comprise in a single word what could not without confusion have been contained in a long discourse. There are evident examples in the use we make of such terms as "substance,"

---

[30] Here is how Locke explains the progress of ideas of this kind. He says: "The ideas that children form of the persons they converse with are only particular like the persons themselves. The ideas they have of their mother and their nurse are well framed in their minds and represent only those individuals, like so many true pictures. The names they first give them are confined to those individuals: thus the names 'nurse' and 'mama' used by children refer to those persons alone. Afterwards when time and a larger knowledge of the world has made them observe that there are a great many other beings which in some common agreement in shape and several other qualities resemble their father, their mother, and other persons with whom they are familiar, they form an idea which they find is equally shared by all those beings and to that they give, with others, the name 'man.' Thus they come to have a general name and a general idea. In doing so they make nothing new but only leave out of the complex idea they had of Peter, James, Mary, and Elizabeth what is particular to each, retaining only what is common to all" [E 3.3.7].

"mind," "body," "animal." If we wish to speak of things merely as in each of them we see a subject that supports its properties and modes, all we need is the word "substance." If we intend to indicate more particularly the kind of properties or modes, we use either the word "mind" or the word "body." If by uniting these two ideas we plan to talk of a living entity that moves of itself and by instinct, we have the word "animal." Finally, as to this last notion we add the ideas that distinguish the different species of animals, usage generally supplies us with the right terms for expressing our thought with brevity.

§3 But we must note that it is less by reference to the nature of things than to our manner of knowing them that we determine the genera and species, or, to speak a more familiar language, that we distribute them in classes by subordination of some to others. If our vision was powerful enough to discover a much larger number of properties in objects, we would soon perceive differences between those that seemed most similar, and we would consequently be able to subdivide them into new classes. Though different pieces of the same metal are, for example, similar in regard to the qualities we recognize in them, it does not follow that they are so in regard to the qualities we do not yet know. If we could make the latter analysis, perhaps we would find as many differences between them as we now find between different kinds of metals.

§4 What makes general ideas so indispensable is the limitation of our mind. God does not need them; His infinite knowledge comprehends all individual things, and it is no more difficult for Him to think of all of them at once than to think of a single one. For us the capacity of the mind is fully occupied not only when we think of an object, but even when we consider it from a particular point of view. Thus to put our thoughts in order, we are obliged to distribute things into different classes.

§5 Notions that stem from such an origin are bound to be very defective, and it would probably be risky to use them if we did not do so with caution. For this reason, philosophers have fallen into a great mistake on this point that has had far-reaching consequences: they have realized all their abstractions, or have regarded them as beings that had real existence independent of that of the things.[31] Here is something which I think has caused a most absurd opinion.

---

[31] At the beginning of the twelfth century, the Peripatetics formed two schools, that of the nominalists and that of the realists. The latter maintained that the general notions which the

§6 All our first ideas were particular; they were certain sensations of light, of color, etc., or certain operations of the mind. All these ideas present a true reality, for properly speaking they are just different modifications of our being, for we cannot perceive anything within us without regarding it as ours, as belonging to our being, or as being our very being existing in such and such a manner, that is, feeling, seeing, etc.: such are all our ideas at the point of their origin.

Since our mind is too limited to reflect simultaneously on all the modifications that can belong to it, it is obliged to distinguish them in order to grasp them successively. The basis of this distinction is that these modifications continually change and succeed each other in its being, which to the mind appears as a secure foundation that always remains the same.

It is certain that these modifications when they are thus distinguished from the being which is their subject no longer have any real existence. The mind, however, cannot reflect on nothing, for that would amount to not reflecting at all. But how then do these modifications become the object of the mind, taken as they are in an abstract manner or separated from the being to which they belong without being part of it except insofar as they are contained in it? By the mind's continuing to consider them as beings, is the answer. Accustomed as it is, whenever it considers these modifications as belonging to itself, to perceive them with the reality of its own being from which they are not at the moment distinct, it preserves for them, as well as it can, this very reality, even when it makes the distinction between them. It is contradicting itself; on the one hand, it considers its modifications as having no relation to its being, and then they are nothing; on the other hand, since what is nothing cannot be grasped, it regards them as something by continuing to attribute to them the same reality it first perceived them to have, even though that reality can no longer belong to them. In a word, when these abstractions were only particular ideas, they were connected with the idea of existence, and this connection is maintained.

schools called "universal nature," "relations," "formalities," and others are real beings distinct from the things. The former, on the contrary, thought that they are only names by which we express different ways of conceiving, and they based themselves on the principle that "nature does nothing in vain." This amounted to supporting a good thesis with a bad reason; for it meant admitting that these real beings were possible, and that, to make them exist, all it took was to find some use for them. Still, this was called the razor of the nominalists. The dispute between these two sects was so heated that they came to blows in Germany, and in France Louis XI was obliged to prohibit the reading of books by the nominalists.

Though this contradiction may be harmful, it is nonetheless necessary. For if the mind is too limited to comprise all at once both its being and modifications, it must distinguish them by forming abstract ideas; and though the modifications in the process lose the reality they had, it must still suppose they have it, for otherwise they could never become the object of its reflection.

It is this necessity that has caused many philosophers to fail to suspect that the reality of abstract ideas is the work of the imagination. They have seen that we were absolutely compelled to consider these ideas to be something real, and they stopped there. But failing to seek the cause that made us perceive them under this false appearance, they have concluded that they were in fact real beings.

All these notions have therefore been realized, but more or less in proportion as the things of which they are partial ideas appeared to have more or less reality. The ideas of modifications have shared fewer degrees of existence than those of substances, and those of finite substances have had still fewer than those of infinite existence.[32]

§7 Realized in that manner, these ideas have been surprisingly fruitful. It is to them that we owe the happy discovery of "occult qualities," "substantial forms," "intentional species," or, to speak only of what is commonly admitted by the moderns, to them we owe those "genera," "species," "essences," and "differences" which are like so many beings that place themselves in each substance to determine it to be what it is. When philosophers use these words "being," "substance," "essence," "genus," "species," we must not imagine that they mean no more than certain collections of simple ideas that come from sensation and reflection; they intend to go deeper by finding specific realities in each of them. If we go into still greater detail by passing in review the names of substances such as "body," "animal," "man," "metal," "gold," "silver," etc., in the eyes of philosophers they all reveal beings that are concealed from the rest of mankind.

One proof that they regard these words as signs of some reality is that, even if a substance has undergone some alteration, they still keep asking if it belongs to the same species to which it belonged before the change, a question that would become superfluous if they placed the notions of

---

[32] Descartes himself made the same argument in the *Meditations* [*in the Third Meditation].

substances and of their species in different collections of simple ideas. When they ask "whether ice and snow are water"; "whether a monstrous fetus is a human being"; "whether God, minds, bodies, or even the vacuum are substances," then it is obvious that the question is not whether these things agree with the simple ideas that are collected under these words "water," "human being," "substance," for that question would resolve itself. The point is to know whether these things contain certain essences, certain realities which, it is supposed, are signified by the words "water," "human being," "substance."

§8 This prejudice has made philosophers believe that we ought to define substances by the nearest difference that is most proper for explaining their nature. But we are still waiting for them to produce an example of these kinds of definitions. They will always be unsound, owing to our own inability to know essences, an inability the philosophers do not suspect, because they have a prior commitment to the abstractions which they realize and afterwards take to be the very essence of things.

§9 The abuse of realizing abstract notions also shows clearly when philosophers, not being content to explain after their manner the nature of what exists, have tried to explain what does not. They have been known to speak of merely possible creatures as if they existed, and to realize everything to the point of including the nothingness from which they emerged. It has been asked, where were the creatures before God had created them? The answer is easy, for that is the same as asking where they were before they were, to which, it seems to me, it is sufficient to answer that they were nowhere.

The idea of possible creatures is only a realized abstraction, which we have formed by ceasing to think of the existence of things in favor of thinking only of the qualities we recognize in them. We have thought about extension, figure, the motion and rest of bodies, but have ceased to think of their existence. That is how we have made the idea of possible bodies for ourselves, an idea that deprives them of all reality because it supposes them in a state of nothingness which, by evident contradiction, saves their reality by representing them as something extended, figured, etc.

Not perceiving this contradiction, philosophers have taken this idea only in the last sense. Consequently they have given to what does not exist the actual qualities of what does exist, and some of them have believed that they were solving the thorniest questions of creation in a sensible manner.

§10 "I suspect" (says Locke [*E 2.21.6]) "that the way people speak of the faculties of the soul has misled many into the confused notion of so many distinct agents in us with different functions and different powers that command, obey, and execute a variety of things like so many distinct beings; which has produced many vain disputes, obscure discourse, and much uncertainty on questions relating to these different powers of the soul." This fear is worthy of a wise philosopher, for why should we treat as important questions "whether judgment belongs to the understanding or to the will"; "whether either one is equally active or equally free"; "whether the will is capable of knowledge, or whether it is a blind faculty"; "whether, finally, it controls the understanding or is itself guided and determined by the latter"? If by "understanding and will" philosophers merely mean the soul considered in relation to certain actions that it produced or can produce, it is evident that judgment, activity, and freedom would either pertain to the understanding or would not pertain to it, depending on whether we considered a greater or lesser number of its actions in speaking of this faculty. The same goes for the will. In cases of this kind, it is sufficient to explain the terms by applying precise analyses to the determination of the notions we form of these things. But having become obliged to represent the soul by abstractions, philosophers have multiplied its modes of being. Both the understanding and the will have suffered the fate of all abstract notions. Even those who, like the Cartesians, have expressly noted that they were not talking about beings distinct from the soul, have discussed all the questions I have mentioned. Thus they have realized abstract notions unintentionally without becoming aware of it. The reason is that, not knowing how to analyze them, they were incapable of recognizing their defects and consequently also failed to use them with all the necessary precautions.

§11 These sorts of abstractions have infinitely darkened everything that has been written on liberty, a question on which many pens have been busy only to make it more obscure. The understanding, say some philosophers, is a faculty that receives ideas, and the will, blind by itself, is a faculty which is determined only as a consequence of the ideas the understanding presents to it. It is not up to the understanding either to perceive or not to perceive ideas and the relations of truth or probability between them. It is not free, it is not even active, for it does not itself produce the ideas of white or black, and it sees by necessity that one is not the other. The will acts, it is true, but being blind in itself it follows the dictates of the understanding, which is the same as saying that it is determined as a result of what is prescribed for it by a necessary cause. But if human beings are free, it would be by one or the other of these faculties. Thus they are not free.

To refute this entire argument, it is sufficient to note that these philosophers turn the understanding and the will into phantoms that exist only in their imagination. If these faculties were what they take them to be, there is no doubt there could be no liberty. I invite them to look into themselves, and my answer to them is that if they would give up their abstract realities and analyze their thoughts, they would see things in a very different light. It is not true, for instance, that the understanding is neither free nor active. Our analyses demonstrate the contrary. But it must be admitted that this difficulty is great, even if not insoluble, in the hypothesis of innate ideas.

§12 After what I have been saying, I am not sure we can ultimately abandon all these realized abstractions; several reasons make me fear the contrary. We must remember that we have said [Section 4] that the names of substances in the mind occupy the place that objects have outside us. They are the bond and support of simple ideas, as the objects are of the qualities in them. That is why we are always tempted to refer them to that object and to imagine that they express its very reality.

In the second place, I have elsewhere [Section 3] observed that we cannot know all the simple ideas of which mixed modes are formed. But the essence of a thing being, according to the philosophers, that which constitutes what it is, it follows that in these cases we would be able to have ideas of essences, and consequently we have given them names. For instance, "justice" means the essence of what is just; "wisdom" the essence of a wise man, etc. That is perhaps one of the reasons that made the scholastics believe that to have names that would express the essence of substances, all they had to do was to follow the analogy of language. Thus they invented the words "corporeity," "animality," "humanity" to designate the essences of "body," "animal," and "man." Once these terms have become familiar to them, it is very difficult to persuade them that they are empty of sense.

In the third place, there are only two ways of making use of words: to use them after fixing in the mind all the simple ideas they ought to signify, or after merely supposing them to be signs of the very reality of things. The first way most often causes confusion because the usage is not always settled enough. Since people see things differently according to the experience they have had, it is not certain that they agree on the number and the quality of ideas of a great many names. Furthermore, even when there is agreement, it is not always easy to grasp the proper extent of the sense of a term; doing that would require time, experience, and reflection. But it is much more convenient to suppose that things have a reality in them of which the words are considered to be the true signs, and to understand by the words "man," "animal," etc. an entity that determines and distinguishes these things, than to pay attention to all the simple ideas that can belong to them. This way our impatience and curiosity are satisfied at the same time. There are perhaps few people, even among those who have worked the hardest to shed their prejudices, who do not feel inclined to refer all the names of substances to unknown realities. That happens even in situations where it is easy to avoid the error because we know very well that the ideas we realize are not true beings. I have in mind moral entities such as "glory," "war," "reputation," to which we have given the denomination of "being" only because, in the most serious discourses as well as in the most familiar conversation, we imagine them under this idea.

§13 That is certainly one of the most extensive sources of our errors. The supposition that words correspond to the reality of things is sufficient to make us take words for things and to conclude that they perfectly explain the nature of things. That is why someone who poses a question asking what such or such a body is, believes, as Locke has noted, that he is asking for something more than a name, and why the person who answers, "It is iron," also believes he is telling him something more. But with that kind of jargon there is no hypothesis, no matter how unintelligible, that cannot be defended. We must no longer be surprised by the prevalence of different sects.

§14 It is therefore very important not to realize our abstractions. To avoid this mistake I know only one remedy, which is to know how to account for the origin and generation of all abstract notions. But philosophers have not known this remedy, and it is in vain that they have tried to make up for it with definitions. The cause of their ignorance in this regard is their perennial prejudice that we must begin with general ideas, for once the way to begin with particular ideas has been blocked, it becomes impossible to explain the most abstract ideas which draw their origin from the former. Here is an example.

Having once defined the impossible as "that which implies contradiction," the possible as "that which does not imply contradiction," and being as "that which can exist," there was no other way to define existence than to say that it is "the completion of possibility." But I ask you if this definition communicates any idea, and whether one would not be justified in casting as much ridicule on it as on some of Aristotle's definitions.

If the possible is "what does not imply contradiction," possibility will amount to the "nonimplication of contradiction." In that case existence becomes "the completion of the nonimplication of contradiction." What language! Closer observation of the natural order of ideas would have shown that the notion of possibility is formed only after that of existence.[P]

I think that definitions of this sort are adopted because people, already otherwise knowing the thing defined, do not bother to consider them very closely. The mind is struck by a certain clarity, attributes it to the definitions, and fails to perceive that they are unintelligible. This example shows how important it is to follow my method, that is to say always to substitute analyses for the philosophers' definitions. I even think that we ought to take the greatest care to avoid using expressions of the sort they cherish the most. The abuse of such expressions has become so widespread that, no matter what care we take, it is difficult to prevent ordinary readers from misconceiving a thought. Locke is an example of that. It is true that he generally makes very proper use of those expressions, but in several places he would have been easier to understand if he had entirely banished them from his style, which, incidentally, I judge only from the translation.

These details show the influence of abstract ideas. If ignorance of their insufficiency has cast all of metaphysics into great obscurity, today when they are known it is up to us to provide the remedy.

[P] See Christian Wolff, *Philosophia prima, sive ontologia methodo scientifico pertractata*, new ed. (Frankfurt and Leipzig, 1736), ed. Jean École (Hildesheim, Olms, 1962), in Part I, Sect. ii, Ch. I "De possibili & impossibili" (pp. 62–87, esp. §79 and §89).

Section 6
Some judgments that have been erroneously attributed to the mind, or the solution of a metaphysical problem

§1 I believe that so far I have not attributed to the soul any operation that everyone is not able to perceive in himself. But to account for visual phenomena, philosophers have believed that we form certain judgments of which we are not conscious. This opinion is so generally accepted that Locke, the most cautious of them all, adopted it. Here is how he explains it:

> On the subject of perception, it is relevant to observe that the ideas we receive by sensation are often altered in grown people by the judgment of the mind, without our taking any notice of it. Thus when we set before our eyes a round body of uniform color, of gold, alabaster, or jet for example, it is certain that the idea that is imprinted in our mind at the sight of this globe represents a flat circle, variously shadowed, with different degrees of light coming to our eyes. But having by use been accustomed to distinguish the sort of images that convex bodies are wont to produce in us and the alterations that occur in the reflection of light, by the sensible difference in the bodies, we right away, for what appears to us, substitute the very cause of the image we see by virtue of a judgment which custom has made habitual with us; so that joining to what we see a judgment that we confuse with it, we make our own idea of a convex figure and a uniform color, though the eyes actually represent to us only a flat surface variously shaded and colored, as it would appear in painting. On this occasion I shall here insert a problem of the learned Mr. Molyneux (. . .) "Suppose a man born blind and now adult who has been taught to

distinguish by touch a cube from a globe made of the same metal and roughly of the same size, so that when he touched one or the other he could say which is the cube and which is the globe. Suppose that the cube and the globe be placed on a table and that the blind man be made to see. The question then is whether by seeing them without touching, he would be able to distinguish them and say which is the cube and which the globe." The acute and judicious proposer of this question at the same time answers: "No. For though this blind person had learned by experience how the globe and the cube affect his touch, he still does not yet know that what affects his touch so or so must affect his eyes so or so, or that the protuberant angle of a cube that presses his hand unequally, must appear to his eyes as it appears in the cube." I entirely share the sentiment of this clever man (. . .) I believe that the blind man will not at first sight be able to say with certainty which was the globe and which the cube so long as he only saw them, though in touching them he could unerringly name and distinguish them by the difference of their figures when he felt them. [E 2.9.8]

§2 This whole argument assumes that the image that is imprinted on the eye at the sight of the globe is merely a flat circle, illuminated and colored differently, which is true. But it further assumes, and that is what seems false to me, that the impression that is consequently made on the mind gives only the perception of this circle; that if we see the globe as a convex figure, it is because, having by the experience of touch acquired the idea of this figure and knowing what sort of image it produces in us by sight, we have become accustomed to judge it convex, a judgment which, to use the expression Locke uses a little later, "changes the idea of the sensation and presents it to us differently than it is in itself."

§3 Among these presuppositions, Locke advances without proof that the sensation in the mind represents no more than the image that we know is imprinted on the eye. As for myself, when I look at a globe, I see something other than a flat circle, an experience it seems entirely natural for me to accept. There are in addition several reasons for rejecting the judgments which this philosopher relies on. First of all, he assumes that we know what sort of images convex bodies produce in us, and what changes occur in the reflection of light depending on the difference of the sensible shapes of bodies, which is a knowledge that the larger part of mankind does not have, though they see figures the same way philosophers do. Secondly, even if we add these judgments to vision, we would never confuse them with it, as Locke assumes, but we will see one way and judge another.

When I see a bas-relief, I know, without any doubt, that it is painted on a flat surface; I have touched it, and yet this knowledge, repeated experience, and all the judgments I can make do not prevent me from seeing convex figures. Why does this appearance persist? Why is it that a judgment that has the power to make me see things quite differently from what they are according to the idea provided by my sensations of them, does not have the power to make me see them in conformity with that idea? We can argue the same way about the apparent roundness we attribute to a distant building which we know and judge to be square and about thousands of other similar examples.

§4 In the third place, one reason that by itself would suffice to overturn this opinion of Locke's is that it is impossible to make us have consciousness of these sorts of judgments. It is useless to base anything on the belief that a good many things seem to occur in the mind of which we take no cognizance. From what I have said in another place [Sect. 2, Ch. 1], it is true enough that we might forget these judgments the moment after we have formed them; but when we make them an object of our reflection, the consciousness of them would be so lively that we could no longer call them into doubt.

§5 Following Locke's opinion in all its consequences, we should reason about distances, situations, magnitudes, and extension as he has done in regard to figures. Thus we might say: "When we see a wide field, it is certain that the idea that imprints itself in the mind at this sight represents a flat surface, shadowed and colored in various ways, with different degrees of light that strike our eyes. But as we are in practice accustomed to distinguish what sort of images are usually produced in us by bodies that differ in regard to situation, distance, size, and extension, and also what sort of changes occur in the reflection of the light in regard to the same differences, we right away replace what appears before us with the cause itself of the images that we see, all of which occurs by virtue of a judgment which familiar usage has made habitual; so that joining the act of seeing to a judgment which we blend with it, we form by ourselves the ideas of different situations, distances, magnitudes, and extensions, even though our eyes actually represent no more to us than a level surface shadowed and colored in different ways."

This version of Locke's argument is the more correct insofar as the ideas of situation, distance, magnitude, and extension we receive from the view of the field are found in miniature in the perception of the different parts of a globe. However, this philosopher has not adopted the consequences. By stipulating in the statement of his problem that the globe and the cube should be of roughly the same size, he makes it clear that sight may, without the assistance of any judgment, give us different ideas of size. But this involves a contradiction, for it is inconceivable how we could have ideas of sizes without also having ideas of figures.

§6 Others have had no difficulty admitting these consequences. Voltaire, who is famous for a large number of works, reports [*Elements of Sir Isaac Newton's Philosophy* (*1738), Ch. 6] and approves of the sentiments of Berkeley, who maintained that neither situations, distances, magnitudes, nor figures would be discerned by a person born blind who suddenly received the use of sight.

§7 I observe, he says, from a good distance through a little hole, a man standing on a roof; the distance and the few light rays at first prevent me from making out whether it is a man; the object appears very small, and I think it is a figure at most two feet high; the object moves, I judge it is a man, and from this moment this man appears to me of ordinary size.

§8 I accept, if you wish, this judgment and the effect attributed to it; but it is still far from proving Berkeley's thesis. There is here a sudden transition from a first judgment to a second one that is opposed to it. This causes greater attention to be fixed on the object in order to see in it the common size of a man. The intense attention probably produces some change in the brain, and then in the eyes so as to produce the sight of a man of about five feet. That is a special case, and the judgment it causes is such that it cannot be denied that it must be accompanied by consciousness. Why would it not be the same on every other occasion if we always, as is assumed, formed similar judgments?

If a man who was four feet from me moves away to eight feet, the image that is imprinted at the back of my eyes will be smaller by half, why do I continue to see him to be of nearly the same size? You perceive him at first, someone will say, at half size; but the connection that experience has effected in your brain between the idea of a man and the idea of a height of five to six feet forces you to imagine, by a sudden judgment, a man of such a height and in actual fact to see such a height. That, I admit, is something I cannot confirm from my own experience. Could a first perception vanish so quickly, to be replaced by a judgment so suddenly that it is impossible to note the transition from one to the other, even when one gave it one's full attention? Furthermore, suppose this man moves away to sixteen feet, thirty-two, sixty-four, and so on in that proportion, why would he not seem to become smaller little by little till at last I did not see him at all? If the perception of seeing is the effect of a judgment by which I have connected the idea of a man to that of a height of five to six feet, this man should either disappear before my eyes all of a sudden, or I would continue to see him of the same size regardless of his distance from me. Why should he diminish more quickly before my eyes than before the eyes of someone else, though we both have the same experience? In short, let them designate at which distance this judgment ought to begin to lose its force.

§9 The people I am opposing compare the sense of seeing to that of hearing and conclude from one to the other. The ear, they say, is struck by sounds; we hear tones and nothing more. In seeing, the eye is struck, we see colors and nothing more. A person who hears the noise of a cannon for the first time would not be able to judge whether it was fired some two miles or thirty paces away. Only experience can habituate him to judge the distance between himself and the place the noise comes from. It is precisely the same thing with the rays of light that come from an object; they do not at all inform us where that object is.

§10 Hearing is not by itself designed to give us the idea of distance, and even with the aid of experience the idea it offers is still the most imperfect of all. There are occasions when it is still pretty much the same with seeing. If I observe an object through a hole, without perceiving the things in between, I will know the distance only very imperfectly. Then I recall the knowledge that I owe to experience, and I judge the object to be more or less distant according to whether it appears more or less below its normal size. There then is a case where it is necessary to add a judgment to the sense of seeing, just as with the sense of hearing. But note well that we are conscious of it and that both after and before we know the distances only imperfectly.

Suppose I open my window and perceive a man at the far end of the street; I see that he is far away from me before I have yet formed any judgment. It is true that it is not the rays of light that come from him that inform me most precisely about the distance, but the rays that come from objects in between. It is natural that the sight of these objects gives me some idea of my distance from the man; it is even impossible for me not to have this idea as often as I perceive them.

§11 You are mistaken, someone will object. The sudden, almost uniform judgments which your mind at a certain age has of distances, sizes, and situations make you think that all you have to do to see the way you do is to open your eyes. But that is not so; you must have the assistance of the other senses. If you had only the sense of seeing, you would never have any means of knowing extension.

§12 What then should I perceive? A mathematical point? No, without doubt. I should certainly see light and colors. But do the light and the colors map out different distances, magnitudes, and situations? If I look in front of me, above, below, to the right, to the left, I see light distributed in all directions and certain colors which are certainly not concentrated in a point; that is all I need. There I find, independent of any judgment and without the assistance of the other senses, the idea of extension with all its dimensions.

Permit me to make a presupposition, though it may seem very bizarre: that of an animated eye. According to the opinion of Berkeley this eye will see a colored light, but it will perceive neither extension, magnitudes, distances, nor figures. It would therefore accustom itself to believing that all of nature is only a mathematical point. Let it be joined to a human body after its soul has long ago contracted the habit of forming this judgment, then one will no doubt believe that this soul only needs to make use of the senses it has just acquired to represent to itself the ideas of magnitudes, distances, situations, and figures. Not at all: the habitual, sudden, and uniform judgments it has formed all along will change the ideas of these new sensations so that it will enter into contact with bodies and confirm that they have neither extension, situation, magnitudes, nor figures.

§13 It would be interesting to discover the laws that God follows when He enriches us with the different sensations of sight, sensations that not only inform us better than all the others about how things relate to our needs and preservation, but that also in a much more striking way proclaim the order, beauty, and grandeur of the universe. However important this study may be, I gladly leave it to others. It is enough for me that those who will open their eyes agree that they perceive light, colors, extension, magnitudes, etc. I do not go beyond that, for it is at this point that I begin to have demonstrative knowledge.

§14 Let us now examine what will happen to a man born blind who is given the sense of sight.

This blind person has formed ideas of extension, magnitudes, etc., by reflecting on the different sensations that he has when he feels bodies by touching. He takes a stick in which he feels that all the parts have the same determination, which gives him the idea of a straight line. He feels another whose parts have different determinations so that if they were continued they would end at different points, from which he draws the idea of a curved line. From there he goes on to the angle, the cube, the globe, and all sorts of figures. Such is the origin of the ideas he has of extension. But we must not believe that at the moment he opens his eyes he can immediately enjoy the spectacle which the wonderful mixture of light and color suffuses over all of nature. That is a treasure which is contained in the new sensations he feels; reflection alone can reveal it to him and give him the full enjoyment of it. When we ourselves fix the eyes on a very composite picture in its entirety, we do not form any determinate idea of it. Properly to see it, we are obliged to consider all the parts in succession. Just imagine what a picture the universe presents to eyes that become open to light for the first time!

I turn now to the moment when this man is capable of reflecting on what strikes his sight. Surely, what appears before him is not like a point, so he perceives an extension in length, breadth, and depth. As he analyzes this extension, he will form the ideas of surface, line, point, and of all sorts of figures; these ideas will be similar to those he has acquired by the sense of touch, for by whatever sense extension enters our cognizance, it cannot be represented in two different ways. If I see or touch a circle or a rule, the idea of the first can never represent anything other than a curved line and the second that of a straight line. This man born blind will thus distinguish the globe from the cube on sight, because he will recognize in them the same ideas which he has formed by touch.

One could, however, induce him to suspend his judgment by presenting the following difficulty to him. This body, we would say, appears to you on sight to be a globe, the other one a cube; but on what grounds will you be convinced that the first is the same one that, when you touched it, gave you the idea of the globe, and that the second is the same one that gave you the idea of the cube? Who has told you that these bodies when touched must have the same figure as when they are seen? How do you know that the one that appears to your eyes to be a globe will not turn out to be the cube when you touch it with your hand? Who can even tell you that there is something similar in the bodies which you recognize when touching them to be a cube and a globe? The argument would be very involved, and I believe that only experience would be able to give an answer; but that is not the thesis of either Locke or Berkeley.

§15 I admit that I still have to solve a difficulty that is not insignificant. It is an experiment which appears in every respect contrary to the opinion that I have been supporting. Here it is as reported by Voltaire in his own words, for it would lose its force if rendered any other way:

> In 1729, Mr. Cheselden, one of those famous surgeons who combine great manual skill with great brilliance of mind, proposed the operation because he thought that sight might be given to a person born blind by removing the cataracts, which he conceived to have been formed almost at the time of birth. The blind person had difficulty in consenting to it. He could not very well conceive that the sense of sight would contribute much to his happiness. Were it not for the desire instilled in him of learning to read or write, he had never desired to see. (. . .) The operation was performed and succeeded. The youth, who was then about fourteen years of age, saw light for the first time. This experiment confirmed all that Locke and Berkeley had rightly foreseen. For a long time he distinguished neither magnitude, distance, situation, nor even figure. An object of an inch placed before his eyes that concealed a house from his sight, appeared to him as big as the house. Everything he saw seemed at first to be upon his eyes, and to touch them as the objects of the sense of touch do the skin. He could not distinguish what he had judged round by the help of his hands, from what he had judged square; nor discern with his eyes whether what his hands had perceived to be above or below, was really above or below. He was so far from knowing magnitudes that after having at length considered by sight that his house was larger than his chamber, he could not conceive how sight could give him that idea. He could not perceive, till after two months' experience,

that pictures only represented solid bodies, and when, after so long a trial of his new sense, he had thought that bodies and not surfaces only were in the painted pictures, he applied his hand to them and was amazed that he did not feel those solid bodies of which he began to perceive the representations. He asked which of the senses deceived him, that of feeling or that of seeing. [Chapter already cited]

§16 Some reflections on what happens in the eye at the presence of light will explain this experiment.

Though we are yet far from knowing the entire mechanism of the eye, we do know that the cornea is more or less convex; that in proportion to the quantity of light that objects reflect, the pupil of the eye contracts or expands to give passage to fewer rays or to receive more. It is believed that the reservoir of aqueous humor successively takes different forms. It is certain that the crystalline lens changes its shape to ensure that the light rays unite precisely on the retina;[33] that the delicate fibers of the retina are agitated and struck in an astonishing variety of ways; that this agitation is transmitted in the brain to other more delicate parts whose springiness is even more surprising. Finally the muscles that serve to turn the eyes toward the objects we want to look at compress the entire globe of the eye, thus more or less changing its form.

Not only must the eye and all its parts submit to all these movements, to all these forms, and to a thousand changes that are unknown to us, with a promptness that is impossible to imagine, but it is furthermore required that all these revolutions occur in perfect harmony so that each of them contributes to the same effect. If, for instance, the cornea were too much or too little convex in regard to the position and to the form of other parts of the eye, all objects would appear confused and inverted, and we would not be able to discern whether *what our hands would have felt to be above or below, would in fact be above or below.* We can convince ourselves of that by using a lens whose form does not agree with that of the eye.

If, in response to the action of light, the parts of the eye modify themselves at every moment with such great variety and vivacity, there can be no other reason than that its modes of reaction have become more pliant and receptive. That was not the case with the young man

---

[33] Or on the choroid, for we do not know for certain whether it is by the fibers of the retina or by those of the choroid that the impression of light is transmitted to the soul.

who had his cataracts removed. For fourteen years his eyes, having grown without any use being made of them, resisted the action of objects. The cornea was too much or too little convex in relation to the situation of the other parts. Once the crystalline lens had become immobile, it always reunited the light rays either short of or beyond the retina; or if it changed situation, it was never to place itself at the point where it should have been. It took many days of exercise to make the springs act in harmony that had become stiff in the course of time. That is the reason this young man was so hesitant for two months. If he owed anything to the assistance of the sense of touch, it is because the efforts he made to find in the objects the ideas he formed of them by handling them, gave him occasion for more frequent exercise of the sense of seeing. If we suppose he would have stopped using his hands whenever he opened his eyes to the light, there can be no doubt that he would have acquired the same ideas, though indeed more slowly.

Those who observed this person born blind at the moment when the cataracts were removed hoped to see the confirmation of an opinion in favor of which they were prejudiced. When they found out that he perceived objects very imperfectly, it did not occur to them that reasons could be advanced other than those Locke and Berkeley had imagined. For them it became an irrevocable conclusion that the eyes, without the help of the other senses, would be unfit to provide us with the ideas of extension, figures, situations, etc.

What causes this opinion, which many readers will no doubt have found astonishing, is on the one hand our eagerness to account for everything, and on the other the insufficiency of the rules of optics. Whatever we do to measure the angles which the light rays form at the back of the eye, we do not find that they bear any relation to the manner in which we see the objects. But I did not believe that it could authorize me to have recourse to judgments that would never enter anyone's mind. I thought that in a work in which I propose to explain the materials of our knowledge, I ought to make it a rule not to advance anything that was not incontestable and that everyone would with the least reflection be able to perceive in himself.

Part II
Language and method

Section 1
The origin and progress of language

Adam and Eve did not owe the exercise of the operations of their soul to experience. As they came from the hands of God, they were able, by special assistance, to reflect and communicate their thoughts to each other. But I am assuming that two children, one of either sex, sometime after the deluge, had gotten lost in the desert before they would have known the use of any sign. The fact I have just stated gives me the right to make this assumption. Who can tell whether some nation owes its origin only to such an event? So that I am permitted to make the assumption. The question[34] is to know how this budding nation made a language for itself.

[34] "Judging only by the nature of things" (says Warburton, *Essai sur les hiérogl.* [*pp. 118–19; *Div. Leg.* 2, 81–2]) "and without the surer instruction of revelation, one would be inclined to accept the opinion of Diodorus Siculus [*Bk. 1, Ch. 8] and Vitruvius [*De Architectura*, Bk. 2, Ch. 1] that the first people lived for some time in caves and forests, like beasts, uttering only confused and indistinct sounds until, joining together for mutual assistance, they came by degrees to form distinct sounds for arbitrary signs or marks on which they mutually agreed so that the speaker could express the ideas he wanted to communicate to others. Hence the diversity of language, for everyone agrees that language is not innate.

"This origin of language is so natural that a father of the church (Gregory of Nyssa) and Richard Simon, a priest of the Oratory, have both made the effort to support it. But they should have known better, for nothing is more evident from Sacred Scriptures than that language had a different origin. They tell us that God taught religion to the first man, which leaves no doubt that He taught him to speak at the same time."[q] (In fact, the knowledge of religion implies many ideas and extensive exercise of the operations of the soul, as I have demonstrated in the first part of this work.) "But though" (Warburton adds later) "God had taught language to men, it is not reasonable to suppose that this language went beyond the immediate human necessities and that he would not by himself have the ability to improve and enrich it. Thus the first language was unavoidably barren and narrow." This entire observation seems very judicious to me. If I suppose two children under the necessity of imagining even the first signs of language, it is because I did not think it was enough for a philosopher to say that something had been achieved

1 The language of action and that of articulated sounds considered from their point of origin

§1 So long as the children I am speaking of lived apart, the exercise of the operations of their soul was limited to that of perception and consciousness, which do not cease so long as we are awake; to that of attention, which occurred whenever some perceptions affected them in a particular manner; to that of reminiscence, when the circumstances which engaged them stayed before their minds before the connections they had formed were destroyed; and to a very limited exercise of the imagination. The perception of a need, for instance, was connected with the object which had served to relieve it. But having been formed by chance and lacking the steady support of reflection, these connections did not last long. One day the sensation of hunger made these children call to mind a tree loaded with fruit which they had seen the day before. The next day this tree was forgotten, and the same sensation called to mind some other object. Thus the exercise of the imagination was not within their power. It was merely the effect of the circumstances in which they found themselves.[35]

§2 When they lived together they had occasion for greater exercise of these first operations, because their mutual discourse made them connect the cries of each passion to the perceptions of which they were the natural signs. They usually accompanied the cries with some movement, gesture, or action that made the expression more striking. For example, he who suffered by not having an object his needs demanded would not merely cry out; he made as if an effort to obtain it, moved his head, his arms, and all parts of his body. Moved by this display, the other fixed the eyes on the same object, and feeling his soul suffused with sentiments he was not yet able to account for to himself, he suffered by seeing the other suffer so miserably. From this moment he

by special means, but that it was his duty to explain how it could have come about by natural means.

[35] What I am now saying about the operations of the soul in the two children cannot be doubted after what has been demonstrated in Part I of this essay, Sect. 2, chs. 1–5, and Sect. 4.

[q] Richard Simon, *Histoire du vieux testament* (Paris, 1678), Bk. I, Ch. 14, which includes a very full report on Gregory of Nyssa. For Gregory, see his "Answer to Eunomius's Second Book" in *Select Writings and Letters of Gregory, Bishop of Nyssa*, tr. William Moore and Henry Austin Wilson = *A Select Library of Nicene and Post-Nicene Fathers of the Christian Church*, Second Series, vol. 5 (Grand Rapids, MI: Eerdmans, n.d.), pp. 276, 290–1.

feels that he is eager to ease the other's pain, and he acts on this impression to the extent that it is within his ability. Thus by instinct alone these people asked for help and gave it. I say "by instinct alone," for reflection could not as yet have any share in it. One of them did not say, "I must bestir myself in that particular way to make the other understand what I need and to induce him to help me"; nor the other, "I see by his motions that he wants to have something and I intend to give it to him." But both acted as a result of the need that was most urgent for them.

§3 The frequent repetition of the same circumstances could not fail, however, to make it habitual for them to connect the cries of the passions and the different motions of the body to the perceptions which they expressed in a manner so striking to the senses. The more familiar they became with the signs, the more readily they were able to call them to mind at will. Their memory began to have some exercise; they gained command of their imagination, and little by little they succeeded in doing by reflection what they had formerly done only by instinct.[36] In the beginning both made it a habit to recognize, by those signs, the sentiments which the other felt at the moment; later they used those signs to communicate the sentiments they had experienced. For example, he who came upon a place where he had become frightened, imitated the cries and motions that were the signs of fear to warn the other not to expose himself to the same danger.

§4 The use of signs gradually extended the exercise of the operations of the soul, and they in turn, as they gained more exercise, improved the signs and made them more familiar. Our experience shows that those two things mutually assist each other. Before the discovery of algebraic signs, the operations of the mind had sufficient exercise to lead to their invention; but it is only after the coming into use of these signs that the operations have had the requisite exercise to carry mathematics to the point of perfection at which we find it today.

§5 These details show how the cries of the passions contributed to the development of the operations of the mind by naturally originating the language of action, a language which in its early stages, conforming to the level of this couple's limited intelligence, consisted of mere contortions and agitated bodily movements.

---

[36] This answers the problem I raised in Pt. I, Sect. 2, ch. 5 of this work [*§49].

§6 Nevertheless, when they had acquired the habit of connecting some ideas to arbitrary signs, the natural cries served as a model for them to make a new language. They articulated new sounds, and by repeating them many times to the accompaniment of some gesture that indicated the objects to which they wished to draw attention, they became accustomed to giving names to things. Still, the first progress of this language was very slow. The organ of speech was so inflexible that it could articulate only very simple sounds with any ease. The obstacles to the pronunciation of other sounds even prevented them from suspecting that the voice could vary beyond the small number of words already imagined.

§7 This couple had a child who, when pressed by the needs he could make known only with difficulty, agitated all parts of the body. His very flexible tongue bent itself in some extraordinary manner and pronounced an entirely new word. The need still persisting again caused the same effects; the child moved the tongue as before and once more articulated the same sound. Full of surprise and having at last figured out what the child wanted, the parents gave it to him while at the same time trying to repeat the same word. The trouble they had pronouncing it showed that they would not by themselves have been able to invent it.

By that sort of procedure, the new language was not much improved. For lack of exercise, the child's vocal organ soon lost all its flexibility. The parents taught him to declare his thoughts by actions, which is a mode of expression whose sensible images were more readily within his reach than articulated sounds. We cannot expect the birth of a new word to occur except by chance, so that any considerable increase in their number would, by this slow process, take many generations. With the language of action at that stage being so natural, it was a great obstacle to overcome. How could it be abandoned for another language whose advantages could not yet be foreseen while the difficulties it posed were so obvious?

§8 As the language of articulated sounds became richer, it was better suited to exercise the vocal organ at an early stage and to preserve its initial flexibility. It then became as convenient as the language of action; either one was used with equal ease until the use of articulated sounds became so easy that they prevailed.

§9 It follows that there was a time when conversation was sustained by discourse that was a mixture of words and actions.

Use and custom, like most other things in life, afterwards changed into ornament what had been due to necessity, but this practice lasted long after the necessity had ceased, especially among the oriental nations whose character naturally inclined them to a mode of conversation which so readily exercised their vivacity by movement and so greatly suited it by a perpetual representation of sensible images.

Sacred Scriptures offer innumerable instances of this sort of conversation. Here are some of them. When the false prophet pushes with horns of iron to note the overthrow of the Syrians [1 Kings 22:11]; when Jeremiah by the order of God hides the linen girdle in the hole of a rock near the Euphrates [Jeremiah 13]; when he breaks the earthen vessel in sight of the people [Ch. 19]; when he puts on bonds and yokes [Ch. 27]; and when he casts a book into the Euphrates [Ch. 51]; when Ezekiel by the order of God delineates the siege of Jerusalem on a brick [Ezekiel 4]; when he weighs the hair of his head and the stubble of his beard [Ch. 5]; when he carries out his household stuff [Ch. 12]; and when he joins together the two sticks of Judah and Israel [37:16]. By these actions the prophets instructed the people in the will of God and conversed with them in signs. [*Hiérogl., p. 120; Div. Leg. 2.83]

Not knowing that the language of action among the Jews was a common and familiar mode of communication, some people have presumed to treat these actions of the prophets as being absurd and fanatic. Warburton effectively rejects this accusation. He says:

The absurdity of an action consists in its being bizarre and meaningless. But usage and custom made those of the prophets wise and pertinent. The fanaticism of an action consists in the turn of mind that delights in making up things that are not at all familiar and in using strange language. But that sort of fanaticism cannot be attributed to the prophets, since it is clear that their actions were ordinary actions and that their discourse conformed to the common speech of their country.

But it is not only in sacred history that we meet with examples of discourse expressed by action. Pagan antiquity is full of them (. . .) The early oracles were given in this way, as we learn from an old saying of Heraclitus, that "the king whose oracle is at Delphi neither speaks nor keeps silent, but reveals himself by signs." This is certain proof that among the ancients the substitution of actions for words was widely used to make oneself understood. [*Hiérogl.*, pp. 123–4; *Div. Leg.* 2.86]

§10 It seems that this language was chiefly preserved to instruct the people in matters that most deeply concerned them, such as government and religion, for the reason that by acting with greater force on the imagination, the impression was more lasting. Its expression even had a strong and noble quality which the languages, being still weak and barren, could not approach. The ancients called this language by the name "dance," which is why it is said that David danced before the ark.

§11 As their taste improved, people gave greater variety, grace, and expression to this "dance." They not only submitted the movements of the arms and the attitudes of the body to rules, but even marked out how the feet should be moved. As a result dancing was naturally divided into two subordinate arts. If you will permit me to use an expression from the language of the ancients, one of them was the "dance of gestures," which was maintained for its contribution to the communication of their thoughts; the other was chiefly the "dance of steps," which was used for the expression of certain states of mind, especially joy; it was used on occasions of rejoicing, pleasure being its principal aim.

The dance of steps therefore stems from that of gestures, whose character it retains. In Italy, where gesticulation is more lively and varied, it is pantomime, while in France, by contrast, it is graver and simpler. If that is an advantage, it seems to me to have the effect that the language of this dance is more limited and less exuberant in the use of pantomime. A dancer, for example, who merely sought to lend grace to his movements and dignity to his postures – would he, when he performed in company, succeed as well as when dancing by himself? Would there not be reason to fear that his dance, owing to its simplicity, would be so limited in its expression as not to provide him with a sufficient repertoire of signs for the language of a figured dance? If that is true, the simpler the art, the more limited the expression.

§12 There are different genres of dance, from the simplest to the one that is least so. They are all good, provided they express something, and the degree of their perfection increases with the variety and scope of the expression. A dance that expresses grace and dignity is good; a dance that creates a sort of conversation or dialogue seems to me better. The least perfect is the dance that merely requires strength, dexterity, and agility, because its aim does not have sufficient interest; still, it should not be despised, for it can cause pleasant surprises. The fault of the French is to limit the arts in order to make them simpler. In doing so they sometimes deprive themselves of what is better merely to hold on to what is good; music is another example of that.

2 The prosody of the first languages

§13 When speech succeeded the language of action, it preserved the character of its predecessor. This new mode of communicating our thoughts could not be imagined except on the pattern of what preceded it. Therefore, to take the place of the violent bodily movements, the voice was raised and lowered by strongly marked intervals.

These languages did not succeed each other all of a sudden, but were for a long time intermixed before speech came to prevail much later. Everyone knows that it is natural for the voice to vary its inflections in conformity with gestural variation. My conjecture is confirmed for a good number of other reasons.

First of all, when people began to articulate sounds, the coarseness of the organs did not permit them to do it with the softness of our inflections.

Secondly, we can observe that inflections and voice are so necessary that we have trouble understanding what is read to us in monotone. If we find it sufficient for the voice to vary only slightly, it is because our mind is busy with the great number of ideas we have acquired and with our habit of connecting them to sounds. This is what was lacking for those people who were the first speakers. Their mind was in its early state of rudeness; notions that today are very common were new to them, so that they could not make themselves understood unless they modulated their voice by very distinct gradations. We ourselves know by experience that the less familiar we are with a language that is being spoken to us, the more we need to linger on each syllable and to distinguish them clearly.

Thirdly, at the origin of languages when they met obstacles that were too great to allow them to imagine new words, people for a long time had no other means for the expression of the sentiments of the soul than the natural signs to which they gave the quality of instituted signs. But the natural cries unavoidably introduced violent inflections, since different emotions are signified by the same sound varied in different tones. Depending on how it is pronounced, "ah," for example, can express admiration, sorrow, pleasure, sadness, joy, fear, disgust, and nearly all the sentiments of the soul.

Finally, I might add that the first names of animals probably imitated their cries, a remark that also goes for those that were given to winds, rivers, and to everything that makes a noise. It is obvious that this imitation implies that the sounds succeeded each other at clearly marked intervals.

§14 One could wrongly give the name of chant to this mode of speaking, as custom indeed gives it to utterances that are strongly accentuated. I refrain from doing so, however, because I will have occasion to use this word in its proper sense. In chant it is not sufficient that the sounds follow each other by distinct degrees; they must also be well enough sustained to bring out their harmony, and their intervals must be such as can be measured. It is not probable that this was generally the quality of the sounds by which the voice varied at the birth of languages, but then again it could not have been far from agreeing with them. However small the relation between two successive sounds, it will be sufficient to lower or raise one of them slightly so as to reveal an interval, as harmony demands. Thus at the origin of languages the manner of articulation allowed inflections of voice that were so distinct that a musician would have been able to record it with all but small adjustments, and so I would say that the manner of articulation partook of the quality of chant.[r]

§15 To the first human beings this prosody would have been so natural that some would have found it easier to express different ideas with the same word when pronounced with different tones of voice than to multiply the number of words in proportion to the number of ideas. This language still exists among the Chinese. They have 328 mono-syllables which they vary in five tones, which amounts to 1,640 signs. It has been noted that our languages are no richer. Other nations, born no doubt with a more fertile imagination, preferred to invent new words. With them prosody little by little grew apart from chant in proportion as the reasons that had kept them together ceased to prevail. But it took a long time before becoming as simple as it is today. It is the fate of established customs to subsist even after the needs that gave birth to them have ceased to operate. If I were to say that the Greeks and

---

[r] I retain the technical term "chant" to avoid dissipating its meaning into a variety of renderings such as "music," "song," "singing," which translation would demand. The entry "Chant" in the *Encyclopédie*, 3 (1753), 141a–142b, explains that chant is one of the two primary, natural modes for the expression of sentiment, the other being gesture. Thus it refers to the entire range of the vocal language of action, as also shown by the cross-references the entry makes to the entries "Gesture," "Accent," "Opera," "Chorus," "Concert," "Precentor," "Ballet." The entry "Gesture" similarly refers to "Chant," "Voice," "Dance," "Declamation," "Music." The word "accent" is the Latin translation of the Greek "prosody."

Romans had a prosody that partook of chant, it would perhaps be hard to guess my grounds for such a conjecture. Still, the reasons for saying so seem both simple and convincing to me; I will explain them in the next chapter.

3 The prosody of the Greek and Latin languages and, *en passant*, the declamation of the ancients

§16 It is well known that the Greeks and Romans had a notation for their declamation, and that it was accompanied by an instrument.[37] Thus it was truly a form of chant. This consequence is obvious to all those who have some knowledge of the principles of harmony. They know (1) that a sound cannot be put down in notation unless it can be measured; (2) that in harmony nothing can be measured except by the resonance of sonorous bodies; (3) and, finally, that this resonance does not give other sounds or other intervals than those that occur in chant.

It is also true that this singing declamation was not at all displeasing to the ancients. We do not learn that they ever complained of its being unnatural, except in particular cases, just as we do when we think that a comedian goes too far. On the contrary, they believed that the quality of chant was essential to poetry. Cicero says that the versification of the better lyric poets would seem like prose if it were not supported by chant. Does that not show that the pronunciation which was then natural in daily discourse partook so fully of the nature of chant that it was impossible to imagine a middle way such as our own declamation?

In fact, our only aim in declaiming is to express our thoughts in the most effective manner, without deviating much from what we consider natural. If the pronunciation of the ancients had been like ours, they would, like us, have been satisfied with a simple declamation. But it must have been very different, since they could not increase the expressiveness without the assistance of harmony.

§17 We also know that Greek and Latin had accents which required that the voice must fall on certain syllables and rise on others, independent of the meaning of a word or of the sense of the entire phrase. There is only one way of understanding how these accents would never be at odds with the utterance of the discourse. We are absolutely bound to assume that in the pronunciation of the ancients, the inflections that expressed the thought were so varied and so evident that they could not conflict with those required by the accents.

§18 Furthermore, no one who places himself in the circumstances of

---

[37] I do not give the evidence, which can be found in the third volume of [Du Bos's] *Réflexions critiques sur la Poésie et sur la Peinture*. I also refer to the same work for most of what I am going to say. The abbé Du Bos, who is the author, is a reliable authority; his erudition is well known.

the Greeks and Romans will be surprised that their declamation was a true chant. The reason we do not find chant very natural is not that its sounds succeed each other according to the proportions required by harmony, but because we find that even the weakest inflections are generally sufficient for the expression of our thoughts. Nations accustomed to conducting their voice by distinct intervals would find our pronunciation monotonous and soulless, while a chant which modified these intervals only so far as was necessary to measure the sounds would, as they saw it, increase the expressiveness of the discourse and would not seem out of the ordinary to them.

§19 For lack of knowledge about the quality of the pronunciation of the Greek and Latin languages, it has often proved difficult to understand what the ancients wrote about their stage performances. Here is an example; a commentator on Aristotle's Poetics [Dacier, *Poet. d'Arist.*, p. 82] says that if tragedy can do without verse,

> it can do better still without music. It must even be granted that we do not understand how music has ever come to be considered as somehow forming part of tragedy, for if there is anything in the world that seems foreign and even contrary to a tragic action, it is chant. I do not wish to displease the inventors of musical tragedies, poems that are as ridiculous as they are novel and would never be endured by people who had the least taste for the stage, had they not been seduced by one of the greatest composers of all time. For if I dare say so, operas are the grotesques of poetry and become still more intolerable by the pretense of making them pass for works that respect the rules. Aristotle would have done us a great favor if he had shown how music could come to be judged necessary to tragedy. Instead, all he did was simply to say that its full strength was known, which merely shows that everybody was convinced of the necessity and felt the wonderful effects that chant produced in the poems, in which it appeared only in the interludes. I have often tried to understand the reasons that induce people so learned and refined as the Athenians to join music and dancing to tragic actions; and after much study to discover how it could ever appear natural and credible to them for a chorus that represented the spectators of an action to dance and sing about such extraordinary events, I have concluded that in all this they followed their natural disposition and sought to satisfy their superstition. For the Greeks were the most superstitious people in the world

and the most in love with dancing and music; and their education enhanced this natural inclination.

"I very much doubt," says the abbé du Bos, "that this argument could excuse the taste of the Athenians if we assume that the music and dancing that ancient authors call absolutely necessary features in the performance of tragedies were the same kind of music and dancing as ours; but as we have already seen, this music was a simple declamation, and the dancing, as we shall see, was only a formal and subordinate form of gesture." [*Crit. Refl.* 3.66–8]

Both these explanations seem to me equally mistaken. Dacier thinks that the Greek mode of pronunciation was like the French and the music of their tragedies like that of our operas, so no wonder he is surprised by the taste of the Athenians; but he is wrong to blame Aristotle. Not being able to foresee the changes that would occur in pronunciation and music, this philosopher counted on being understood by posterity as he was by his contemporaries. If he seems obscure to us, let us blame our habit of judging the customs of the ancients by our own.

The source of the abbé Du Bos's error is the same. Since he did not understand how the ancients could have introduced music similar to that of our operas as the most natural practice in their theaters, he has chosen to say that it was not music but merely plain declamation according to notation.

§20 First of all, in what he is saying it seems to me that he does violence to many passages by the ancients. This is especially clear in the trouble he has explaining those that deal with the chorus. Secondly, if the learned abbé could have known the principles that govern harmony, he would have seen that plain declamation according to notation is a demonstrated impossibility. To demolish the system he has created in this matter, it will be sufficient to relate how he tries to establish it.

I have asked several musicians, he says, if it would be very difficult to invent characters with which one could record in notation the declamation that is practiced on our stage (. . .) These musicians have answered that the thing was possible and even that one could note declamation by using the scale of our music, provided that one did not give the notes more than half the usual intonation. For example, the notes that have a semitone of intonation in music would only have a quarter-tone in declamation. Thus one could note the smallest elevations of voice that are discernible at least to our ears.

French versification does not carry its measure along with it like the Greek and Roman meter. But I have also been told that it would be possible to use it in declamation for the value of the notes as well as their intonation. Thus a half-note would be given the value of a quarter-note and the latter in turn the value of an eighth-note, and other notes would be valued proportionally.

I know very well that it would not be easy to find people who could read this kind of music from the page and intone the notes properly. But if this intonation were taught to fifteen-year-olds for six months, they would succeed. Their organs would submit to this intonation or pronunciation of notes done without singing, just as they submit to the intonation of our ordinary music. Exercise and the habit that comes from exercise are to the voice what the bow and the hand of the violinist are to the violin. How then can anyone think that this intonation would be difficult? All it will take is that the voice becomes accustomed to do by method what it does all the time in conversation. Sometimes our speech is quick and sometimes slow. We use all sorts of tones, and we make progressions by raising or lowering the voice by all possible intervals. Notated declamation will be nothing but the tones and movements of the pronunciation written in notes. Certainly the difficulty of performing such a notation would not approach the difficulty of simultaneously reading words one had never seen, and of singing and accompanying on the harpsichord the words on a sheet of music one had never studied. And still even women learn by practice to perform all three operations at the same time.

As for the means of writing declamation in notation, whether the one we have indicated or some other, it would be no more difficult to reduce it to fixed rules and to put the method into practice than to produce the art of notating the steps and figures of a ballet entrée by eight dancers, especially with the steps being as varied and the figures as interlaced as they are today. Nevertheless Feuillée[s] has succeeded in notating this art, and his notation even tells the dancers how to hold their arms. [*Crit. Refl.* 3.113–15]

§21 What I have quoted is a very evident example of the pitfalls and the hazy arguments that become unavoidable in speaking of an art

[s] Raoul-Auger Feuillet, *Choréographie, ou l'art de décrire la danse par caractères, figures, et signes démonstratifs* (Paris, 1700 and 1701).

whose principles one does not know. The passage can justly be criticized from beginning to end. I have given it at length to show that the mistakes of a writer, who is moreover as estimable as the abbé Du Bos, teach us that, whenever we speak in terms of inaccurate ideas, we run the risk of deceiving ourselves in our conjectures.

No one who knows the formation of sounds and the artifice by which their intonation becomes natural would ever imagine that one could divide them in quarter-tones and that their scale would soon become as familiar as the one that is used in music. The musicians who are the abbé Du Bos's warrant may be excellent in practice, but it would seem that they did not at all know the theory of an art whose true principles were first laid down by Rameau.[t]

§22 His *Génération harmonique* shows (1) that a sound cannot be measured unless it is sustained long enough to reveal its harmonic structure; (2) that the voice cannot sing several sounds in sequence, with distinct intervals between them, unless it is guided by a ground bass; (3) that no ground bass can yield a succession of quarter-tones. But in our declamation the sounds are for the most part rarely sustained, and they succeed each other by quarter-tones or even slighter intervals. The task of putting them into notation is therefore not feasible.

§23 It is true that the fundamental succession by a tierce gives the semitone minor, which is a quarter-tone below the semitone major. But that occurs only in the changes of modes, so that it can never produce a scale of quarter-tones. Furthermore, this semitone minor is not natural, and the ear is so unfit to measure it that on the harpsichord it is not distinguished from the semitone major, for the same key is used for both.[38] The ancients undoubtedly were familiar with these two semi-tones, and that is what made the abbé Du Bos and others believe that the ancients divided their scale by quarter-tones.

§24 No inference can be drawn from choreography or from the art of written notation for the steps and figures of a ballet interlude. Feuillée had only signs to contrive, for in dancing, all the steps and movements are measured, at least those he knew how to put into notation. In our declamation, sounds for the most part cannot be measured; they

---

[38] See in *Génération harmonique*, Ch. 14, Art. 1 for the way in which the voice passes to the semitone minor.

[t] Jean-Philippe Rameau (1683–1764), French composer and the author of important treatises on musical theory.

correspond to what in ballets are particular expressions, which choreography cannot record in writing.

I put in a note my discussion of certain passages from the ancients which the abbé Du Bos has cited in support of his opinion.[39]

---

[39] He cites some passages in which the ancients speak of their ordinary pronunciation as being simple and with continuous sound; but he should have noted that they were speaking of it only in comparison to their music, so that it was not absolutely simple. In fact, when they considered it in itself, they assigned prosodic accents to it, which do not at all occur in our pronunciation. A Gascon who did not know any pronunciation that was simpler than his own would hear only a continuous sound when he compared it with vocal music. The ancients were in the same situation.

Cicero makes Crassus say that when he listens to Laelia he believes he is hearing a recitation from the plays of Plautus and Naevius, because her pronunciation is uniform and does not feign the accents of foreign languages [*De oratore, III, 45]. That is true, but at the time of Plautus and Naevius the pronunciation of Latin already partook of chant, because the declamation of these poets' plays had been notated. Thus Laelia's pronunciation was uniform only because she did not use the new accents which custom had made fashionable.

Comic actors, says Quintilian [*II, x, 13], do not deviate from nature in their pronunciation, at least not so much that we would fail to recognize it; but by the ornamentations which their art permits they enhance the usual manner of speaking. Can that be called singing? asks the abbé Du Bos. Yes, if we assume that the pronunciation which Quintilian calls natural would be so charged with accents that it came close enough to chant to be put into notation without being much altered. But that is especially true of the time when this rhetorician was writing, for the accents of the Latin language had then greatly increased in number.

Here is a fact which at first would seem still more favorable to the abbé Du Bos's opinion. In Athens they ordered the declamation of the laws to be formalized and that the man who proclaimed them be accompanied by an instrument. But is it likely that the Athenians had their laws sung? I answer that they would never have thought of establishing such a custom if their pronunciation had been like ours, because the simplest chant would not have been sufficiently different from the pronunciation. But we must put ourselves in their place; their language still had more accents than Latin, so that declamation only slightly charged with singing could do justice to the inflections of the voice without seeming to vary from the ordinary pronunciation.

Thus it would seem evident, concludes the abbé Du Bos, that the chant of the plays that were recited in the ancient theaters had neither transitions, nor rhythmical portamento, nor sustained tremolo, nor the other features of our vocal chant.

Either I am mistaken or this writer did not have a very clear idea of what chant is. It seems that he conceives of it only in terms of our operas. Having mentioned Quintilian's complaint that some orators pleaded at the bar as if they recited on the stage, can one believe, he adds, that these orators were singing as in our operas! I answer that the succession of tones that form the chant can be much simpler than in our opera, and that it does not need to have the same transitions, the same rhythmical portamento, and the same sustained tremolo.

In addition, in the ancients we find many passages which prove that their pronunciation was not continuous sound. "Such is," says Cicero in his *Orator* [*57], "the marvellous power of the voice, that three tones, acute, grave, and middle, form all the variety, all the sweetness and the harmony of chant; for we must understand that pronunciation contains a sort of chant, not a musical chant or such as is used by the Phrygian and Carian orators in their perorations, but a less accentuated chant of the sort Demosthenes and Aeschines had in mind when they reproached each other with their inflections of voice, and when Demosthenes, to push the irony a step further, admitted that his adversary had spoken in a soft, clear, and reasonable tone of voice" (from the translation of M. l'abbé [*Hyacinthe] Colin).

Quintilian observes that this reproach of Demosthenes and Aeschines should not be taken as a condemnation of those inflections of the voice, since it shows that they both use them.

§25 The same causes that produce the variation of voice by distinct intervals will necessarily also cause a difference in the time allotted for the pronunciation of each syllable. It would therefore be unnatural for people whose prosody partook of chant to give equal time to each syllable, for such a mode of pronunciation would not sufficiently imitate the language of action. At the beginning of languages some sounds followed each other very rapidly, others very slowly. That is the source of what the grammarians call "quantity," or the marked difference between long and short syllables. Quantity and pronunciation by distinct intervals went together and changed at pretty much the same rate. Roman prosody was still close to chant, so their words were composed of very unequal syllables. We have not preserved quantity except insofar as the weak inflections of our voice have made it necessary.

§26 Just as inflections by perceptible intervals had introduced a singing declamation, so the marked inequality of the syllables added a difference of time and measure. Thus ancient declamation had the two features that characterize chant: I mean modulation and movement.

Movement is the soul of music, and it is no wonder that the ancients considered it absolutely essential in declamation. Their theaters had a man who marked it by tapping with his feet, and comic actors were constrained by the measure just as much as musicians and dancers are today. It is obvious that this kind of declamation was so different from our pronunciation that it would seem unnatural to us. Far from requiring the actor to follow a certain movement, we do not allow him

"The great actors," says the abbé Du Bos [*Crit. Refl. 3.198], "would never speak a word in the morning before, if I may say so, having unfolded the voice with care by letting it emerge little by little, giving flight to it gradually, in order not to damage the organs by deploying them with precipitous violence. They even made sure they were lying down during this exercise. When they had finished acting, they sat down, and in this posture they again folded up their organs, so to speak, by respiring on the highest tone they had reached in their declamation and afterward successively on all the other tones until they finally came to the very lowest" [*De oratore*, I, 251]. If the declamation had not been a chant that admitted all the tones, would the comic actors have taken the precaution to exercise their voices every day on the whole series of tones they could produce?

Finally, "the writings of the ancients," says the abbé Du Bos [*Crit. Refl.* 3.200], "abound with facts which show that the attention they paid to everything that could strengthen or embellish the voice went to the point of superstition. In the third chapter of the eleventh book in Quintilian we read that with regard to all kinds of eloquence, the ancients engaged in deep musings on the nature of the human voice and on all the practices that would help strengthen it by exercise. The art of teaching to strengthen and manage the voice even became a special profession." Could a form of declamation that was the result of so much care and so much thought have been as simple as ours?

to make us aware of the measure of the lines, or we even insist that he break it so that he seems to be speaking in prose. Thus everything confirms that the pronunciation of the ancients in everyday conversation came so close to chant that their declamation may be called a chant in the strict sense.

§27 In our theater performances, we often observe that singers have great difficulty making their words distinctly understood. Someone will surely ask me if the declamation of the ancients caused the same problem. My answer is no, and I find the reason in the nature of their prosody.

Since our language has little quantity, we are pleased by the musician so long as he keeps the short syllables short and the long ones long. Provided this difference is respected, he is free to shorten or lengthen as he wishes, for example lingering one, two, or three measures on the same syllable. The absence of prosodic accent gives him the same liberty, for he can raise or lower the voice on the same sound, his own taste being the rule. All this will naturally cause some confusion in words that are set to music.

In Rome the artist who composed the declamation of dramatic performances was obliged to conform to the prosody in every respect. He was not free to lengthen a short syllable more than one measure and a long syllable more than two, or the audience would have hissed him. The prosodic accent often determined whether he should pass to a higher pitch or to a lower; he was not free to make his own choice. Finally, it was his duty to make the movement of the chant conform both to the measure of the verse and to the thought expressed in it. This ensured that the declamation, while conforming to rules more fixed than our own, contributed to making the words distinctly understood even though set to music.

§28 It would be a mistake to think that ancient declamation was like our recitatives; its chant was not so musical. As to our recitatives, we have so heavily charged them with music because no matter how simple they might have been, they would never have seemed natural to us. Wishing to introduce chant on the stage and seeing that it could not come close to our ordinary pronunciation, we have chosen, as compensation for these charms, to charge it with what it took away, not from nature but from a habit we mistake for nature. The Italians have a recitative that is less musical than ours. Being used to accompanying

their speaking with more movement than we do and with a pronunciation that values accents as much as we avoid them, they found that
simple music was natural enough. That is why they prefer to use it in
the plays that might require to be declaimed. We would find our
recitative diminished if it became too simple, because it would have
fewer charms without being more natural to our taste. But for the
Italians, their recitative would lose if it became less simple, because it
would not gain in charming qualities what it would lose in regard to
nature, or rather what they took to be nature. The conclusion is that the
Italians and the French ought to stick to their particular manner, and
that on this subject they are wrong to criticize each other.

§29 In the prosody of the ancients, I also find the reason for a fact
that no one, I believe, has explained. The question is how the Roman
orators who delivered their orations in the public forum could be heard
by the entire crowd.

The sounds of our voice carry easily to the limits even of a large
square; the only difficulty is in preventing the sounds from becoming
confused. But this difficulty will lessen in proportion as the syllables of
each word, owing to the prosodic quality of the language, are more
clearly distinguished. In Latin they differed by the quality of sound; by
the accent which, independent of the sense, required the lowering or
raising of the voice; and by the quantity. We have no accents, our
language has hardly any quantity, and many of our syllables are mute. A
Roman could therefore make himself understood in a public space
where a Frenchman could do so only with difficulty and perhaps not at
all.

4 Progress of the art of gesture among the ancients

§30 Today everyone knows the progress which the art of gesture had made among the ancients, and chiefly among the Romans. The abbé Du Bos has collected the most interesting things the authors of antiquity had to say on this matter.[u] But no one has explained the reason for this progress, which is why the public performances of the ancients seem to be marvels we do not understand, with the consequence that we often find it hard to withhold the ridicule we so willingly confer on whatever differs from our own customs. Coming to their defense, the abbé Du Bos shows the immense cost the Greeks and Romans paid for the staging of their plays and the progress they made in poetry, oratory, painting, sculpture, and architecture. From this he concludes that we ought to form a favorable opinion of those arts that leave no monuments, so that, if we believe him, we should give the same high praise to their dramatic performances that we give to their buildings and writings. I believe that to develop a taste for such performances, they would need to have been prepared by customs far removed from ours, and that, as a result of those customs, the ancient theater deserves our praise and may even be superior to our stage. This is what I shall try to explain in this and the following chapter.

§31 If, as I have said, it is natural for the voice to vary its inflections in step with an increasing variety of gestures, it is also natural for people who speak a language whose pronunciation is much like chant to have a greater variety of gestures, for these two things will go together. In fact, if we in Greek and Roman prosody find traces of the quality of the language of action, we have still greater reason to find it in the bodily movements with which they accompanied their discourse. That means that their gestures could be sufficiently distinct to be measured. We therefore should have no difficulty understanding that they prescribed rules for the gestures, and that they had discovered the secret of

---

[u] Condillac's references to Du Bos's *Crit. Refl.* are all to Part III, "which contains a dissertation on the theatrical representations of the ancients" (this is also vol. 3 in all but the first edition, 1719). He is especially drawing on pp. 160–225 with these telling titles: Ch. 13, "Of saltation, or the art of gesticulation, called by some authors the hypocritical music"; Ch. 14, "Of the theatrical dance or saltation. How the player that gesticulated, could act in concert with the other who recited. Of the dance of the chorus"; Ch. 15, "Observations concerning the manner in which the dramatic pieces of the ancients were represented. Of the passion which the Greeks and Romans had for theatrical entertainment; as also of the study the actors made of their art, and the recompences they received"; and Ch. 16, "Of the pantomimes, or players who acted without speaking."

providing a notation for them. Today this part of declamation has become as simple as the rest. We do not value an actor except so far as he commands the art of expressing all the emotions of the soul by a slight variation of gestures, and find him unnatural if he deviates too much from our usual gesticulation. For that reason we can no longer have fixed principles to regulate all the attitudes and movements that are used in declamation, so that the observations we can make on this subject become limited to particular cases.

§32   When gestures were reduced to an art and put down in notation, it became easy to submit them to the movement and measure of declamation, as the Greeks and Romans did. They even went farther by dividing the chant and the gestures between two actors. This practice may seem extraordinary, but we see how one actor, by a measured movement, could appropriately vary his attitudes to make them agree with the narrative of the other who did the declamation, and why they would be as shocked by a gesture out of measure as we are by the steps of a dancer who does not keep time.

§33   The manner in which the Romans introduced the practice of dividing chant and gestures between two actors shows how greatly the Romans appreciated a gesticulation that would seem exaggerated to us. It is said that the poet Livius Andronicus, who acted in one of these plays, having become hoarse by several times repeating passages the audience liked, thought it proper that one of his slaves would recite the lines while he himself made the gestures. His action gained in liveliness because his energies were not divided, and when his acting was applauded, this practice came to prevail in the monologues. It was only in scenes of dialogue that the same comic actor continued to do both gestures and narration. Would movements that required all the energy of one person be applauded on our stage?

§34   The practice of dividing the declamation naturally led to the discovery of the art of pantomimes. All it took was for the actor who did the gestures to put so much expression into them that the role of the actor who did the narration could be dispensed with. The earliest writers tell us that the first pantomimes tested their skill in monologues, which were, as I have said, scenes in which the declamation was divided. These comic actors first appeared under Augustus and were soon able to perform entire plays. Compared with our gesticulation, their art was what the chanting declamation of narratives is to our declamation. By a long process, this is how they came to imagine, as an entirely new invention, a language which had been the first that mankind spoke, or which at least differed from it only by being suitable for the expression of a much larger number of thoughts.[v]

§35 The art of pantomimes would never have come into being in a nation such as ours. The slight gesticulation that accompanies our discourse is too far removed from the lively, varied, and characteristic movements of the kinds of actors we are talking about. For the Romans these movements were part of the language, and especially the language used in their theaters. They had made three collections of gestures, one for tragedy, another for comedy, and a third for the dramatic pieces that were called "satires." That is where the first Roman mimes, Pylades and Bathyllus, learned the gestures of their art. If they invented new gestures, they no doubt did so on the analogy of those that everyone already knew.

§36 What I have been saying about ancient declamation is confirmed by the following considerations: that the progress which the comic actors had made in their art naturally gave birth to pantomimes; that their gestures were borrowed from the collections made for the performance of tragedies, comedies, and satires; that there was a close relation between strongly marked gesticulation and the distinct variation of the inflections of the voice. Furthermore, if we also bear in mind that the mimes could not rely on facial expression because, like other actors, they wore masks, we can realize how animated their gestures had to be and, consequently, how musical the declamation must have been in the scenes from which those gestures had been borrowed.

§37 The competition that Cicero and Roscius sometimes engaged in shows us the importance of gestural expression even before there were mimes. Cicero spoke a passage he had just written, and the comedian repeated the meaning by silent acting. Cicero then changed the words or the phrasing without weakening the sense, and Roscius again expressed it as before with new gestures.[w] Now, I ask you if such gestures could ever find their match in the sort of declamation that is as simple as ours.

---

[v] This remark about ancient theatrical practice inventing something close to what communication was at its origin points to the core of Condillac's argument in *Origin*, with its reliance on rhetorical expressivism. Cicero and Quintilian often treat the affinity between the skills of the orator and the actor.

[w] The source of this competition is Macrobius, *Saturnalia*, Bk. 3, ch. 14. See Macrobius, *The Saturnalia*, tr., with introd. and notes, Percival Vaughan Davis (New York, Columbia University Press, 1969), p. 233.

§38 The art of mimes charmed the Romans from the beginning; it spread to the farthest provinces, and it lasted as long as the empire. The people wept at their performances as they did at those of other actors; these performances even had the advantage of giving greater pleasure, because the imagination is more deeply affected by a language that is all action. The passion for this sort of performance finally went so far that the senate, during the first years of the reign of Tiberius, was obliged to enact a statute forbidding the senators to frequent the schools of mimes and the Roman knights to pay any respect to them in the streets.

The abbé Du Bos has good reason to say that

> the art of the pantomimes would have had great difficulty succeeding among the northern nations of Europe whose natural gesticulation is not very eloquent and not sufficiently distinct to be easily understood when seen without hearing the discourse which should be its natural accompaniment (. . .) But (. . .) conversations of all kinds carry along with them more outward show and speak much more to the eyes, if I may be permitted that expression, in Italy than in our part of the world. When a Roman wishes to quit his formal bearing to give free rein to his natural vivacity, he abounds in gestures and outward show that signify nearly as much as entire phrases. His actions make many things intelligible which our action would not make it possible to figure out, and his gestures are so distinct that they are easy to recognize when we see them a second time. For a Roman who wishes to tell a friend a secret about some important business, it is not enough to make sure he is not overheard; he also takes the precaution of not being seen, being for good reason afraid that his gestures and facial expressions would reveal what he is about to say.
>
> From this we learn that the same vivacity of mind, that the same fire of imagination which by a natural movement causes gestures that are animated, varied, expressive, and distinct, also make it easy to grasp the meaning when we need to understand the sense of the gestures that other people make. We easily understand a language we speak (. . .) If to these observations we add the familiar consideration that there are nations whose disposition has more sensibility than that of other nations, we shall have no difficulty understanding that the mute comic actors could so deeply touch the Greeks and Romans whose natural gesticulation they imitated. [*Crit. Refl.* 3.216–17]

§39 The details given in this and the preceding chapter show that ancient declamation differed from ours in two respects: by the chant which ensured that the actor was understood by those who were farthest from the stage, and by the fact that the gestures, owing to their greater variation and liveliness, were understood at a distance. That made it possible for them to build theaters so vast that the entire people could attend the show. Owing to the remoteness of the greater part of the spectators, the actors' faces could not be seen clearly, a fact that also prevented them from illuminating the stage as much as we do. So they had good reason to introduce the use of masks. They were perhaps first used to hide some deformity or tic, but later they were used to amplify the voice and to give to each actor the particular physiognomy that suited his character. In that respect, masks were extremely useful; their only drawback was that they covered up the facial expression, but to so few spectators that the loss could be ignored.

Today declamation has become simpler, so that the actor cannot make himself understood from so far away, and the gestures are less varied and distinct. It is with the facial expression and with the eyes that the good comedian takes pride in expressing the sentiments of his soul, which means he must be seen from close up without a mask. For that reason our theaters are much smaller and better illuminated than those of the ancients. That is how prosody, by assuming a new quality, has changed even things with which it would at first seem to have no connection.

§40 From the difference between our mode of declamation and that of the ancients, we can conclude that it is today much more difficult to excel in this art than it was in their time. Since we permit less deviation in voice and gesture, we demand greater subtlety in acting. Still, I have been told that there are more good comedians in Italy than in France. That may be, but it must be understood with reference to the tastes of the two nations. For the Romans, Baron would have seemed cold, while Roscius would seem deranged to us.

§41 The love of declamation was the favorite passion of the Romans; most of them, says the abbé Du Bos, had become declaimers [*Crit. Refl.* 3.188–202]. The reason is obvious, especially in the time of the republic, when the talent for eloquence was especially prized by the citizens because it opened the way to the greatest careers, for which the cultivation of eloquence was an indispensable prerequisite. This art was one of the chief aims of education, and it was easier to teach to children by virtue of rules that were as fixed as they are today in dancing and music. That is one of the principal reasons for the passion the ancients had for public spectacles.

The taste for declamation was taken up by the theater audiences. They easily became accustomed to a manner of recitation that did not differ from what was natural to them, except by following rules which heightened the expression. Thus it lent a refinement to their knowledge of the language which we do not find today except among the better sort of people.

§42 By a series of changes that it has undergone, prosody has become so simple that it can no longer be reduced to rules. Today it is almost wholly a matter of instinct and taste. With us it cannot form part of education, and it is neglected to such a degree that we have orators who do not seem to believe that it could be an essential element in their art, something that would have seemed as inconceivable to the ancients as their most astonishing achievements are to us. Because we do not study declamation at an early age, we do not hasten to public shows with the same eagerness as they did, and eloquence has less power over us. The oratorical speeches they have left us have preserved only part of their expressiveness. We know neither the intonation nor the gesticulation which must have made such a powerful impression on the soul of the audience.[40] In short, we hardly feel the thunder of Demosthenes or the harmony of Cicero's sentences.

---

[40] In *De oratore* [*III, 213] Cicero writes: "Have we not often seen mediocre orators carry off all the honour and prize of eloquence by the mere dignity of their action, while very learned orators were considered mediocre because they lacked the graces of pronunciation; so that Demosthenes was right to give action the first, the second, and the third rank of importance. For if eloquence is nothing without this talent and if action without eloquence has so much force and efficacy, must we not admit the extreme importance of action in public discourse?" The ancient manner of declamation must have had much more power than ours for Demosthenes and Cicero, who excelled in the other parts, to have judged that eloquence is nothing without action. Today our orators would not share that judgment, and is it not true that the abbé Colin says that Demosthenes' sentiment is an exaggeration? But if that were true, why would Cicero approve it without qualification?

5 Music

So far I have been obliged to assume that the ancients were familiar with music. It is now appropriate to treat its history, at least insofar as this forms a part of language.

§43 At the origin of languages, when prosody varied greatly, all the inflections of voice were natural to it. Consequently chance was bound sometimes to introduce some passages that pleased the ear. As they were noticed and habitually repeated, the first idea of harmony came into being.

§44 The diatonic order, that is to say the order in which sounds succeed each other by tones and semitones, today seems so natural that one would think it was the first to be known. But if we find sounds whose relations are much more perceptible, we would be right to conclude that their succession was noted earlier.

It has been demonstrated that the progression by a third, a fifth, and an octave immediately depends on the principle on which harmony is based, that is to say on the resonance of sonorous bodies, and that the diatonic order develops from this progression. From this it follows that the sounds must be much more perceptible in a harmonic succession than in the diatonic order. By differing from the harmonic principle, the diatonic order cannot preserve the relations between sounds except insofar as they are transmitted by the succession that produces it. For example, "re" is connected with "do" only because "do," "re" is produced by the progression "do," "sol"; and the connection of the last two is based on the principle of sonorous bodies, of which they form a part. This argument is confirmed by the ear, which more easily feels the relation of the sounds "do," "mi," "sol," "do" than that of the sounds "do," "re," "mi," "fa." Therefore the harmonic intervals were noted first.

There are still other progressions to be observed here, for since the harmonic sounds form intervals that are more or less easy to intone and have more or less perceptible relations, it is not to be expected that they would have been perceived and understood at the same time. Thus it is probable that the entire progression "do, mi, sol, do" was found only after several experiments. Once it was known, others were made on the same pattern, such as "sol, si, re, sol." As for the diatonic order, it was only discovered little by little and after many uncertain efforts, because its generation has only been worked out very recently [see Rameau's *Génération harmonique*].

§45 The first progress of this art was therefore the product of long experience. Its principles were multiplied to such a degree that the true principles remained hidden. Rameau is the first to have found the origin of all harmony in the resonance of sonorous bodies and to have reduced the theory of this art to a single principle. Neither the Greeks, whose music is so highly praised, nor the Romans knew composition in parts. It is likely, however, that they early on practiced some chords, either because they would have noticed them by chance in the coincidence of the voices or because the plucking of two strings of an instrument at the same time would have made them aware of harmony.

§46 The progress of music having been so slow, it took a long time before the ancients thought of separating music from words, for it would have seemed entirely without expression. Furthermore, with prosody having regulated all the tones of the human voice and having by itself provided occasion to note their harmony, it was natural to regard music merely as an art that could make discourse more agreeable or forceful. Here we see the origin of the ancient prejudice against separating music from words. For those among whom music first arose, it was pretty much what declamation is for us; it taught them to regulate the voice whose use had formerly been subject to chance. It would have seemed as ridiculous to separate chant from words as it would be today to separate the sounds of our declamation from our verse.

§47 In the meantime the art of music improved, so that little by little it came to equal the expression of words, which in turn it tried to surpass. At this point it became apparent that music was by itself a potential means of much expression, with the result that it no longer seemed ridiculous to separate it from words. The expression of sounds in the prosody that partook of chant and in musical declamation prepared the way for their expression when they were heard without words. Two factors ensured the very success of those who, if they had any talent, experimented with this kind of music. The first is that they undoubtedly chose passages to which the usual declamation had routinely joined a particular expression, or at least they imagined something of that kind. The second is the surprise that this music was bound to produce by its very novelty. The greater the surprise, the more readily one would give in to the impression it made. Furthermore, they saw that the people who were most easily moved by the very forces of the sounds were transported by stages from joy to gloom or even to fury. At the sight of this change, others who had not reacted were moved almost to the same degree. The effects of this music became much discussed, and the imagination was kindled at their very mention. Everyone was eager to judge for himself, so that people, by their eagerness to share the confirmation of extraordinary things, hastened to hear this music in the most receptive frame of mind. Given these opportunities, it often performed the same marvels.

§48 Today our prosody and declamation offer no preparation for the effects which our music ought to produce. For us, chant is not a language that is as familiar as it was to the ancients; and music separated from words no longer has the air of novelty that alone can have a powerful effect on the imagination. Furthermore, while it is being performed, we stay as cool as we can, we do not let the musicians disturb our composure, so that our sentiments derive entirely from the action of the sounds on the ear. But when the imagination does not by itself react on the senses, the sentiments of the soul are usually so weak that we should not be surprised that our music does not come up to the astonishing effects of ancient music. To judge its power we would need to play compositions before people with much imagination so that for them the music would carry the benefit of novelty, and its declamation, by virtue of respecting a prosody that partook of chant, would itself be musical. But this experiment would be nugatory if we were as much inclined to admire things that are near as those that are distant.

§49 Today our chant set to words is so different from our customary pronunciation and declamation that the imagination has a hard time submitting to the illusion of our musical tragedies. The Greeks, by contrast, surpassed us in sensibility because they had a livelier imagination. The musicians chose the most favorable moments to stir their sentiments. Alexander, for example, was at a table and (as Burette reports)[41] most likely overheated with wine, when music fit to inspire fury made him take up arms. I have no doubt that we have soldiers who

---

[41] *Hist. de l'Acad. des Belles-Lettres*, vol. 5.[x]

[x] Pierre-Jean Burette, "Dissertation où l'on fait voir, que les merveilleux effets, attribués à la musique des anciens, ne prouvent point qu'elle fut aussi parfaite que la nôtre." *Académie Royale des Inscriptions et Belles-Lettres, Mémoires de littérature tirés des registres de cette académie*, 5 (1729), 142. (Read 28 July 1718.)

would do as much at the sound of drums and trumpets. We should not, therefore, judge ancient music by the effects we attribute to it, but by the instruments they used; if we do that, we will have reason to presume that their music must have been inferior to ours.

§50 There is reason to believe that music without words grew among the Greeks owing to a development that was similar to the one that gave the Romans the art of pantomime; and that these two arts at the outset caused the same surprise and produced equally astonishing effects in these two nations. I find this concurrence very interesting and also a confirmation of my conjectures.

§51 Like so many other writers on this subject, I have said that the Greeks had a livelier imagination than we do. But I am not sure we know the true reason for this difference; to me at least, it seems wrong to attribute it exclusively to the climate. If we suppose that the Greek climate had always remained the same as it was, then the imagination of the people must little by little have weakened. We shall see that this is a natural effect of the changes that occur in language.

I have elsewhere observed [Pt. 1, Sect. 4, §21] that the imagination has the keenest effect in people who do not know the use of instituted signs. With the language of action being the immediate effect of this imagination, it follows that it must be more ardent. In fact, to those who are familiar with it, a single gesture is often equivalent to a long sentence. For that reason languages that are made on the pattern of this language must also be the liveliest, while other languages will lose their vivacity in proportion as they preserve fewer of its qualities in the process of moving away from it. But what I have said about prosody shows that Greek more than any other language felt the influence of the language of action, and what I shall later say about inversions will prove that this was not the only effect of that influence. This language was therefore especially suitable for the exercise of the imagination. French, by contrast, is so simple both in construction and prosody that it hardly requires more than the exercise of memory. In speaking of things, all we do is to recall their signs but rarely the ideas. Thus as the imagination is less often called into action, it naturally becomes difficult to arouse it. Therefore our imagination is not so lively as that of the Greeks.

§52 The prejudice in favor of custom has always been an obstacle to the progress of the arts, and music has especially suffered under it. Six hundred years B.C.E., Timotheus was banished from Sparta by a decree of the Ephori for adding three strings to the lyre in contempt of ancient music, that is to say, for intending to make it fit to execute more varied and extensive chants. Those were the prejudices of that time. We have them too, and so will those who come after us, without ever suspecting that they could some day be found ridiculous. Lully,[y] whom we consider so simple and natural, seemed extravagant in his day. They said his ballet music spoiled dance and that he reduced it to buffoonery. "One hundred and twenty years ago," says the abbé Du Bos, "the chants that were composed in France were, generally speaking, only a series of long notes (. . .) and (. . .) eighty years ago all the ballet tunes had only a slow movement, and their chant, if I may say so, marched sedately even when it was most joyful" [*Crit. Refl.* 3.127–8]. That is the kind of music that was missed by those who blamed Lully.

§53 Since everyone considers himself a good judge of music, the number of bad judges is very large. There is no doubt, in this art as in the rest, a point of perfection from which it must not vary; that is the principle, but how vague! Who has so far determined that point? And if no one has, who will? Is it the least-practiced ears because they are in the majority? Thus there was a time when Lully's music was justly condemned. Is it the ears of those who know music, though in the minority? Thus today we have a music that is no less beautiful for being different from Lully's music.

Music must have been criticized as it got better, especially if the progress was striking and sudden, for when that happens it is less like what people are used to hearing. But as we become more familiar with it, we gain a taste for it, and it ceases to be the object of prejudice.

§54 Since we cannot know the quality of the instrumental music of the ancients, I shall limit myself to making some conjectures on the chant of their declamation.

It probably differed from their usual pronunciation almost the way our declamation differs from ours, and was likewise varied to suit the plays and the scenes. In comedy it must have been as simple as the prosody allowed. The usual pronunciation was altered no more than was needed to measure the sounds and to lead the voice by certain intervals.

In tragedy the chant was more varied and extensive, chiefly in the monologues, which were called canticles. Those are usually the most

[y] Jean-Baptiste Lully (1633–87) established opera as an art in France; appointed superintendent of music at court by Louis XIV.

passionate scenes, for it is natural that the actor, while he restrains himself in the other scenes, when alone will let loose all the impetuosity of the sentiments that move him. That is why the Romans had their monologues set to music by professional composers. Sometimes they even put them in charge of composing the declamation for the rest of the play. That was not the case among the Greeks, for their poets knew music and did not entrust that task to others.

Finally, in the choruses the chant was more elaborate than in the other scenes, for those were the places where the poet gave the greatest flight to his genius, and there is no doubt that the musicians followed his example. These conjectures are confirmed by the different instruments that accompanied the voices of the actors, for their range followed the character of the words.

We cannot form an idea of the ancient choruses by comparing them to those of our opera. Their music was very different because they did not have composition in parts, and their dancing was perhaps still more removed from any resemblance to our ballets. "It is easy to imagine," says the abbé Du Bos [*Crit. Refl.* 3.184], "that those dances were nothing but gestures and signs by which the characters of the choruses expressed their sentiments, whether they spoke or by a silent show made evident how strongly they were moved by the incident in which they were involved. This declamation often obliged the choruses to walk on the stage, and as the movements of several people on the stage at the same time must be coordinated in advance to prevent giving the appearance of a giddy multitude, the ancients prescribed specific rules for the steps of the choruses." In the vast theaters of antiquity, these movements could create delineations that properly expressed the sentiments of the chorus.

§55 The art of marking the declamation and accompanying it with an instrument was known at Rome from the early days of the republic. In the beginning their declamation was simple, but later it changed owing to contact with the Greeks. The Romans could not resist the charms of the harmony and expression of this nation's language. This cultured nation became the school in which they formed their taste in literature, the arts, and the sciences, and the Latin language conformed to the nature of the Greek language to the extent its genius allowed.

Cicero tells us that accents borrowed from foreigners had changed the Roman pronunciation to an appreciable degree. They no doubt caused corresponding changes in the music of their dramatic performances, for one is a consequence of the other. In fact, both Horace and Cicero observe that the instruments used in the theaters in their time had a much wider range than those that had been used earlier; that the actor, to keep up with them, was obliged to declaim in a greater number of tones; and that the chant had become so impetuous that it was impossible to observe the measure without great agitation. I refer to those passages as they are quoted by the abbé Du Bos, so that the reader can judge if they can possibly mean only a simple declamation [*Crit. Refl.* 3.116–31].

§56 Such is the idea we can form of musical declamation and of the causes that have created it or introduced variations. It remains to examine the circumstances that have given rise to a declamation as simple as ours and to public spectacles that are so different.

The climate did not make it possible for the cold and phlegmatic nations of the north to preserve the accents and the quantity which necessity had introduced at the birth of languages. When the barbarians invaded the Roman Empire and had conquered the western part, Latin lost its character as it became mixed with their forms of speech. That is the source of the lack of accent which we consider the most beautiful feature of our pronunciation, but the origin is not to its credit. Under the domination of these rude nations, letters declined; theaters were destroyed; and many arts were lost, such as the art of miming; the art of marking the declamation and dividing it between two actors; the arts which contribute to the scenery such as architecture, painting, sculpture; and all the arts which in one way or another depend on music. At the time of the Renaissance the genius of languages was so different and customs had changed so radically that it became impossible to understand what the ancients had written about their public spectacles.

Perfectly to understand the cause of this revolution, we must remember what I have said about the influence of prosody. Roman and Greek prosody was so distinct that it followed fixed rules, and so well known that people even without study of the rules were shocked by the slightest slips in pronunciation. Those are the factors that provided the means for developing an art of declamation and recording it in notation; in due course, this art became part of education.

With declamation thus made perfect, it produced the art of dividing chant and gestures between two actors, and as it extended its influence even to the shape and the dimensions of the theaters, they became so large, as we have seen, that they could accommodate huge crowds.

Here we have the origin of the ancient taste for spectacles, for stage scenery, and for all the related arts such as music, architecture, painting, and sculpture. For the ancients no talent was lost, for each citizen at every moment confronted objects that could engage his imagination.

Since our language is almost devoid of prosody, our declamation cannot have fixed rules, and we have been unable both to record it in notation and to learn the art of dividing it between two actors. For the same reason the art of miming has little appeal to us, and dramatic performances have had to be enclosed in theaters which left no room for the common people. From this follows the saddest part, our limited taste for music, architecture, painting, and sculpture. We believe that we alone resemble the ancients, but in this regard the Italians come much closer than we do. Thus we see that if our shows are so different from Greek and Roman spectacles, it is all a natural effect of the changes that have occurred in prosody.

6 Musical and plain declamation compared

§57 Our declamation sometimes allows intervals that are as distinct as in chant. If we altered them as much as would be necessary to measure them, they would be no less natural and could be expressed in notation. I even believe that good taste and the ear would make the comedians prefer harmonic sounds so long as they did not clash too much with our usual pronunciation. Undoubtedly, it is for sounds of this kind that Molière had invented a notation [*Crit. Refl.* 3.234–44]. But it is impossible to make a notation for the rest of the declamation, for there the inflections of voice are so feeble that to measure the tones it would be necessary to change the intervals so much that the declamation would violate what we call nature.

§58 Though our declamation, unlike chant, does not have a succession of distinct sounds, it does express the sentiments of the soul with sufficient force to move those who are familiar with it, provided their language has little life and variation in its prosody. It no doubt produces this effect because its sounds pretty nearly preserve the same mutual proportions as in chant. I say "pretty nearly" because, not being measurable, they cannot have exact relations.

Our declamation is therefore naturally less expressive than music. In fact, what is the sound that is best suited to express a sentiment of the soul? In the first place, it must be the sound which imitates the cry that is its natural sign and is the same for declamation and music. Next, it is the overtones of the first, for they are closely connected. Finally, it is all the sounds that can arise from this harmony, as they vary and combine in the movement that characterizes each passion, for every sentiment of the soul determines the tone and movement of the chant which is most proper for its expression. But these last two kinds of sounds are rarely found in our declamation, which in any event does not imitate the movements of the soul as chant does.

§59 This defect of our declamation is, however, remedied by the advantage it has of appearing more natural to us. It gives an air of truth to the expression which makes a stronger impression on the imagination, even if a weaker one on the senses. That is why we are often more touched by a well-declaimed passage than by a beautiful recitative. But it is within everyone's experience that, in moments when it does not destroy the illusion, music makes a much deeper impression.

§60 Though our declamation cannot be put into notation, it seems to me that it may be somehow reduced to method. It would be sufficient for a musician to have enough skill to observe pretty much the same proportions in the chant as the voice in declamation. Those who had made themselves familiar with this chant would, with a good ear, be able to recognize in it the declamation that has been the model for it. Would not someone thoroughly familiar with the recitatives of Lully declaim the tragedies of Quinault as Lully himself would have declaimed them? But to make the matter simpler, however, it would be desirable that the melody was extremely simple and that the inflections of the voice were distinguished only so far as would be necessary to measure them. The declamation would be much easier to recognize in Lully's recitatives if he had not put so much music into them. It follows that we would have reason to believe that we might here find great assistance for those who have a gift for good declamation.

§61 The prosody of different languages does not differ equally from chant. It may strive to have few or many accents, even to squander them to excess, or avoid them altogether, because the variety of temperaments means that people who live in different climates do not feel alike. That is why languages, all depending on their quantity, have different genres of declamation and music. It is said, for instance, that the tone the English use for anger is in Italy only the expression of surprise.

The vast size of the theaters, the money the Greeks and Romans spent on their decoration, the masks that gave each actor the physiognomy of the character he portrayed, the fixed-rule declamation which was more susceptible to expression than ours, all these taken together seem to prove the superiority of the performances of the ancients. In compensation we have greater refinement, the expression of the face, and some fine points of acting which our mode of declamation alone makes it possible to perceive.

7 Which is the most perfect prosody?

§62 Everyone is surely tempted to decide in favor of the prosody of his own language, but to guard against this prejudice, let us try to sharpen our ideas.

That prosody is the most perfect which is, by its harmony, best suited to express the whole range of human qualities. Three things contribute to harmony: the quality of the sounds, the intervals of their succession, and movement. A language must therefore have soft, less soft, and even harsh sounds, or in a word every kind of sound; it must have accents that determine the lowering or raising of the voice; and it must finally, by the inequalities of its syllables, be able to express all sorts of movements.

To produce harmony the cadences must not be placed at random. Sometimes harmony should be suspended, at other times end in a sensible pause. Consequently, in a language with perfect prosody, the sequence of sounds must be subordinated to the pause of each period, so that the cadences are more or less abrupt and the ear encounters no pause that leaves anything more to be expected until the mind is entirely satisfied.

§63 We can understand how much closer Roman prosody came to perfection than ours if we consider the great surprise with which Cicero spoke of the effect of metrical rhythm in oratory [*Orator*, 212–15]. He describes the people as being enraptured by the cadence of harmonious periods; and to show that the rhythm is the sole cause, he changes the word order in a period that had received great applause, and assures us that the harmony was felt to vanish immediately. Neither in the mixture of long and short syllables nor in the variety of accents did the second construction preserve the order which is necessary to satisfy the ear. Our language has softness and openness, but harmony takes more than that. I do not find that our orators, with the different turns authorized by harmony, have ever found anything similar to the cadences that so greatly affected the Romans.

§64 Another reason that confirms the superiority of Latin prosody is the Roman taste for harmony and the sensitivity even of the people in this regard. The moment comic actors lengthened or shortened a syllable, the entire audience, including the common people, rose in protest against their false pronunciation.

We can only read such accounts with surprise, for we see nothing to confirm it in our own nation. That is because the pronunciation of the better sort of people today is so simple that those who violate it even slightly are not found out except by a few, because there are not many who have made it a point to know the right pronunciation. Among the Romans, the pronunciation was so distinct and the cadence so evident that ordinary ears were cognizant of it, with the effect that any alteration in the harmony could not fail to offend them.

§65 Now, to extend my conjectures, if the Romans were more sensitive to harmony than we are, the Greeks must have been more sensitive than the Romans, and the Asiatics still more than the Greeks, for the older the languages are, the closer they approach chant. There is also reason to think that Greek was more harmonious than Latin, since Latin borrowed its accents from Greek. As for the Asiatics, they had a fondness for harmony which the Romans found excessive. Cicero makes this clear when he, after blaming those who, to make the discourse more cadenced, spoil it by the transposition of terms, calls the Asiatic orators greater slaves to rhythm than the others. Perhaps he would today find that the quality of our language makes us fall into the opposite vice; but if we find that we in that regard have somewhat fewer disadvantages, we shall see elsewhere that we are compensated in other respects.

What I said at the end of the sixth chapter of this section is very evident proof of the superiority of ancient prosody.

8 The origin of poetry

§66 If prosody at the origin of languages was close to chant, then, in order to copy the sensible images of the language of action, the style was a virtual painting, adopting all sorts of figures and metaphors. For example, to give the idea of a man being frightened, the language of action had no means other than to imitate the cries and movements of fright. When they wished to communicate this idea in articulated sounds, they used all the expressions that presented it in corresponding detail. A single word that does not portray anything would have been too feeble to be the next step after the language of action. This language was so adjusted to the rudimentary quality of their minds that articulate sounds could not replace it unless the expressions were piled up one after the other. The poverty of languages made it impossible to speak any other way. Since they rarely had the proper term, they could not impart a thought except by repeating similar ideas. That is the origin of pleonasm, a defect especially prevalent in the ancient languages. In fact, examples occur very often in Hebrew. They only slowly became accustomed to connecting a single word to ideas which before were expressed by multiple movements, and diffuse expressions were un-avoidable before languages had become sufficiently copious to furnish proper and familiar terms for all the ideas they needed. Stylistic precision became known much sooner among the northern nations. Their cold and phlegmatic temperament made it easier for them to give up the remnants of the language of action. Elsewhere the influences of this manner of communicating thoughts persisted for a long time. In parts of Southern Asia pleonasm is even today considered elegant in speech.

§67 At its origin, style was poetic because it began by painting ideas in the most sensible images and in addition was marked by its strongly rhythmic quality. But as languages became more copious, the language of action gradually dissolved, variation of voice became more moderate, and, for reasons that I will explain, a taste for figures and metaphors imperceptibly declined as the style began to resemble our prose. But writers all the same preferred the old language, as more forceful and better suited to inscribe itself on the memory, as the sole means they then had of passing their works on to posterity. They devised different forms for this language, making a particular art of inventing rules to increase its harmony. The need to follow these rules gave rise to the lasting belief that all composition must be in verse. So long as mankind lacked letters to write down their thoughts, this belief was based on the fact that verse is easier to learn and retain than prose, but this bias persisted long after it had lost its rationale. At long last a philosopher who did not wish to submit to the rules of poetry became the first who ventured to write in prose.[42]

§68 Unlike meter, figures, and metaphors, rhyme does not owe its origin to the birth of languages. The cold and phlegmatic northern nations could not retain such a strictly measured prosody when the initial conditions for it no longer prevailed. Their remedy was the invention of rhyme.

§69 It is not difficult to imagine the progress of poetry into art. Having noted the uniform and regular cadences that accidentally appear in discourse, the different movements caused by the inequality of syllables, and the agreeable impression made by certain inflections of the voice, people formed patterns of rhythm and harmony from which they little by little derived all the rules of versification. Music and poetry were therefore naturally born together.

§70 These two arts allied themselves with gesture, which is older than either and called by the name of dance. This leads to the conjecture that some form of dance, music, and poetry has always existed in all nations. The Romans inform us that the Gaelic and Germanic nations had their musicians and poets, and in our own time we have the same information about the African, Caribbean, and Iroquois nations. Thus it is among barbarian nations that we find the seeds of the arts which have developed among the civilized nations, and which today, when they are used to feed the luxury of our cities, seem so far removed from their origin that the first source is hardly recognizable.

§71 The intimate relation of the arts to their birth is the real reason the ancients lumped them together under a single generic term. For them the term "music" comprises not only the art it signifies in our language, but also the art of gesture, dance, poetry, and declamation. It is therefore to the union of these arts that we must refer the greater part of the effects of their music, and then they are no longer so surprising.[43]

---

[42] Pherecydes from the island of Scyros is the first who is known to have written in prose.

[43] It is said, for instance, that the music of Terpander quelled a revolt; this music was not a simple chant, however, but verses declaimed by this poet.

§72 The aim of their first poems is obvious. At the first institution of societies, mankind could not concentrate on mere amusement, because the needs that obliged people to join together limited their outlook to what they found useful and necessary. Poetry and music, therefore, were cultivated only to proclaim religion and laws and to preserve the memory of great men and the services they had rendered to society. For that purpose nothing was better than poetry, or rather it was the only means they had, since they did not yet have writing. All the monuments of antiquity prove that these arts at their beginning were intended for public instruction. The Gallic and Germanic nations used them to preserve their history and laws, and for the Egyptians and Hebrews they somehow formed part of religion. This explains why the ancients made music the principal object of their education, taking that term in the full sense they gave it. For the Romans music belonged to every age of life, because they thought it taught children what they ought to learn and adults what they ought to know. The Greeks found it so shameful not to know music that a musician and a scholar were the same thing to them, and an ignorant person in their language was called a person who did not know music. This nation did not think that music was a human institution, but believed that they owed their marvellous instruments to the gods. Surpassing us in imagination, they were more sensitive to harmony, and in addition their veneration for laws, religion, and the great men they celebrated in their songs became a part of the music which preserved the tradition of those things.

§73 As prosody and style became simpler, prose moved farther and farther away from poetry. On the other hand, as poetry with the progress of mind gained new images, it distanced itself from the language in common use, thereby losing contact with the people and becoming less suited for instruction.

In addition, facts, laws and all the things mankind must know multiplied so rapidly that memory was not up to carrying the burden; societies became so populous that it became hard to secure the promulgation of the laws to their citizens, and it became necessary to find new means of instructing the people. It was then that writing was first invented, and I shall soon give an account of its progress [Ch. 13 of this section].

With the birth of this new art, poetry and music began to change their aims; they were divided between use and pleasure, but in the end confined themselves almost entirely to amusement. As they became less necessary, they more eagerly sought occasions to please, and both made considerable progress.

Hitherto inseparable, poetry and music, as soon as they had reached perfection, began to split into two separate arts, but those who first ventured to separate them were accused of abuse. The effects they could produce without mutual support were not yet clear enough, their future course could not yet be foreseen, and in addition this new practice conflicted too strongly with customary ways. Appeal was made, just as we have made it, to the old days which had never practiced one without the other, and people believed that tunes without words or verse that was not sung was something so bizarre that it would never succeed. But when experience proved otherwise, the philosophers began to fear that the arts would demoralize the people. Thus it is not without having had to overcome many obstacles that music and poetry have changed their aims and become distinguished as two separate arts.

§74 It is tempting to think that the predisposition toward respect for antiquity began with the second generation of mankind. The more ignorant we are, the more we need guidance, and the more likely we are to believe that everything our predecessors did, they did well, so that all we need to do is to imitate them. The experience of many centuries ought surely to have cured us of that prejudice.

What reason cannot bring about, time and circumstance will, but often only to end up at the other extreme, as we see in the case of poetry and music. With our prosody having become as simple as it is now, these two arts have become so entirely different that the plan to bring them together on the stage seemed ridiculous to everyone, and seemed even more so – people are bizarre – to several of those who applauded the realization of the plan.

§75 The aims of the most ancient poems indicate their character. It is probable that they celebrated religion, laws, and heroes in song only to evoke sentiments of love, admiration, and emulation in the citizens. These poems were psalms, canticles, odes, and ballads. As for epic and dramatic poems, they became known later. We owe their invention to the Greeks, and their history has been told so often that everyone knows it.

§76 We can judge the style of the earliest poems by the genius of the first languages.

In the first place, the practice of leaving out words which are to be supplied was then very prevalent. Hebrew is the proof, and the reason is the following:

Introduced by necessity, the custom of mixing together the language of action and the language of articulate sounds continued a long time after there was no longer any need for it, especially in nations with a very active imagination, such as the nations of the Orient. This had the effect that when a word was new, they understood each other just as well when they used it as when they did not. For this reason they often omitted it in order to express their thought with greater force or to include their thought within the measure of a verse. This freedom was all the more readily tolerated because tone and gesture took the place of the omitted word, which was a consequence of the fact that poetry was made to be sung and could not yet be written down. But when a word, by a process of long habituation, had become the most natural sign of an idea, it was no longer easy to make something take its place. This explains why the subaudition of words has grown increasingly rare in the course of moving in time from the ancient to the modern languages. French rejects subaudition so strongly that one might say it sometimes mistrusts our acuteness of mind.

§77 In the second place, the first poets would have been strangers to exactness and precision. Therefore, to complete the meter of their verse, they would often insert useless words or repeat the same thing in different ways, which is another reason for the frequent pleonasms in the classical languages.

§78 Finally, poetry was extremely figurative and metaphorical, for we are informed that the Oriental languages allow figures even in their prose that are rarely used in Latin poetry. It is therefore among the Oriental poets that enthusiasm created the greatest deviations from order; it is in their poetry that the passions displayed themselves with colors that would seem exaggerated to us. But I am not sure we have the right to blame them. They did not feel things as we do, so it follows that their expressions would not be the same as ours. To appreciate their works, we must take into account the temperaments of the nations for whom they wrote. There is much talk about *la belle nature*,[z] and every

---

[z] *La belle nature* is a term also used in English in the history of art. It refers to an idealized view of nature that regards only its pleasant and conventionally pleasing features. At the time, it was coming under attack in favor of the view that nature could also be harsh, threatening, unpleasant, and even ugly.

cultured nation takes pride in its imitation, but every individual thinks he finds the model in his own mode of feeling. We need not be surprised therefore that this model of *la belle nature* is so difficult to seize; its outward face changes too often, or at least assumes the air of each country. I am not even sure that the way I am now talking about that model is not somehow tinged with the quality it has recently assumed in France.

§79 As poetic style and ordinary language moved apart, they left a middle range between them where eloquence took its origin, sometimes moving closer to the tone of poetry, at other times to that of conversation. It does not differ from the latter except in rejecting all expressions that are not sufficiently dignified, and from the former except insofar as it is not subject to its meter and, depending on the character of the languages, does not allow certain figures and turns of phrase which appear in poetry. For the rest, these two arts are so mixed together that it is no longer possible to distinguish between them.

9 Words

I could not allow any interruption of what I wished to say about the art of gestures, dance, prosody, declamation, music, and poetry: all these are too closely interrelated as a whole and to the language of action which is their underlying principle. I shall now look into the progress which the language of articulate sounds has followed to gain perfection and to become the most convenient of all languages.

§80 To understand how mankind came to agreement among themselves about the signification of words they wished to put into use, it is sufficient to observe that they pronounced them in circumstances in which everyone was obliged to refer to the same perceptions. By that means they fixed the meaning with greater exactness in proportion as the circumstances, by frequent repetition, habituated the mind to connect particular ideas to particular signs. The language of action removed the ambiguities and double meanings which in the beginning would occur very often.

§81 The objects that are designed to meet our needs sometimes easily escape our attention, but we find it difficult not to take note of those that can produce sentiments of fear and pain. Thus, as people sooner or later would have to name things according as they claimed their attention, it is plausible that hostile animals were named before the fruits which were their nourishment. As for other objects, they imagined words to distinguish them in light of their suitability for meeting their most urgent needs and of the forcefulness of the impressions they received from them.

§82 For a long time languages had words only for the objects that fall under the senses, such as "tree," "fruit," "water," "fire," and others they often had occasion to talk about. Complex notions of substances, being the first to become known, since they come directly from the senses, must have been the first to be named. As they gradually learned to analyze these notions by reflecting on the perceptions they comprise, they imagined signs for simpler ideas. Given, for instance, the sign for "tree," they added those for "trunk," "branch," "leaf," "verdure," etc. Later they little by little distinguished the various sensible qualities of objects; they noted the circumstances in which they could be identified and made words to express these things, which brought adjectives and adverbs into being. But they found it very difficult to give names to the operations of the mind, because we naturally have little inclination to reflect on ourselves. For a long time they had no other means of communicating the ideas "I see," "I hear," "I wish," "I love" and similar ideas than to pronounce the names of things in particular tones of voice and by some action to mark approximately the condition in which they found themselves. This is how children, who do not learn these words until they can already name the objects that relate most closely to them, make known what is going on in their minds.

§83 As they acquired the habit of communicating these kinds of ideas by action, they became used to delimiting them, and from then on they began to find it easier to connect them to other signs. The names they chose for this purpose were called verbs. Thus the first verbs were imagined only to express the state of mind when the mind acts or is acted upon. On this pattern they later made words to express the state of each particular thing. They had this in common with adjectives: that they designated the state of a being, and in particular that they marked that state insofar as it consists of what we call "action" and "passion." "To feel," "to move" were verbs; "large," "small" were adjectives; as for adverbs, they served to indicated the circumstances which were not expressed by adjectives.

§84 Before people had the use of verbs, the name of the object they wished to talk about was pronounced at the very moment when by some action they indicated the state of their minds; that was the best means of being understood. But when they began to replace the action with articulate sounds, the name of the thing naturally came to mind first as being the most familiar sign. This mode of expression was most convenient both for the speaker and the hearer; for the former because it made him begin with the idea that was easiest to communicate, for the latter even more so because it, by fixing his attention on the object of the speaker's intention, prepared the hearer more easily to understand a little-used term, whose signification would not be so evident for him. Thus the most natural order of ideas caused the object to be placed before the verb, as in "fruit to desire."

This can be further confirmed by a simple consideration. Since only the language of action could serve as model for that of articulate sounds, the latter would, in the beginning, have had to maintain the ideas in the same order which usage had made the most natural in the former. But the language of action could not disclose the state of one's mind except by showing the object to which that state related. The movements of the body that expressed a need were understood only when some gesture pointed to what could meet that need. If they came too early, their point was lost and they would have to be repeated, for the people to whom someone intended to communicate his thoughts still had too little practice to think of remembering those movements in order to interpret their sense. But the effortless attention given to the indicated object made the action easy to understand. It seems to me that even today this would be the most natural way of using this language.

With the verb coming after the object, the word which governed it, that is the nominative, could not be placed between the two, for that would have obscured the relation between them. It also could not stand at the head of the phrase, for that would have made its relation to the verb less evident, so it was placed after the verb. By that means the words were construed in the same order in which they were governed, which was the only way to make them easy to understand. So they said "fruit to desire Peter" instead of "Peter desires fruit," and the first construction was no less natural than the second is today. That is proved by Latin, which admits both equally. It would seem that this language occupies a sort of middle position between the ancient and the modern languages, sharing the qualities of both.

§85 At the beginning verbs expressed the state of things only vaguely, as for example the infinitive "to go," "to act." The action which accompanied verbs supplied the rest, that is tense, mood, number, and person. When saying "tree to see," some gesture indicated whether they spoke in the first or third person, about a singular or plural, in the past, present, or future, and finally whether in the indicative or a conditional sense.

§86 The practice of connecting these ideas to such signs having facilitated their connection to sounds, words were for this purpose invented and in discourse placed after the verb, for the same reason that verbs had been placed after the nouns. They consequently ranged their ideas in this order: *fruit manger à l'avenir moi* in order to say *je mangerai du fruit*.[aa]

[aa] Condillac's French examples cannot be usefully translated into English, since they work only in the context of French grammar. There is no solution, therefore, but to leave them as they stand. *Je mangerai du fruit* is the first-person future of the verb *manger*, "to eat": "I shall eat some fruit." *Fruit manger à l'avenir moi* can be rendered "fruit to eat in the future me."

§87 Since the sounds which gave determination to the verb were always added to it, they soon formed a single word with different endings for the various meanings. Then the verb came to be considered a name which from its indeterminate beginning had, by virtue of its tense and moods, become adapted to express the active and passive states of everything in a determinate manner. This was the way mankind gradually came to imagine the conjugations.

§88 When words had become the most natural signs of our ideas, the need to range them in an order so contrary to the order in which we now place them no longer prevailed. The old order was nevertheless maintained, because, the character of languages having been formed by these constraints, it did not allow any change of usage; only after several languages had succeeded each other did people begin to approach the way we think. These changes were very slow, because younger languages always retain part of the genius of their predecessors. Latin contains quite evident remnants of the character of older languages, from which they have been transmitted into our conjugations. When we in French say *je fais, je faisais, je fis, je ferai*, etc., we mark tense, mood, and number only by changing the verb endings, which has its source in the fact that our conjugations have been formed on the model of Latin. But when we say *j'ai fait, j'eus fait, j'avais fait*, etc., we follow the order we now find the more natural, for here *fait* is the true verb because it is the term which indicates the state of action, while *avoir* merely corresponds to the sound which at the beginning of languages came after the verb to designate tense, mood, and number.

§89 The same observation can be made about the word *être* which renders the participle to which it is joined sometimes the equivalent of a passive verb, sometimes the equivalent of the compound preterite of an active or neuter verb. In the phrases *je suis aimé, je m'étais fait fort, je serais parti, aimé* expresses the passive state, while *fait* and *parti* express the active state; but *suis, étais*, and *serais* only mark the tense, mood, and number. These words found little use in Latin conjugations, and they were, as in the first languages, placed after the verb.

§90 Since in French, to signify tense, mood, and number, we have terms we place before the verb, we could by placing them after the verb form an idea of the conjugations in the first languages. Thus instead of *je suis aimé, j'était aimé*, etc., we would have *aimésuis, aimétais*, etc.

§91 People did not multiply words beyond immediate need, especially when they first began to use words, for the effort to imagine and retain them was too great. The same vocable which served as the sign of a tense and mood was therefore placed after each verb, which had the effect of making each mother language have only a single conjugation. If their number increased, it was either owing to the mixture of several languages or because the words designed to indicate tenses, moods, etc. were sometimes altered, depending on their ease of pronunciation with the preceding verbs.

§92 The different qualities of the mind are only an effect of the states of action and passion it undergoes or of the habits it acquires when it acts or is acted upon repeatedly. To know these qualities we must therefore form some idea of the different ways in which this substance acts and is acted upon. From this it follows that adjectives, which express these different ways, could not gain currency until after verbs were known. The words "to speak" and "to persuade" must have been in use before the word "eloquence," an example that will suffice to show what I mean.

§93 In speaking of the names given to the qualities of things, I have so far mentioned only adjectives, for the good reason that abstract substantives could not become known until much later. When people began to pay attention to the different qualities of objects, they did not see them in their naked state, as it were, but as something that clothed a subject. Consequently, the names they gave them would have to include some idea of this subject, as in the words "great, vigilant," etc. Later, when they took a second look at the notions they had formed, they became obliged to decompose them so as to make them more convenient for the expression of new thoughts. At this point they began to distinguish the qualities from their subjects by creating such abstract substantives as "greatness," "vigilance," etc. If we could reach all the way back to the primitive names, we would find that all abstract substantives derive from some adjective or verb.

§94 Before verbs came into use, people had, as we have seen, adjectives for the expression of sensible qualities, because the ideas that are the most easily determined must have been the first to be named. But not having a word to connect the adjective to its substantive, they put one next to the other. "Terrible monster" signified "this monster is terrible," for the action or gesture made up for what was not expressed by the sounds. To this we may add that the substantive was sometimes placed before and sometimes after the adjective, depending on where they wished to place the emphasis. A man who was surprised by the tallness of a tree would say "tall tree," while on all other occasions he would say "tree tall," for the idea we find most striking we are naturally inclined to place first.

As soon as they had the use of verbs, they easily observed that the word they had added to them to indicate person, number, tense, and mood also had the property of connecting the verbs to the noun that governed them. They therefore used this same word to connect the adjective with its substantive, or at least they imagined something similar to it. This is the function of the word "to be," except that it did not suffice to denote the person. This way of connecting two ideas is, as I have said elsewhere [Pt. I, Sect. 2], what we call "to affirm." Thus it is the nature of this word to mark affirmation.

§95 When they used this word to connect the substantive to the adjective, they joined it to the latter because the affirmation was felt to fall chiefly on the adjective. It was not long before the same thing was repeated that had earlier happened to verbs, namely that the two came to form a single word. Thus adjectives now became susceptible to inflection, being distinguished from verbs because the qualities they expressed pertained neither to acting nor to being acted upon. So, to put all these names in the same class, they considered the verb only "as a word which, by virtue of being susceptible to conjugation, affirms a quality of some kind about a subject." Thus there were three kinds of verbs: some active or signifying actions; others passive or signifying being acted upon; and finally neuter verbs or those which denote other qualities. Later the grammarians changed these categories or thought up new ones because they found it more useful to distinguish verbs by reference to grammatical government than to meaning.

§96 With adjectives having been changed into verbs, the construction of languages was somewhat altered. The placing of these new verbs varied as much as the placing of the nouns from which they were derived; thus they were sometimes put before the substantive they governed, sometimes after it. This practice was later extended to other verbs. This is the epoch which was preliminary to the construction we find so natural.

§97 People were now no longer constrained always to place their ideas in the same order; from several adjectives they took away the word formerly added and conjugated it apart; and after they had for a long time placed it anywhere they pleased, as in Latin, they fixed it in French either after the governing noun or before the noun it governs.

§98 Not being the sign of any quality, this word could not have been counted among the verbs if they had not for its sake extended the notion of a verb as they had already done for adjectives. This term therefore came to be considered as "a word which signifies affirmation with distinctions of persons, numbers, tenses, and moods." At that point, "to be" became the only true verb. Since grammarians had not taken the progress of these changes into account, they found it difficult to agree on the idea or conception they ought to have of the terms of this kind.[44]

§99 The Latin declensions must be explained like their conjugations, for they cannot have a different origin. To express number, case, and gender, they made up words which were placed after the nouns, thus giving them terminations. On this it is relevant to observe that our declensions in French have been made in part on the pattern of the Latin language insofar as their endings differ, and in part by following the order in which we now range our ideas, for the articles, which are the signs of number, case, and gender, are placed before the nouns.

It seems to me that the comparison of French with Latin makes my conjectures quite plausible, and, further, that there are grounds for assuming that they would come close to the truth if we could reach all the way back to a first language.

§100 The Latin conjugations and declensions have the advantage over French in that they have greater variety and precision. The frequent use we are forced to make of auxiliary verbs and articles makes our style diffuse and tiresome, which becomes still more noticeable because we are overscrupulous in the repetition of articles beyond any necessity. We do not, for example, say *c'est le plus pieux et plus savant homme que je connaisse* ["he is the most pious and most learned man I know"], but *c'est le plus pieux et le plus savant* ["he is the most pious and the most learned"], etc. It is also true that, given the nature of our declensions, we lack the words which the grammarians call comparatives, something we can only remedy by using the word *plus*, which requires the same repetitions as the article. Since the conjugations and

---

[44] Of all the parts of speech, says the abbé Regnier, none has so many definitions as the verb. *Gramm. Franc.*, p. 325 [*François-Séraphin Regnier-Desmarais, *Grammaire française* (Paris, 1706)].

the declensions are the parts of our grammar which occur most often in discourse, it is obvious that French is less precise than the Latin.

§101 But our conjugations and declensions also have an advantage over those of Latin, because they make it possible for us to distinguish meanings which are confounded in Latin. French has three preterites, *je fis, j'ai fait, j'eus fait*, but Latin has only one, *feci* [all meaning "I did"]. The omission of the article sometimes changes the sense of a clause; *je suis père* ["I am a father"] and *je suis le père* ["I am the father"] have two different meanings which are confounded in the Latin *sum pater* ["I am a/the father"].

10 The same subject continued

§102 Since it was not possible to make up names for every individual object, it early on became necessary to have general terms. But think of the cleverness it took to size up the circumstances in order to ensure that everyone formed the same abstractions and gave the same names to the same ideas! The reading of works on abstract matters shows that even today it is not easy to succeed in that enterprise.

To grasp the order in which abstract terms were invented it is sufficient to observe the order of general ideas, for the origin and purpose are the same in either case. My point is that if it is certain that our most general notions derive from ideas we receive immediately from the senses, it is equally certain that the most abstract terms derive from the first names that were given to sensible objects.

Insofar as it is in their power, people relate their most recently acquired knowledge to some of the knowledge they have already acquired. In this process the least familiar ideas connect with the better-known ones, thus offering great assistance to memory and the imagination. When circumstances brought new objects to their attention, people would examine what the new ones had in common with better-known objects and put them in the same class, and the same names served for both. This is how the ideas of signs became more general, but that happened only little by little, for the most abstract notions were arrived at only gradually, and the terms for "essence," "substance," and "being" were acquired very late. There can be no doubt that some nations have not yet enriched their language with those terms,[45] but if they are more ignorant than we are, I do not think it is in this respect.

§103 With the increasing acceptance of abstract terms, it also became apparent how appropriate articulate sounds were even for the expression of thoughts which seem to bear the least relation to sensible things. The imagination endeavored to find, in objects that struck the senses, images of what occurred inside the mind. People have always perceived motion and rest in matter; they have observed the leaning or inclination of bodies; they have seen the air become agitated, darkened, and clear; that plants grow, mature, decay – with all these things before their senses, they began to speak of "the movement," "the rest," "the inclination

---

[45] That is confirmed by the account of La Condamine.

and the leaning" of the soul; they spoke of mind becoming "agitated," "darkened," "enlightened," of its "growing," "maturing," and "decaying." In short, they were happy to find some relation between a mental and a physical action in order to give the same name to both.[46] For where does the word *esprit* ["mind"] come from if not from the idea of very rarified matter, of a vapor, of a breath that cannot be seen? This is an idea which several philosophers have so far made their own as to imagine that a substance composed of innumerable parts is capable of thinking. I have refuted this error [Pt. I, Sect. 1, Ch. 1].

It is obvious how all these names had a figurative origin. Among the more abstract terms we may find examples in which this truth is not entirely evident, among them the French word for thought, *pensée*.[47] But we will soon see that this is no exception.

It is our needs that provided mankind with the first occasions to observe what occurred within themselves and to express it first by actions before, later, by names. Thus these observations took place only in relation to our needs, and no distinction was made among many things unless our needs required that it be made. But our needs were related only to the body, from which it follows that the first names that were given to what we are capable of feeling signified sensible actions alone. Later, as mankind gradually became familiar with abstract terms, we became capable of distinguishing mind from body, and of con-

---

[46] "I do not doubt," says Locke, Book III, Ch. 1, §5, "that if we could trace all words to their source, we would find in all languages that the words we use to stand for things that do not fall under the senses, have had their first origin from sensible ideas. By which we may give some kind of guess what kind of notions filled their minds who were the first speakers of languages, and how nature unawares to men suggested the origin and principle of all their knowledge, by the very names they gave to things."

[47] I think this is the most challenging example one can choose. Of this we may judge by an objection which the Cartesians believe will reduce to absurdity what is maintained by those who believe that all our knowledge derives from the senses. "By which sense," they ask, "could the most spiritual ideas, that of thought, for example, and that of being have come into the understanding? Are they luminous or colored to enter by sight? a grave or acute tone to enter by hearing? a good or bad odor to enter by smell? Cold or hot, hard or soft to come by touch? Since no reasonable answer can be given, it must be admitted that spiritual ideas, such as those of being and thought, cannot by any means have their origin in the senses, but that our mind has the faculty of forming them by itself." *The Art of Thinking* (. . .). This objection is from Augustine's *Confessions*. It might have seduced some before Locke, but today, if there is anything less likely to stand up, it is the objection itself.[bb]

[bb] Condillac is referring to the so-called Port-Royal *Logic*, that is, Antoine Arnauld and Pierre Nicole's *La Logique ou l'art de penser* (Paris, 1662, and thereafter in new editions with important additions and revisions). Condillac is giving a condensed summary of Pt. I, Ch. 1. The relevant passages in Augustine's *Confessions* are chiefly in Bk. x, Chs. 6–10.

sidering the operations of these two substances separately. They then perceived not only what the action of the body is when we say, for example, "I see," but they separately observed the perception of the mind and began to regard the term "I see" as being appropriate for both kinds of actions. It is even plausible that this practice came about so naturally that they did not notice the extension of the word's meaning. This shows how a sign which initially was limited to an action of the body, became the name of an operation of mind.

The more they reflected on the operations which by this process had furnished the ideas, the more they felt the need to refer them to different classes. To this end they did not imagine new terms, for that would not have been the readiest way to be understood; but they gradually, according to need, extended the signification of some of the names which had become signs of the operations of mind until one of them finally became so general that it expressed them all, namely the word *pensée*. We ourselves do likewise when we wish to denote an abstract idea which practice has not yet determined. Thus all this confirms what I have said in the preceding paragraph, that "the most abstract terms derive from the first names that were given to sensible objects."

§104 But as soon as their usage became familiar, people forgot the origin of these signs so that they fell into the error of believing that they were the most natural signs of spiritual things. They even believed that those signs perfectly explained the nature and essence of those things, though they in fact only expressed imperfect analogies. This abuse is evident in the ancient philosophers, it is still with us even in the best modern philosophers, and it is the principal cause of our slow progress in the conduct of reasoning.

§105 Since people, especially at the beginning of languages, were ill suited to reflect on themselves or had only signs hitherto applied to altogether different things to express the little thinking on self of which they were capable, we can form an idea of the obstacles they had to overcome before giving names to particular operations of mind. The particles, for instance, which connect the different parts of speech, must have been imagined very late. They express the manner in which objects affect us and the judgments we make on them with a delicacy which for a long time was not within the reach of the crudeness of mind which kept mankind strangers to reason. To reason is to express the relations between different propositions, but it is evident that only conjunctions provide the necessary means to do so. The language of action had inadequate remedies for the lack of these particles, and people were not capable of using names to express the relations of which they are the signs until those names had become established under distinct conditions and many repetitions. We shall later on see that this was the origin of the apologue or fable.

§106 People never understood each other better than when they gave names to sensible objects, but the moment they wished to do the same for ideas of mixed modes, they began to have much difficulty understanding each other because they usually lacked patterns, found themselves in situations that constantly changed, and were not all equally good at conducting the operations of their minds. They brought together under a single name a few or many simple ideas, but often ideas that were entirely incompatible, resulting in disputes over words. In this regard it rarely occurred that terms in two different languages showed perfect conformity. On the contrary, even in the same language, one could very often find terms whose sense was not clearly determined, with the consequence that they were open to a thousand applications. These defects have shown up even in philosophical works and are the source of many errors.

In treating the names of substances, we have seen that those of complex ideas were created before the names of simple ideas [above, §82]. Quite a different procedure was followed in giving names to ideas of mixed modes. Since these notions are nothing but collections of several simple ideas which we have put together, it is evident that we would not have been able to form them until after we had already, by particular names, determined each of the simple ideas we wished to include. For example, the name "courage" could not have been given to the notion of which it is a sign until other names had been given to the ideas "danger," "knowledge of danger," "obligation to expose oneself to it," and "resolution to fulfill this obligation."

§107 The pronouns were the last words to be imagined because their lack was the last to be felt, and it is even likely that it took a long time to get used to them. Since minds were habituated each time to revive the same idea by the same word, they had difficulty getting used to a name which took the place of another and sometimes of an entire sentence.

§108 To lessen these difficulties, they put pronouns before the verbs in discourse, thus making their relations more obvious by putting the pronoun in the space of the noun it replaced. French even makes a rule on that point; the only exception is when a verb is imperative, signifying a command, as in *faites-le* ["do it"]. This usage has perhaps been introduced only to make a clearer distinction between the present tense and the imperative. But if the imperative signifies a prohibition, the pronoun keeps its natural place, as in *ne le faites pas* ["don't do it"]. The reason seems obvious to me. The verb signifies the state of a thing, and the negation marks the absence of this state; for the sake of clarity it is therefore natural not to separate it from the verb. But since *pas* completes the negation, there is greater need for *pas* than for *ne* to stand next to the verb. It even seems to me that this particle never likes to be separated from the verb, but I do not know whether the grammarians have taken note of that.

§109 The nature of words was not always taken into account when they were assigned to different classes, which is why some words have been classified as pronouns though they are in fact not pronouns. If we say, for example, *voulez-vous me donner cela?* ["will you give me that?"], then *vous, me, cela* signify the person speaking, the person spoken to, and the thing asked for. Those are, strictly speaking, nouns which were known long before pronouns, and they have been placed in the discourse like other nouns, that is before the verb when it governed them and after when they governed it; the old form was *cela vouloir moi* ["that to want me"] where we say *je veux cela* ["I want that"].

§110 I believe that all that remains for us to speak of is the distinction of genders. But it is obvious that it owes its origin entirely to the difference of sex and that the assignment of nouns to two or three genders has been introduced to bring greater order and clarity to language.

§111 What I have said is pretty much the order in which words have been invented. In the true sense languages did not begin to have a style until they had names for all the different kinds of things and had established fixed principles for the construction of discourse. Before that time they had only a certain number of terms which could not express a sequence of thoughts without the assistance of the language of action. We must note, however, that pronouns were necessary only for the sake of stylistic precision.

11 The signification of words

§112 To see why the names of simple ideas are the least open to ambiguity, it is enough to consider how names were first created, for the circumstances clearly determine the perceptions to which they are related. I cannot doubt the meaning of the words "white" and "black" when I observe that they are used to designate particular perceptions which I now experience.

§113 The same is not true of complex notions, for they are sometimes so compounded that the simple ideas they consist of can be assembled only very slowly. A few sensible qualities that were easy to see made up our first notion of substance; later the notion became more complex as people became better at singling out new qualities. It is probable, for instance, that the notion of gold at first was merely that of a yellow and very heavy body, but one day, sometime later, experience caused malleability to be added, and next ductility and fixity, and so on, successively adding all the qualities which enter into the idea which the best chemists have formed of this substance. Everyone could see that the newly discovered qualities had the same right to become part of the notion that had already been formed as those that were discovered first. This explains why it became impossible to determine the number of simple ideas that might compose the notion of any particular substance. Some held it was higher, others that it was lower, all depending entirely on the experience and insight of the chemists. For that reason, the signification of the names of substances has unavoidably been very uncertain, causing much dispute over words. We are naturally inclined to believe that other people have the same ideas as we do because they use the same language, which often has the effect that we believe ourselves to hold a contrary opinion when we uphold the same beliefs. On these occasions it would suffice to explain the sense of the terms to resolve the disputed issues, thus clearly showing the frivolity of many questions we think are important. Locke gave an example which deserves to be cited:

> I was once in a meeting of very learned and ingenious physicians, where by chance there arose a question whether any "liquor" passed through the filaments of the nerves. Opinions were divided and the dispute lasted a good while, both sides proposing different arguments to support its position. As I had for a long time been of the opinion that the greater part of disputes were more about the

signification of words than about any real difference in the conception of things, it occurred to me to suggest to these gentlemen that
before they went any further in this dispute, they would first
examine and establish among themselves what the word "liquor"
signified. They were at first very surprised at this proposal, and if
they had been less polite, perhaps they might have regarded it with
scorn as being frivolous and extravagant since there was no one in
this meeting who did not think he understood very perfectly what
the word "liquor" stood for, which I believe is actually not one of
the most obscure names of substances. However that may be, they
were pleased to comply with my request and upon examination
found that the signification of this word was not so settled and
certain as they had all hitherto imagined and that, on the contrary,
each of them made it the sign of a different complex idea. This
made them perceive that the heart of their dispute was about the
signification of that term and that they differed very little in their
opinions, namely that some fluid and subtle matter passed through
the conduits of the nerves, though it was not easy to agree whether
this matter should be called by the name liquor or some other
name, a thing which when considered by each of them, was
thought not worth disputing. [E 3.9.16]

§114 The signification of words for ideas of mixed modes is still more
uncertain than that of substances, either because we rarely encounter
the model of the collections to which they pertain, or because it is often
very difficult to observe all the parts, even when we have their model;
the most essential are the very ones which are most likely to escape us.
To form the idea of a criminal action, for instance, it is not enough to
observe what is exterior and visible in it, for we must also grasp things
which do not appear before our eyes. We must examine the intention of
the perpetrator, discover the relation of the crime to the law, and
sometimes even know many circumstances that preceded it. All that
requires a degree of care which we can rarely muster owing to our
negligence and limited insight.

§115 It is interesting to observe people's confidence in the use of
language at the very moment when they are abusing it. They believe
they understand each other, though they take no measures to ensure
that they do. We have become so familiar with the use of words that we
have no doubt others grasp our thought the moment we speak the
words, as if the ideas would necessarily be the same in speaker and

hearer. Instead of remedying these abuses, philosophers have themselves shown a partiality for obscurity. Every sect has been eager to think up terms that are ambiguous or without sense. By that means they have tried to cover up the weak parts of many frivolous and ridiculous systems, and cleverness in succeeding in that has, as Locke remarks [E 3.10], passed for penetration of mind and true learning. Ultimately people have emerged who, by making their language a composite of the jargon of all sects, have maintained the pros and cons on all sorts of subjects, a talent that has been and perhaps still is admired, but which would be treated with sovereign contempt if people knew better. To prevent all these abuses, here is what the precise signification of words ought to be:

§116 We should never make use of signs except to express the ideas we actually have in our minds. If it is a question of substances, the names we give them should refer only to the qualities we have observed in them and of which we have made our collections. Names of mixed modes must designate only a certain number of simple ideas, which we must be ready to specify. We must especially avoid the careless assumption that others attach to the same words the same ideas that we do. In debating a question, our first care must be to consider whether the complex notions of our interlocutors contain a greater number of simple ideas than our own notion. If we suspect it is greater, we must find out how many and what kind of ideas. If it seems less, we must get to know which simple ideas should be added.

In regard to general names, we must treat them only as signs that distinguish the different classes into which we distribute our ideas; and when we say that a substance belongs to a particular species, we should merely understand that to mean that it contains the qualities contained in the complex notion of which a particular word is the sign.

In every case, except that of substances, the essence of the thing coincides with the notion we have formed, so that, consequently, the same name is equally the sign of either. A space bounded by three lines is at the same time the essence and the notion of a triangle. The same is true of what mathematicians comprehend under the general name "magnitude." Having observed that in mathematics the notion of the thing entails knowledge of its essence, philosophers have overhastily concluded that the same is true in physics, which has made them imagine they know the very essence of substances.

Since mathematical ideas are determined by evidence, the confusion of notion and essence has no ill effect, but in the branches of knowledge which deal with mixed modes, people are often less on their guard against verbal disputes. They may ask, for instance, what is the essence of the dramatic poems we call comedies, and whether certain plays so called deserve the name.

To this I say that the first person to have imagined comedies did not have a model, so that consequently the essence of poems of this sort was solely in the notion he framed of it. His successors one after the other have added something to this first notion, thus changing the essence of comedy. We have the right to do likewise, but instead we consult the models we have today and form our idea on those that please us the most. Consequently, we admit only certain plays and exclude all the rest. If someone later asks whether a particular poem is or is not a comedy, each of us answers in terms of the notions we have formed, with the result that since these are not the same for all, we will seem to be of different opinions. If we were to substitute the ideas in place of the words, we would soon find that we differed only in the way we expressed ourselves. Instead of thus limiting the notion of something, it would be much more reasonable to extend it in step with the discovery of new genres that can be made subordinate to the original notion. It would in turn be an interesting and well-defined task to examine which genre is superior to the rest.

What I have said about comedy also goes for the epic poem, since whether *Paradise Lost*, *Le Lutrin*,[cc] etc. are epic poems is debated as absorbing questions.

It is sometimes sufficient to have inadequate ideas, provided that they are determinate, while at other times it is absolutely necessary that they be adequate; it all depends on the aim one has in view. We must be especially careful to distinguish between whether we are speaking of things to explain them or merely to learn more about them. In the first case, it is not enough to have just some idea of them; we must know them in depth. But it is a common error to settle the mind on everything using a small number of ideas, even badly determined ones.

When I treat of method, I shall indicate the means we can always use to determine the ideas we connect with different signs.

[cc] Mock-heroic poem by Boileau published in parts in 1674 and 1683.

12 Inversions

§117 We flatter ourselves that French has the advantage over the ancient languages of arranging words in our discourse as ideas arrange themselves in the mind, because we think that the most natural order demands that we proclaim the subject we speak of before saying what we affirm about it; that is to say, that the verb is preceded by its nominative and followed by its object. We have seen, however, that in the beginning of languages, the most natural construction required an entirely different order.

What is here called natural necessarily varies with the genius of the languages, and in some it covers more than it does in others. Latin is our evidence. It unites contrasting constructions, which nevertheless seem equally in conformity with the arrangement of ideas, as in these instances: *Alexander vicit Darium, Darium vicit Alexander* [both meaning "Alexander overcame Darius"]. If we in French [*and English] accept only the first, "Alexander overcame Darius," it is not because that order alone is natural, but because our declensions do not permit us to reconcile clarity with a different order.

On what is the opinion based of those people who claim that in this proposition, "Alexander overcame Darius," the French construction alone is natural? Whether they consider the matter in light of the operations of mind or in light of the ideas, they will find that they are caught in a preconception. Taking it in light of the operations of the mind, we can assume that the three ideas which make up this proposition come to life all of a sudden in the mind of the speaker, or that they are evoked successively in the mind. In the first case they have no order; in the second case the order may vary, for it is just as natural that the ideas "Alexander" and "overcame" should arise on the occasion of the idea "Darius" as that the idea "Darius" should follow on occasion of the other two.

The error is just as evident if we look at the matter from the point of view of the ideas, for the subordination among them equally authorizes the two Latin constructions *Alexander vicit Darium* and *Darium vicit Alexander*, for this reason:

In discourse ideas are modified when one idea explains another and when it extends or limits it. By that means they are naturally subordinated among themselves, but more or less directly depending on whether their connection is more or less direct. The nominative is connected to the verb, the verb to its object, the adjective to its substantive, etc. But the connection between the object of the verb and the nominative is not so close, because these two names receive modification only by means of the verb. The idea "Darius," for example, is immediately connected to the idea "overcame," that of "overcame" to that of "Alexander," and the subordination among these three ideas preserves the same order.

This observation shows that to avoid violating the natural arrangement of ideas, it is sufficient to conform to the greatest connection between them. But this is what is equally satisfied by the two Latin constructions *Alexander vicit Darium* and *Darium vicit Alexander.* Therefore one is as natural as the other. The mistake we make is that we take a particular order to be natural, though it is in fact only a habit we have contracted from the character of our language. Yet even French has constructions that would have made it possible to avoid this error, for in them the nominative is much better placed after the verb, as for example in *Darius que vainquit Alexandre* ["Darius whom Alexander overcame"].

§118 The subordination of ideas is altered as we reduce conformity with their greatest connection, for then the constructions cease to be natural. This is the case with *Vicit Darium Alexander*, for here the idea of Alexander is separated from that of *vicit* with which it ought to be immediately connected.

§119 Latin authors offer examples of all kinds of constructions. *Conferte hanc pacem cum illo bello*; here is one that is analogous with French: *Hujus praetoris adventum, cum illius imperatoris victoria; hujus cohortem impuram, cum illius exercitu invicto; hujus libidines, cum illius continentia*; these are all as natural as the first, since the connection of ideas is not altered, and yet our language would not allow those constructions. Finally, the period ends with a construction which is not natural: *Ab illo, qui cepit, conditas; ab hoc, qui constitutas accepit, captas dicetis Syracusas. Syracusas* is separated from *conditas, conditas* from *ab illo*, etc., all of which is contrary to the subordination of ideas.[dd]

§120 When they do not conform to the greatest connection of ideas,

---

[dd] The passage is from Cicero's *Orator*, 167: "Compare this peace with that war, the arrival of this praetor with the victory of that general, this abandoned retinue with that invincible army, the praetor's lust with the general's restraint; you will say that Syracuse was founded by its conqueror, and captured by its governor."

inversions would have drawbacks if the Latin language did not provide the remedy by the relation which the grammatical endings establish between the words which ought naturally not be separated. This relation is such that the mind easily joins the ideas that stand farthest apart so as to place them in their proper order. If these constructions do some violence to the connection of ideas, they also have advantages it is important to recognize.

The first is to give greater harmony to the discourse. In fact, since the harmony of a language consists in the mixture of sounds of all sorts, in their movement, and in the intervals by which they succeed each other, we can appreciate the harmony that can be produced with judiciously chosen inversions. As a model Cicero gives the period I have cited above [*Orator*].

§121 Another advantage is that inversion increases the force and liveliness of the style, which comes about by the freedom it gives us to place each word where it will naturally produce the greatest effect. Perhaps someone will ask why a word has greater force in one place than in another.

To understand this, we need only compare a construction in which the terms follow the connection of ideas with one in which they depart from it. In the first, the ideas present themselves so naturally that the mind sees the entire sequence with hardly any exercise of the imagination. In the other, the ideas that ought to follow each other immediately are placed too far apart to be grasped in the same way; but if it is done right, the most distant words will meet up without effort owing to the relation which the endings establish between them. Thus the small obstacle of their being placed apart seems to have been designed in order to exercise the imagination, and the ideas are dispersed only so that the mind when obliged to join them will feel the connection or the contrast with greater liveliness. By this artifice all the force of a sentence is sometimes concentrated in the last word. For example:

> *Nec quicquam tibi prodest*
> *aërias tentasse domos, animoque rotundum*
> *percurrisse polum, morituro.* [Horace, *Odes*, Bk. I, no. 28]

[it profits you nothing
to have explored the airy dwellings and to have

traversed in thought the round vault of heaven,
for you were to die.]

This last word (*morituro*) concludes with force because the mind cannot connect it with *tibi* without heeding everything that separates them. If you transpose *morituro*, in conformity with the connection of ideas, and say *nec quicquam tibi morituro*, etc., the effect will no longer be the same, because the imagination is not exercised to the same degree. These sorts of inversions partake of the character of the language of action, in which a single sign is often equivalent to an entire sentence.

§122 The second advantage of inversions gives rise to a third, which is that they create a picture [*tableau*], that is, that they in a single word unite the circumstances of an action, much as a painter unites them on the canvas. If they merely came plodding one after the other, it would be only a plain narrative. An example will cast light on what I have in mind:

Nymphae flebant Daphnim extinctum funere crudeli is a plain narrative. We learn that Nymphs wept, that they wept for Daphnis, that Daphnis was dead, etc. Thus with the circumstances coming one after the other, they make only a slight impression on me. But if we change the order and say:

> *Extinctum Nymphae crudeli funere Daphnim*
> *Flebant* [Vergil, *Eclogues* 5, line 20]

then the effect is entirely different, because after reading *extinctum Nymphae crudeli funere* ["cut off by a cruel death"] without understanding anything, at *Daphnim* I encounter the first stroke of the painter's brush, and with the second at *flebant* ["they wept"], the picture is completed. The nymphs in tears, Daphnis dying, and this death attended by the attributes of a doleful fate strike me all of a sudden. Such is the power of inversions over the imagination.

§123 The last advantage I find in constructions of this sort is that they render the style more precise. By habituating the mind to relate a term to those from which it stands farthest apart in the same phrase, they also give the mind the habit of avoiding repetition. Our language is so ill suited to foster this habit in us that one could say that we do not see any relation of two words unless they immediately follow each other.[ee]

§124 If we compare French and Latin, we find advantages and draw-

---

[ee] The points Condillac makes about the advantages of inversion are clearly prefigured in what Quintilian says about hyperbaton (VIII, vi, 62–7).

backs in both. Of two arrangements of words that are equally natural, our language normally allows only one; in this respect, then, it has less variation and is less suitable for harmony. It rarely tolerates those inversions in which the connection of ideas is altered; it is thus by its very nature less lively. But it compensates with its simplicity and by the clarity of its turns of phrase. It makes a point of ensuring that its constructions always conform to the greatest connection of ideas. Thus it early on accustoms the mind to grasp this connection, naturally makes the mind more precise, and gradually lends it this character of simplicity and clarity which makes the language itself so superior in many genres. We shall later [last chapter of this section] see how these advantages have contributed to the progress of philosophical thought, and how greatly we are compensated for the loss of some of the beautiful qualities of the ancient languages. To forestall any notion that I am advancing a paradox, I wish to note that it is natural for us to be used to connecting our ideas in conformity with the genius of our native language, and that we acquire precision in proportion to its presence in the language itself.

§125 The simpler our constructions are, the more difficult it becomes to grasp their particular quality. It seems to me that it was much easier to write in Latin. Their conjugations and declensions could by their nature prevent many bothersome problems which we can guard against only with much difficulty. A large number of ideas were without confusion united in a single period, sometimes even with the effect of beauty. By contrast, in French we cannot be careful enough to include in the sentence only the ideas that can most naturally be construed together in it. It takes extraordinary attention to avoid the ambiguities occasioned by the use of pronouns. And as we protect ourselves against these errors, think of the resourcefulness we need not to resort to those out-of-the-way turns of phrase that produce weary discourse. But when these obstacles have been overcome, is there anything more beautiful than the constructions of our language?

§126 But in the end I dare not flatter myself that I can settle the preference for Latin or French to everyone's satisfaction in regard to the subject of this chapter. There are people who strive only for order and the greatest measure of clarity, while others prefer variety and liveliness. On these occasions it is natural that everyone rely on his judgment. For my part, I believe that the advantages of these two languages differ so greatly that they cannot be compared.

13 Writing[48]

§127 Once mankind were able to communicate their thoughts by sound, they felt the need to find new signs to make those thoughts remembered and to make them known at a distance.[49] At that time the imagination presented to them only the same images which they had already expressed by actions and words and which had, from the beginning, made the language figurative and metaphorical. The most natural means was therefore to sketch the images of things. To express the ideas of a man or a horse, they represented the form of one or the other, so that the first effort at writing was a mere picture.

§128 It is probably to this need to sketch our thoughts that painting owes its origin, and this need has undoubtedly contributed to the preservation of the language of action as being the easiest to depict.

§129 In spite of the deficiencies of this method, the most cultured people in America did not find a better one.[50] The Egyptians, being more ingenious, were the first to use a more concise method, which has been called by the name hieroglyphics.[51] From the greater or lesser artifice of the methods they devised, it would seem that they did not invent letters till they had followed writing through its stages of progress.

The problem caused by the enormous amount of space required induced them to make a single figure the sign of several things. By this means, from being a simple depiction, writing became depiction and also character, which is what truly constitutes a hieroglyph. This was

---

[48] This section was nearly finished when I came upon the *Essai sur les hiéroglyphes* translated from the English of Warburton, a work equally informed by philosophical spirit and erudition. I was pleased to see that he and I agreed that language must at the beginning have been highly figurative and metaphorical. My own thoughts had also led me to observe that writing at first was merely a simple picture; but I had not yet tried to discover by what progress mankind had arrived at the invention of letters, and I found success hard to attain. This task has been perfectly accomplished by Warburton; from his work I have borrowed practically all I say about this subject.

[49] I gave the reasons in Chapter 7 of this section.

[50] That is all the savages of Canada have.

[51] Hieroglyphics are of two kinds, proper and symbolic. The proper are subdivided into curiological and tropical hieroglyphics. The curiological hieroglyphs substituted part for the whole, and the tropical represented one thing with another which had some known resemblance or analogy with it. Both of these kinds were used to make things known to the people. The symbolic hieroglyphs were used to keep things secret, and were also of two kinds, tropical and enigmatical. To form tropical symbols, they used the least-known qualities of things, and the enigmatical were composed of a mysterious assemblage of different things and of parts of a variety of animals. See *Essai sur les hiérogl.* §20ff. [*Hiérogl.*, pp. 144–55; *Div. Leg.* 2.105–15].

the first step in the improvement of this cumbersome means of preserving the ideas of mankind. They followed three different avenues which, by the nature of the task, would seem to have been found by degrees at three different times. The first consisted in employing the principal feature of the subject to stand for the whole. Two hands, for example, one holding a shield and the other a bow, represented a battle. With greater art, the second consisted in substituting the real or metaphorical instrument of the thing for the thing itself. An eye given striking prominence was intended to represent God's infinite knowledge, and a sword stood for a tyrant. Finally, in their third method of writing, to represent one thing they used another in which they saw some resemblance or analogy to the first. The universe, for example, was represented by a serpent, and its motley spots indicated the stars.

§130 The first aim in the creation of hieroglyphs was to preserve the memory of events and to proclaim laws, ordinances, and whatever related to the governance of society. In the beginning they therefore took care to use only figures with an analogy that was as much as possible within the reach of everyone; but this method led them into refinements when philosophers began to apply themselves to matters of speculation. As soon as they thought they had found the most abstruse qualities in things, some of them, whether owing to eccentricity or in order to conceal their knowledge from the people, took pleasure in choosing their written characters from figures whose relation to what they wished to express was unknown. For a while they limited themselves to figures that have some pattern in nature, but later they found that these figures were neither numerous nor convenient enough for the large number of ideas furnished by their imagination. So instead they formed their hieroglyphs from the mysterious assemblage of different things or from parts of a variety of animals, which made them altogether enigmatic.

§131 Finally, the custom of expressing thoughts by analogous figures, sometimes with the intent of secrecy or mystery, induced them to represent the very qualities of basic conceptions by means of sensible images. Openness was expressed by a hare, impurity by a wild goat, impudence by a fly, knowledge by an ant, etc. In short, they thought up symbolic marks for all the things that do not have material forms. On these occasions, they were satisfied with any sort of relation whatever;

that was the manner in which they had already acted when they gave names to ideas that do not fall under the senses.

§132 Until that time the animal or the thing chosen for representation was drawn after nature. But when the study of philosophy, which had occasioned symbolic writing, had inspired Egyptian scholars to write much on a variety of subjects, this exact delineation became too voluminous and thus tedious. They therefore gradually began to employ another form of writing, which may be called the running hand of hieroglyphics. It resembled Chinese characters which, at first having been formed by the mere outline of each figure, became at length like marks. One natural result of this cursive writing was that its use greatly diminished the attention given to the symbols, instead fixing it on the thing signified by it. By this means the study of symbolic writing was much abbreviated, there being then little to do but to remember the power of the symbolic mark, whereas before it had been necessary to learn the properties of the thing or animal used as a symbol. In a word, this sort of writing was reduced to the present state of Chinese writing. [*Hiérogl.*, p. 155; *Div. Leg.* 2.115]

§133 Since these characters had gone through so many variations, it was not easy to figure out how they derived from a form of writing which had been a mere picture. That explains why some scholars have fallen into the error of believing that Chinese writing did not have the same origin as Egyptian writing.

§134. That is the general history of writing, followed by degrees from picture to letter. For letters are the very next step to take after Chinese marks, which on the one hand partake of the nature of Egyptian hieroglyphs and on the other of letters, precisely as the hieroglyphs equally partook of Mexican pictures and Chinese characters. These characters are close to our writing, insofar as an alphabet is only a concise abridgment of their troublesome multiplicity. [*Hiérogl.* p. 114; *Div. Leg.* 2.78]

§135 In spite of the advantage of letters, the Egyptians still continued to use hieroglyphics for a long time after letters had been invented, because all the learning of this nation had been committed to that kind of writing. The veneration they had for their books was transferred to the characters whose use the scholars perpetuated. But those who had no learning were not tempted to extend the use of that kind of writing. On them the authority of the scholars merely had the effect of making them respect these characters as suitable for the embellishment of public monuments, on which their use was continued. Perhaps the Egyptian priests themselves were happy to see that little by little they were becoming the only ones who had the key to the writing which preserved the secrets of their religion. This is what caused the error of those who have imagined that the hieroglyphics contained the most sublime mysteries.

§136 From what has been said we see how it happened that what had its origin in necessity came in time to be employed for secrecy and was cultivated as ornamentation. But as a result of the incessant revolution of things, these same figures which had at first been invented for clarity and later converted into mystery, at length resumed their first usage. In the flourishing ages of Greece and Rome they were used on their monuments and medals as the best means to propagate their thought, so that the same symbol which in Egypt was pregnant with profound wisdom was understood by the common people in Greece and Rome. [*Hiérogl., pp. 173–4; Div. Leg. 2.142]

§137 In its progress, language has had the same fate as writing. At the beginning, as we have seen, figures and metaphors were necessary for the sake of clarity. We shall now examine how they transformed themselves into mysteries, later to serve as ornament, and at long last to be understood by everyone.

14 Origin of the fable, the parable, and the enigma, with some details about the use of figures and metaphors[52]

§138 From everything that has been said, it is evident that at the origin of languages it was necessary for people to combine the language of action with the language of articulate sounds, and to speak only with sensible images. In addition, knowledge that today is altogether ordinary they found so subtle that they could bring it within their reach only to the extent that it bore a close relation to the senses. And not least, without the use of conjunctions, it was not yet possible to give form to an argument. For instance, those who wished to prove the advantages of obeying the laws or of following the advice of the best informed had no simpler method than to imagine circumstantial facts of an event which they presented as being adverse or favorable, depending on their point of view, with the double advantage of instruction and persuasion. This is the origin of the apologue or fable. Its first aim was evidently instruction, and consequently the subjects were chosen from the most familiar things, closely related to the senses. At first the subjects were human beings, then animals, and soon also plants, until the spirit of refinement, which in all ages has its partisans, induced them to draw from the most distant sources. They studied the oddest properties of beings in order to draw intricate and delicate allusions, with the effect that the fable was gradually changed into parable, and finally made so mysterious that a mere enigma was all that remained. These enigmas became increasingly fashionable because sages, or those who wished to pass for sages, believed they were obliged to conceal part of their knowledge from ordinary people, with the result that the language which had been created to ensure clarity was changed into a mystery. We have no better vestige of the taste of the first ages than people who have no smattering of letters; they take pleasure in everything that is figurative and metaphorical, no matter how obscure. They have no idea there could be any choice in these matters.

§139 Another cause has contributed to make style increasingly figurative, namely the use of hieroglyphics. These two modes of communicating our thoughts have unavoidably influenced each other.[53] Speaking of a thing, it was natural to use the name of the hieroglyphic

---

[52] The greater part of this chapter is also drawn from the *Essai sur les hiéroglyphes*.

[53] See in Warburton the ingenious parallel he draws between apologue, parable, enigma, figures,

figure which was its symbol, just as it had, at the beginning of hieroglyphics, been natural to depict the figures which usage had made current in the language. Hence we find that

> in hieroglyphic writing the sun, the moon, and the stars were used to represent states, empires, kings, queens, and nobility; that the eclipse and extinction of these luminaries indicated temporary disasters; that fire and flood signified the desolation of war and famine; and that plants and animals indicated the qualities of particular persons, etc. Similarly, we find that the prophets give the names of these celestial luminaries to kings and queens; that their misfortunes and overthrow are represented by the eclipse and extinction of the same luminaries; that the stars falling from the firmament are used to designate the destruction of the nobility; that thunder and tempestuous winds mark hostile invasions; that lions, bears, leopards, goats, and high trees designate army generals, conquerors, and founders of empires. In a word, the prophetic style seems to be a speaking hieroglyph. [*Hiérogl.*, p. 183; *Div. Leg.* 2.152]

§140 As writing became simpler, so did style. As they forgot the meaning of hieroglyphs, they little by little lost the use of many figures and metaphors, but it took centuries for these changes to become evident. The style of the ancient Asiatic authors was prodigiously figurative; even in spoken Greek and Latin we find traces of hieroglyphic influence on the language;[54] and the Chinese, who still use a character of writing similar to hieroglyphics, load their discourse with allegories, comparisons, and metaphors.

§141 Finally, after all these revolutions, figures were employed to embellish discourse when people had acquired so exact and extensive a knowledge of the arts and sciences as to draw images from them which, without ever doing harm to the clarity, were as cheerful, dignified, and sublime as the subject required. Thereafter languages could only lose in the course of the revolutions they underwent. We even find that the epoch of their decadence occurred at the time when they seemed to aspire to the greatest beauties. We see figures and metaphors piling up and overloading the style with ornamentations, to the point where the

and metaphors on the one hand and the different kinds of writing on the other [*Hiérogl.*, pp. 125–32; *Div. Leg.* 2.87–94].

[54] *Annus* ["year"], for example, comes from *annulus* ["ring," "circlet"] because the year revolves upon itself. [*The proper spelling is *anulus*.]

foundation merely seems accessory. When this time comes, we can slow down, but we cannot prevent, the decline of a language. In things moral as well as physical there is a peak of growth after which they decay.

This is how the figures and metaphors first invented by necessity and later chosen to serve the ends of mystery became the ornament of discourse so long as they could be used with discretion; and this is also how, in the decadence of languages, they caused the first damage by the abuses made of them.

15 The genius of languages

§142 Two things contribute to the formation of a nation's character – climate and government. Climate makes people tend either toward the vivacious or toward the phlegmatic, thus disposing them to one form of government rather than another. But these dispositions are changed by a thousand circumstances. The barrenness and fertility of a country and its location; the respective interests of its inhabitants as well as those of their neighbors; the impatient minds who cause trouble as long as the government does not have a solid basis; the extraordinary men whose imagination surpasses that of their fellow citizens – all of those and many other causes contribute to alter and sometimes even to change entirely the first inclinations a nation owes to its climate. For this reason, the character of a people often undergoes nearly the same variations as its government, and it does not become settled until the latter has taken permanent form.

§143 Just as the government influences the character of nations, so the character of nations influences that of languages. Always being pressed by needs and agitated by some passion, people naturally do not speak of things without revealing their interest in them. They must always insensibly link their words to accessory ideas which indicate how they are affected and what their thoughts are. This is easily known, for there is hardly an individual who by his discourse does not ultimately disclose his true character, even in moments when he does his best to conceal it. We need only a short acquaintance with someone to learn his language; I say "his language," for everyone has his own, depending on his passions. I make an exception only of cold and phlegmatic people, who are more difficult to size up, since they readily conform to the way other people speak.

The character of nations shows still more openly than the character of individuals. A multitude cannot act in concert to conceal their passions. Furthermore, we never dream of making a mystery of our preferences when they are shared by our compatriots. On the contrary, we are proud of them and happy that they point to our native country, in favor of which we are always prejudiced. Thus everything confirms that the language of each nation expresses the character of the people who speak it.

§144 In Latin, for example, agricultural terms imply ideas of nobility, unlike in our language. The reason is obvious. When the Romans laid the foundations of their empire, they as yet knew only the most necessary arts. They put a high value on them because it was in equal measure essential for all members of the republic to apply themselves to those arts; and they early became accustomed to look with the same eye on agriculture and the lord who cultivated the fields. The terms of this art therefore appropriated the accessory ideas which gave them the air of nobility. They still retained them when the Roman republic fell into excess of luxury, for the character of a language does not change as easily as the customs of a nation, especially if it has become settled by celebrated writers. In France the general outlook has been quite different since the establishment of the monarchy. The Frankish respect for military art, to which they were indebted for a powerful empire, could only make them contemptuous of the arts they were not themselves obliged to cultivate but left in the care of slaves. From that time, the accessory ideas attached to agricultural terms were bound to differ greatly from what was the case in the Latin language.

§145 Though the genius of languages initially depends on that of nations, its development does not reach completion without the contribution of eminent writers. To trace its progress, we must resolve two questions which have often been discussed but have never, I think, been well explained: to know why the arts and sciences are not evenly distributed among all countries in all ages; and why eminent figures in all genres are much like contemporaries.

The difference of climate has given one answer to these two questions. If there are nations that are strangers to the arts and sciences, some have claimed climate as the true cause; and if there are others where they are no longer cultivated with success, it is claimed that the climate has changed. But there is no basis for assuming a climate change that is as sudden and comprehensive as revolutions in the arts and sciences. The influence of climate is on our organs; even the most favorable can produce only better-organized machines and probably produce pretty nearly the same number in all ages. If it were everywhere the same, we would not fail to see the same variety among nations; some, as at present, would be enlightened and others would stagnate in ignorance. What we need, therefore, are conditions that foster the talents of gifted individuals by directing them to things for which they have a native endowment. Otherwise they would resemble those excellent automatons we let go to ruin because we do not know how to maintain the mechanism and make the springs work. Climate therefore is not the cause of the progress of the arts and sciences, but only necessary as the essential condition.

§146 The conditions that are favorable to the development of geniuses are present at the time when a language begins to acquire fixed principles and a settled character. This time, therefore, is the epoch of eminent men. This observation is confirmed by the history of the arts, but I will give a reason for it that is drawn from the very nature of the thing.

The first turns of expression introduced into a language are neither the clearest nor the most precise and elegant; only long experience can gradually enlighten people in this choice. Languages which are formed out of the leftovers of several other languages even face great obstacles to their progress. Having chosen something from each, they are nothing but a bizarre heap of heterogeneous expressions. They do not have the analogy that instructs writers and gives character to a language. That was the state of French when it was first established. This is why it was so long before we wrote in the vernacular, and why those who made the first efforts to do so were unable to give their style a sustained character.

§147 If we recall that the exercise of the imagination and memory depends entirely on the connection of ideas and that it is formed by the relation and analogy of signs [Pt. I, Sect. 2, Chs. 3 & 4], we will also understand that the poorer a language is in analogous expressions, the less assistance it gives to memory and imagination, which means that it is ill suited to foster talent. It is with languages as with geometrical signs; they give new insights and enlarge the mind in proportion to their degree of perfection. Newton's success was prepared by the choice of signs that had been made before his time and by methods of calculation already contrived. If he had come sooner, he might have been a great figure for his century, but he would not have become the admiration of ours. The same is true in other disciplines. The success of the most gifted geniuses depends altogether on the progress of the language in regard to the age in which they live; for words correspond to the signs used by geometricians, and the way in which they are used corresponds to methods of calculation. In a language short of words or without sufficiently convenient constructions, we should therefore expect to meet the same obstacles as they faced in geometry before the invention of algebra. The French language was for a long time so unfavorable to the progress of mind that if we could imagine Corneille successively at different times during the monarchy, we would gradually find less genius in him as we moved away from the century in which he lived, and in the end we would come to a Corneille who could not give any proof of his talent.

§148 Perhaps it will be objected that men such as this great poet might in the learned languages have found the support which the vernacular withheld.

I answer that having been accustomed to conceive of things in the same way as they were expressed in the language they had grown up with, their minds were naturally constrained. The lack of precision and correctness would not shock them, because it had become habitual with them. Thus they were not yet capable of grasping all the advantages of the learned languages. In fact, if we go back through the centuries we will find that the more uncultivated our language was, the farther we were from knowing the Latin language, and that we did not begin to write well in Latin until we were able to do so in French. Furthermore, it would be showing very slight understanding of the genius of languages to believe that the advantages of the most perfect languages could in a flash be introduced into the most unrefined; this can only be the work of time. Why does Marot,[ff] who knew Latin, not have a style as well formed as that of Rousseau,[gg] who took Marot for his model? It is solely because French had not yet made sufficient progress. Perhaps with less talent, Rousseau gave a more regular character to the Marotic style because he lived in more favorable conditions; had he come a century earlier, he would not have succeeded. The comparison that can be made between Régnier[hh] and Boileau-Despréaux also confirms this argument.

§149 We must note that in a language which is not formed from the scattered parts of several other languages, this progress must be much faster because it has a character from the very beginning, which is why Greece very early had excellent writers.

§150 Let us suppose a highly gifted person who is born in a nation

---

[ff] Clément Marot (1496–1544), French poet who exercised a varying influence over the next two hundred years.
[gg] Jean-Baptiste Rousseau (1671–1741), French poet who was highly regarded in his time.
[hh] Mathurin Régnier (1573–1613), French satiric poet and critic.

still uncultivated though living in a climate which is favorable to the arts and sciences; I believe that he can acquire a mind that is good enough to make him a genius in the midst of these people, but it is obvious that he could never equal some of the eminent writers of the century of Louis XIV. Presented in this light, the matter is so plain that it cannot be called in doubt.

If the language of these unrefined people is an obstacle to the progress of mind, let us give it one degree of perfection, or even two, three, and four; the obstacle would still subsist and would diminish only in proportion to the grades of perfection that were added to the language. The obstacle therefore would not be entirely removed until this language had acquired about as many degrees of perfection as ours had when it first began to produce good writers. On these grounds, it is demonstrable that superior geniuses cannot arise in nations until their languages have already made considerable progress.

§151 Here, in ranked order, are the causes that contribute to the development of talented artists: (1) the climate is an essential condition; (2) the government must have taken permanent form, so that a nation's character is settled; (3) this character must form the character of the language by multiplying the turns of phrase that express the prevailing taste of a nation; (4) this occurs slowly in languages formed on the ruins of several other languages, but once these obstacles have been overcome, the rules of analogy become established, the language makes progress, and good talents develop. Thus we see why great writers are not born at the same rate in all ages, and why they arise sooner in some nations and later in others. It remains for us to examine why superior figures in all genres are nearly contemporaries.

§152 When a genius has discovered the character of a language, he gives it forceful expression and upholds it in all his writings. With this support, other talented men, who before were unable to grasp that character on their own, now clearly perceive it and, following his example, express themselves in it, each in his particular genre. The language is gradually enriched with many new turns of phrase which, by their relation to its character, develop it more and more, and analogy becomes like a torch whose light constantly grows brighter to enlighten a greater number of writers. Then everybody naturally focuses on those who stand out, with the result that their taste becomes the prevailing taste of the nation. Each writer brings to his own subject matter the discernment he has borrowed from them; new talents spring up; all the arts assume their proper character; and superior artists arise in all genres. All this shows why great talents, of whatever kind, do not appear until after the language has already made considerable progress. This is so true that, even though the conditions favorable to military arts and governments occur very often, generals and ministers of the first rank belong all the same to the age of great writers. This is a measure of the influence of men of letters on state affairs; it seems to me that its full extent has not yet been rightly understood.

§153 If great talents owe their growth to the evident progress of language before their time, the language in turn is indebted to men of talent for the further progress which raises it to its ultimate phase. This is what I shall now explain.

Though eminent men in some respect share the character of their nation, they always have something that sets them apart from it. They see and feel in their own particular way, and to express their manner of seeing and feeling they are obliged to imagine new expressions within the rules of analogy or with as little deviation from those rules as possible. Thus they conform to the genius of the language while at the same time adding their own. Corneille writes about the affairs of great men, about the politics of ambitious men, and about all the movements of the soul with a dignity and force that are entirely his own. Racine gives expression to love, its fears and excitements, with the tenderness and elegance characteristic of the gentle passions. Languor guides Quinault's brush in his portrayal of pleasure and sensual delight. And there are several other writers of the past or prominent today, each of whom has a character which our language has gradually absorbed. It is to the poets that we owe the first and perhaps also the greatest obligations. Being bound by rules which constrain them, their imagination strives with increased effort, thus of necessity creating new expressions. Indeed, the sudden progress of a language always occurs in the age of some great poet. Philosophers carry it to perfection only much later. It has been their achievement to give our language the correctness and clarity that constitute its principal quality, and that, by providing the most useful signs for the analysis of ideas, give us the ability to discern what is most exquisite in every object.

§154 Philosophers seek the reasons of things, they formulate the rules of art, they explain what escapes us, and by their instruction they increase the number of good judges. But if we turn our attention to the aspects of the arts which require the most imagination, then philosophers cannot flatter themselves that they contribute as much to their progress as they do to the progress of the sciences; on the contrary, they seem to have a negative effect. That is because our attention to knowledge of the rules and fear of seeming not to know them dampen the fire of the imagination, which prefers to be guided by feeling and by the vivid impressions of the objects that engage it, rather than by the exercise of reflection which combines and calculates everything.

It is true that knowledge of the rules is very useful for those who, in the moment of composition, let their genius soar so high that they forget the rules or remember them only when they revise their works. But for a mind that feels some insufficiency, it is very hard not to invoke the rules. And yet can we expect to succeed in works of the imagination if we do not know when to refuse such assistance? Ought we not at least to be mistrustful of our productions? Generally speaking, in an age when philosophers lay down the precepts of the arts, the works are as a rule better made and better written, but at the same time artists of genius appear less often.

§155 Since the character of languages is formed little by little in conformity with the national character, it must necessarily have some dominant quality. It therefore cannot happen that the same advantages are shared to the same degree by several languages. The most perfect would unite them all insofar as they were compatible, for it would surely be a defect for a language to excel so strongly in one particular genre that it was unfit for any other. Perhaps the character of our language as shown in the works of Quinault and La Fontaine proves that we will never have a poet who equals Milton's intensity and that the intense quality of *Paradise Lost* proves that the English will never have poets like Quinault and La Fontaine.[55]

§156 Analysis and imagination are two operations that are so different that they usually raise obstacles to the progress of each other. It takes a special temperament for these advantages to lend each other mutual assistance without at the same time doing harm, and this temperament is the middle between two extremes which I have already had occasion to deal with [Pt. I]. It would therefore not be easy for the same

---

[55] I venture this conjecture on the basis of what I have heard about Milton's poem, for I do not know English.

languages equally to favor these two operations. By the simplicity and clarity of its constructions, French early on lends a correctness to the mind which gradually becomes habitual, greatly smoothing the way for the progress of analysis, but it is quite opposed to the imagination. By contrast, the inversions of the ancient languages were an obstacle to analysis insofar as they, by facilitating the exercise of the imagination, made that exercise more natural, to the detriment of the other operations of mind. There I think is one of the reasons for the superiority of the modern over the ancient philosophers. A language as discriminating as French in the choice of figures and expressions ought to be even more so in its conduct of reasoning.

To be clear about all this, we need to imagine two languages: one would give so much freedom of exercise to the imagination that the people who spoke it would talk nonsense incessantly; the other, by contrast, would practice analysis so fiercely that the people for whom it was natural would conduct themselves even in their pleasures like geometricians seeking the solution to a problem. Between these two extremes we could imagine for ourselves all the languages that are possible and see how they assume different qualities, depending on their closeness to one of the extremes, and how they would compensate for the advantages they lost on one side by those they gained on the other. The most perfect language lies in the middle, and the people who speak it will be a nation of great men.

Someone might ask me this question: if the character of a language is a reason for the superiority of modern over ancient philosophers, does it not follow that the ancient poets are superior to our modern poets? My answer is no. Since analysis draws assistance from language, it cannot occur unless it is favored by language. But we have seen, by contrast, that the causes which favor the progress of the imagination are much more extensive, for there is in fact nothing that is not conducive to the exercise of this operation. If the Greek and Roman poets in certain genres are superior to ours, we have poets who in other genres are superior to their poets. Does antiquity have any poet who can be compared to our Corneille or Molière?

§157 The simplest way of deciding which language excels in the largest number of genres would be to take a count of the original authors in each. I doubt that our language, French, would show any disadvantage in that respect.

§158 Now that I have shown the causes of the ultimate progress of language, it is relevant to look into the causes of its decline; they are the same, and they produce opposite effects only owing to the nature of circumstances. Here it is much the same as with what pertains to the body, in which the same movement that has been a source of life also becomes the source of destruction.

When a language has original writers in every genre, then the more genius a writer has, the more readily he sees obstacles to surpassing them. To equal them does not satisfy his ambition; like them, he wants to be the first in his genre. Thus he tries to break a new path. But since all the styles analogous to the character of the language and to his own have already been used by his predecessors, he has no choice but to keep his distance from the analogy. Thus in order to be original he is obliged to contribute to the ruin of a language whose progress a century sooner he would have hastened along.

§159 Though writers such as this man are criticized, they have too much talent not to be successful. Being free to copy their faults, mediocre minds soon persuade themselves that it is within their reach to gain an equal reputation. It is at this point that we see the emergence of a preponderance of subtle and twisted conceits, of overdone antitheses, eye-popping paradoxes, frivolous turns of phrase, far-fetched expressions, newfangled words, and in short the jargon of would-be clever minds spoiled by bad metaphysics. The public applauds, we have a plethora of trivial and ridiculous works with a short life, poor taste infects the arts and sciences, and gifted people become more and more rare.

§160 I have no doubt there will be disagreement about what I have been saying on the character of languages. I have often met people who believe all languages are equally qualified for all genres and who hold that a person with Corneille's gifts would have given the same evidence of his talents regardless of the age in which he might have lived or the vernacular in which he wrote.

The fact that signs are arbitrary the first time they are used is perhaps the source of the belief that they cannot have a character; but I wonder whether it is not natural for each nation to combine its ideas according to its particular genius and to join different accessory ideas to a certain stock of principal ideas, depending on the different ways in which nations are affected. Now, being authorized by usage, these combinations are truly what constitutes the genius of a language. It can be more or less pervasive; that depends on the number and variety of accepted expressions and on the analogy which provides the means of inventing them according to need. No one has the power to change this character entirely. The moment we no longer stay close to that character, we speak a foreign language and cease to be understood. Only time can bring about changes of such magnitude by placing an entire nation in conditions which induce the people to envisage things in ways that are altogether different from what they did before.

§161 Of all writers, it is with poets that the genius of languages finds its strongest expression. This is the source of the difficulty of translating the poets, which is such that it is often easier for a man of talent to surpass than to equal them. Strictly speaking, one can even say that it is impossible to give good translations of poetry, for the reasons that prove that two languages cannot have the same character also prove that the same thoughts can rarely be expressed in both with the same beauties.

In speaking of prosody and inversions, I have said a number of things which are relevant to the subject of this chapter, but I do not intend to repeat them here.

§162 From this account of the progress of language, it can be understood that for anyone who knows languages well, they are like a painting of the character of each nation's genius. He will see how the imagination has combined the ideas in accordance with the preconceptions and passions; he will see how each nation formed a different mind in proportion to its degree of isolation from other nations. But if customs have influenced the language, the language in turn has influenced customs and for a long time preserved the character of the people, once eminent writers had fixed the rules of the language.

§163 Perhaps this entire history will be taken for a romance, but at least its plausibility cannot be denied. I cannot easily believe that the method I have used has often caused me to fall into error, for it has been my aim to propose nothing that does not rest on the supposition that every language has always been imagined on the model of its immediate predecessor. For me the language of action is the seed of the languages and of all the arts that can be used to express our thoughts; I have examined the circumstances that have been conducive to the development of this seed; and from this seed I have not only discovered the birth of these arts, but I have also followed their progress and explained their different characters. In a word, it seems to me that I have demonstrated, on the basis of evidence, that things which appear most unusual to us were the most natural in their time, and that nothing happened except what we had reason to expect.

Section 2
Method

It is from the knowledge we have gained of the operations of mind and of the causes of their progress that we must learn how to conduct ourselves in the search for truth. Before we arrived at this point we could not conceive of a good method, but now it actually seems to reveal itself as a natural consequence of our researches. It will be sufficient to enlarge upon some of the thoughts that occur in this work.

1 The first cause of our errors and the origin of truth

§1 Many philosophers have eloquently told us about the large number of errors we attribute to the senses, the imagination, and the passions; but they cannot flatter themselves that their works have produced all the benefits that were promised in those works. Their very imperfect theory is ill qualified to instruct us in practice. The imagination and the passions work in such intricate ways and depend so much on people's temperaments, on times and circumstances, that it is impossible to discover all the springs they set in motion, and, by the same token, they make it natural for everyone to flatter himself that he is not among those they have led into error.

Instead of quitting its errors, often the mind merely takes up new error, much like an ailing person who recovers from one illness only to contract a new one. For a person of weak constitution to be cured of all his illnesses, it would be necessary to provide him with an entirely new temperament; for our mind to be cured of all its debilities, it would be necessary to give it new ways of looking at things, without lingering over its maladies, but going directly to their true source without hesitation.

§2 We find this source in our habit of reasoning on things of which we either have no ideas or have ill-determined ideas. It is appropriate to seek the source of this habit here so that we can have a convincing understanding of the origin of our errors and to know what sort of critical spirit we must bring to the reading of philosophy.

§3 While still children and incapable of reflection, we are wholly occupied by our needs. At that time, objects make impressions on our senses with a force that is inversely proportional to the resistance they meet. Our organs develop slowly, our reason even more slowly, and we fill our minds with ideas as they come to us by chance and poor education. When we reach the age when the mind begins to put some order in its ideas, we still see only things which have been familiar to us for a long time. Therefore we do not waver in our belief that they exist and that they have a particular nature, because it seems natural to us that they should exist and be what they are. They are so strongly imprinted on our brain that it would not occur to us to think that they might not exist or that they might exist in some other way. Hence our indifference to knowing about things we are used to, and our surges of curiosity for everything that seems new.

§4 When we begin to reflect, we do not understand how the ideas and maxims we find in ourselves have gotten to be there, for we do not recall ever having been without them, so we are secure in their enjoyment. However defective they may be, we take them to be self-evident notions, and we call them "reason," "the light of nature or born with us," or "principles engraved, imprinted on the soul." We rely all the more willingly on these ideas because we believe that if they deceive us, God is the source of our error, since we regard them as the only means He has given us to arrive at the truth. This is why some notions with which we have only a passing acquaintance appear to us to be principles of the utmost certitude.

§5 Our mind becomes used to this lack of care about correctness by the way we grow into language. We reach the age of reason only long after contracting the habit of speech. If we except words for the expression of our needs, it is usually by chance that we have occasion to hear certain sounds rather than others, just as chance has determined what ideas we connect with the sounds. The moment we reflect on the children we see around us, we remember the state we passed through and recognize that our ordinary use of words is far from precise. This is not surprising. As children we heard expressions whose meaning, though well determined by usage, was so complex that we had neither enough experience nor enough insight to grasp it; we heard others which never twice expressed the same idea or were altogether without sense. To appreciate how impossible it was for us to use words with discrimination, we need only consider the trouble we still often face in their right use.

§6 The habit of connecting signs to things became so natural to us at a time when we were not capable of understanding what we were doing, that it became habitual with us to relate names to the very reality of objects, believing that they perfectly explained their essence. We imagined that there were innate ideas, because some are the same in all mankind; we would not have failed to believe that our language is innate if we had not known that other nations speak different languages. It seems that in our strivings, all our efforts aim at finding new expressions, which as soon as we have them make us believe we have acquired new knowledge. Our pride easily persuades us that we know things when we have long sought to know them and have talked much about them.

§7 By tracing our errors to the origin I have indicated, we enclose them within a single cause of which we cannot deny that it has hitherto played a large role in our judgments. Perhaps we may oblige even the most prejudiced philosophers to admit that this unique cause is the foundation of their systems, provided we put the question the right way. In fact, if our passions lead us into error, it is because they cause the misuse of a vague principle, of a metaphorical expression and an equivocal term, so that we can deduce opinions we find flattering to ourselves. If we fool ourselves, then those vague principles, metaphors, and equivocations are causes that precede our passions. Consequently, to do away with the trickery of this error, all we need to do is to renounce this empty language.

§8 If the origin of the error is in the lack of ideas or in ill-determined ideas, then the origin of truth must be in well-determined ideas. For this we have the evidence of mathematics. If we have exact ideas, regardless of the subject, they will also be sufficient to make us perceive the truth; if on the contrary we do not, we will always get everything mixed up no matter what precautions we take. In a word, in metaphysics we proceed securely with well-determined ideas, while without them we get lost even in arithmetic.

§9 But how do the arithmeticians get their exact ideas? The reason is that, by knowing how ideas are generated, they are always able to compose and decompose them in order to compare them in regard to all their relations. It is only by reflecting on the generation of numbers that they found the rules of combination. Those who have not thought about this generation are able to calculate with as much correctness as others because the rules are sure; but, not knowing their rational foundation, they do not know what they are doing, thus being incapable of discovering new rules.

§10 Now, in arithmetic as in all the sciences, the truth can be discovered only by composition and decomposition. If we do not for the most part reason with the same correctness in the other sciences, it is because we have not yet found dependable rules always to compose and decompose our ideas correctly, which has its source in the fact that we have not even been able to define them. But perhaps our reflections on the origin of knowledge will provide the remedy.

2 The manner of determining ideas or their names

§11 It is an old and received opinion that words should be taken in the sense that usage gives them. Indeed, it seems at first that there is no other means of being understood than to speak like other people, but I have thought I ought to take a different path. I have observed that to attain true knowledge we should start afresh in the sciences without allowing ourselves to become biased in favor of trusted opinions, and for this reason it has seemed to me that to make the language exact, we must reform it without regard to usage. This does not mean that I intend to make it a law always to connect our terms to ideas that are all different from the ideas they usually signify; that would be a puerile and ridiculous affectation. For the names of simple ideas and for many familiar notions common among mankind, usage is uniform and stable; in those cases no change is needed, but when it comes to complex ideas, especially those pertaining to metaphysics and moral philosophy, nothing is more arbitrary and often even capricious. This has made me believe that to invest language with clarity and precision, we need to take a new view of the materials of knowledge and make new combinations without regard for those which have already been made.

§12 In our examination of the progress of languages, we have seen that usage fixes the meaning of words only by means of the circumstances in which we speak [Pt. II, Sect. 1, Ch. 9]. In truth, these circumstances are arranged by chance, but if we ourselves knew how to choose them, we could on every occasion do what chance makes us do on some occasions, namely determine the signification of words exactly. There is no other means of always giving precision to language than the means that have always been the source whenever language has been precise. We must therefore at the outset place ourselves in receptive circumstances, so that we can make signs expressive of the first ideas we will acquire by sensation and reflection. Now, as by reflection on these we acquire new ideas, we will make new names whose meaning will be determined by placing other people in the same circumstances in which we found ourselves, thus making them entertain the same reflections we made. Then the expressions would always follow the ideas, with the effect that they would be clear and precise, because they would express only what everybody had experienced.

§13 In fact, a person who began making a language for himself and who decided not to communicate with others until he had fixed the meaning of his expressions by the circumstances in which he had placed himself would not have fallen into any of those mistakes we have so often landed in. The names of simple ideas would be clear, for they would not signify anything except what he perceived in the chosen conditions; the names of complex ideas would be precise, because they would comprise nothing but the simple ideas which particular circumstances united in a determined manner. Finally, when he wished to add to these first combinations or retract something, the signs he employed would preserve the clarity of the first signs, provided that what he added or contracted was indicated by new circumstances. If he afterwards wished to communicate his thoughts to others, he would merely need to place them in the same situation he had been in when he imagined the signs, thereby inducing them to connect the same ideas as he did to the words he had chosen.

§14 Furthermore, when I speak of making words, I do not mean to suggest that we should plan to make entirely new terms. Those that are authorized by usage seem to me usually sufficient for conversation about all kinds of subjects. It would even be harmful to the language, especially to the sciences, to invent words without necessity. I therefore use the phrase "to make words," not because I wish to propose that we should begin by explaining the terms only to define them afterwards, as is commonly done, but because it would be necessary, after placing ourselves in the circumstances in which we felt or saw something, to give names we borrowed from usage to what we saw and felt. This procedure seemed quite natural to me and also better suited to show the difference that exists between the way in which I would suggest that the signification of words be determined and the definitions of the philosophers.

§15 I believe it would be useless to restrict our plan to using only expressions authorized by the language of the learned; perhaps it would even be to our advantage to take them from our common language. Though one is no more exact than the other, I do all the same find one defect less in the latter, namely that the better sort of people, who have not otherwise reflected on the sciences, will quite freely admit their ignorance and the inexactness of the words they use. But, being ashamed of their useless meditations, philosophers are always stubborn partisans of the pretended benefits of their long nights of study.

§16 To have a better understanding of this method, we must go into greater detail by applying what we have been saying in a general way to different kinds of ideas. Let us begin with the names of simple ideas.

The obscurity and confusion of words stem from our giving them a more or less extensive scope, or even from using them without our having connected any idea to them. There are many whose signification we only partially grasp; we consider it piecemeal, adding or subtracting, thus forming different combinations with only one sign, with the result that it can happen that the same words have very different meanings when spoken by the same mouth. Furthermore, as the study of language, no matter how little effort is put into it, demands some reflection, we take a shortcut and refer signs to realities for which we have no ideas. Among these are, in the language of the philosophers, such terms as "being," "substance," "essence," etc. It is obvious that these defects can belong only to ideas which are the work of the mind. As to the meaning of the names of simple ideas, which are derived immediately from sense, it is known at once; its object cannot be imagined realities, since it refers directly to simple perceptions, which are in fact in the mind such as they appear in the perceptions. Terms of this kind cannot, therefore, be obscure. Their sense is so clearly identified by all the circumstances in which we naturally find ourselves, that even children cannot be mistaken. However little they know their language, they do not confound the names of sensations, and their ideas are as clear as ours of the words "white," "black," "red," "movement," "rest," "pleasure," "pain." With regard to the operations of the mind, they also understand their names, provided they are simple and that the circumstances turn their reflection in that direction, for it is evident by the way they use the words, "yes," "no," "I will," "I will not," that they grasp their true meaning.

§17 Perhaps someone will object that it is demonstrable that the same objects produce different sensations in different individuals, that we do not attribute the same ideas of magnitude to objects, and that we do not perceive the same colors in them, etc.

I answer that we all the same always understand one another well enough in regard to the aim we have in view in metaphysics and moral philosophy. As for the latter, we need not assure ourselves, for instance, that the same punishment produces the same feelings of pain in all people, and that the same rewards are accompanied by the same feelings of pleasure. Whatever the variety in the ways the causes of pleasure and pain affect people of different temperaments, it is sufficient that the words "pleasure" and "pain" are so well settled that no one can be mistaken about them. The circumstances in which we find ourselves all the time do not permit us to be mistaken in our use of these terms.

As for metaphysics, it is sufficient that the sensations represent extension, figure, and color. The difference in the perceptions of two individuals cannot cause any confusion. If, for instance, what I call "blue" constantly appears to me as what others call "green," and what I call "green" constantly appears to me as what others call "blue," we will understand one another as well when we say "the meadows are green," "the sky is blue," as if we had the same sensations. This is because we do not intend to say anything more than that the sky and the meadow come to our cognizance as appearances which enter the mind by sight, called "blue" and "green." If we wished to make these words signify that we have precisely the same sensations, these propositions would not become obscure, but they would be false, or at least they would not be sufficiently well founded to be regarded as certain.

§18 I believe, then, that I can conclude that the names of simple ideas, of sensations as well as of operations of mind, can be very well determined by circumstances, since they are already so exact that even children are not mistaken about them. In regard to sensations, a philosopher must take care to avoid two errors which people habitually commit owing to precipitous judgments; one is believing that sensations are in the objects; the other, which we have talked about, is believing that the same objects produce the same sensations in everyone.

§19 When the terms which are the signs of simple ideas are exact, nothing stands in the way of determining those that belong to other ideas. To that end, we must settle the number and the quality of simple ideas from which complex ideas can be formed. What on these occasions raises numerous obstacles to fixing the sense of terms, even after many efforts leaving much equivocation and obscurity behind, is that we take words as we find them in the usage to which we absolutely intend to conform. Moral philosophy especially is full of intricately composed expressions, and the usage we consult is so inconsistent that this method will unavoidably make us speak with little exactness and cause us to fall into a great many contradictions. A person who at first applied himself to the consideration of nothing but simple ideas and who collected them under signs only as he became familiar with those ideas surely would not face the same danger. The most compounded words he would be obliged to use would constantly have a determined signification because he delimited the sense of each within precise bounds, since he had himself chosen the simple ideas and determined their number as he connected them to the words.

§20 But if we do not renounce the empty science of those who refer words to realities they do not know, there is no point in thinking that we can make language precise. All parts of arithmetic are demonstrable because we have an exact idea of unity and because, by the art of using signs, we determine how many times unity is added to itself in the most compounded numbers. In other sciences we pretend to reason on complex ideas with vague and obscure expressions and to discover their relations. To realize how unreasonable this procedure is, we need only consider where we would be if people could have thrown arithmetic into the same state of confusion which now prevails in metaphysics and moral philosophy.

§21 Complex ideas are the work of the mind; if they are defective, it is because we have done a poor job in making them; the only way to make them right is to remake them. We must therefore start over again with the materials of knowledge and put them to work as if they had never before been used. To this end it is appropriate, in the beginning, to attach to sounds only the smallest possible number of simple ideas; to choose only those which everyone can easily perceive by placing himself in the same circumstances as ourselves; and not to add new ideas till we are familiar with the first and to make sure we find ourselves in the right circumstances to ensure they enter the mind with clarity and precision. Doing all that, we will become used to connecting words with all sorts of simple ideas, however numerous they may be.

The connection of ideas with signs is a habit that cannot be acquired all of a sudden, especially if the result is richly compounded notions. Children only late form precise ideas of the numbers 1,000, 10,000, etc. They acquire them only by long and frequent practice as they learn to multiply unity and fix each collection by a particular name. In regard to the large number of complex ideas pertaining to metaphysics and moral philosophy, it is equally impossible for us to ensure precision for the terms we have chosen if, the first time and without any precaution, we insist on loading them with simple ideas. The result will be that we one moment take them in one sense and the next in another, because we, owing to our having only superficially imprinted our collections of ideas on the mind, often add or subtract something without being aware of it. But if in the beginning we add only a few ideas to the words and proceed to the largest collections in a very orderly fashion, we will become increasingly familiar with the compounding of notions without making them less fixed and secure.

§22 That is the method I intended to follow, chiefly in the third section of this work. I did not begin by explaining the names of the operations of mind to define them later, but I made an effort to place myself in the circumstances best suited to make me perceive the progress of these operations; and as I framed ideas which made an addition to the previous ideas, I secured them with names, in conformity with usage whenever possible.

§23 We have two sorts of complex ideas: the first are those we form on the basis of patterns, the others are certain combinations of simple ideas which the mind puts together voluntarily.

In practice, it would be a useless and even dangerous method to try to make notions of substances by arbitrarily making a collection of certain simple ideas. Such notions would represent substances nowhere to be found, would be gathering together properties nowhere existing together, and would separate those that were united, and it would be pure chance if they sometimes conformed to any model. To render the names of substances clear and precise, we must therefore consult nature, so that the names signify only simple ideas we find existing together.

§24 There are still other ideas belonging to substances, called abstract ideas. As I have already said, these are more or less simple ideas to which we pay attention by ceasing to think of other simple ideas coexisting with them. If we cease to think of the substance of bodies as being actually colored and figured, looking on it only as something mobile, divisible, impenetrable, and having an indeterminate extension, we shall have the idea of matter, an idea simpler than that of body, of which it is only an abstraction, though many philosophers may have had the fancy to reify it. If afterwards we cease to think of the mobility of matter, its divisibility and impenetrability, in order to reflect only on its indeterminate extension, we will form the idea of pure space, which is still simpler. This goes for all abstractions, which shows that the names of the most abstract ideas are as easy to determine as those of substances themselves.

§25 In the determination of the notions of mixed modes, that is to say the ideas we have of human actions and everything pertaining to the realm of moral philosophy, jurisprudence, and the arts, things are very different from what they are with substances. Legislators did not have patterns when for the first time they united certain simple ideas from which they composed their laws, any more than when they spoke of a number of human actions before they had considered whether there were any examples of them. So also the patterns of the arts are found nowhere except in the mind of the first creators. As we know them, substances are mere collections of properties which it is not in our power to join or separate and which we need not know except insofar as they exist and in regard to their manner of existence. Human actions are constantly changing combinations of which it is often useful to have ideas before we have seen patterns for them. If we formed notions of them only as experience instructed us, it would often be too late. We are therefore obliged to go about things differently, by voluntarily uniting or separating certain simple ideas, or by adopting the combinations others have already made.

§26 There is this difference between notions of substances and notions of mixed modes, that we regard the latter as patterns to which we refer exterior things and that the former are mere copies of what we perceive outside ourselves. For the truth of the first, the combinations made by the mind must conform to what we observe in things; for the truth of the second, it is sufficient that the combinations may be externally such as they are in the mind. The notion of justice would be true even if there were no such thing as a just action, because its truth consists in a collection of ideas, which does not depend on external things. The idea of iron is true only so far as it conforms to this metal, which must be its model.

With these details about mixed modes, it is easy to understand that it is entirely up to us to fix the meaning of their names, because it is our task to decide on the simple ideas which we have ourselves put together in the collections. We also understand that other people will share our thoughts, provided they are placed in the circumstances in which the same simple ideas are the object of their minds as of ours, and in which they are induced to unite them under the same names under which we have collected them.

Those are the means I wish to propose for investing language with all the clarity and all the precision of which it is susceptible. I have not found it necessary to change anything in the names of simple ideas, for their sense seems to me to be sufficiently determined by usage. As for complex ideas, they are formed with so little accuracy that we have to reconsider their elements and put them together in new combinations without regard for those already formed. They are all the work of the mind, both the most and the least exact. If we have had success with some, we can succeed with the rest if we always conduct ourselves with the same skill.

3 The order we ought to follow in the search for truth

§27 It seems to me that a method that has led to one truth can lead to another, and that the best method must be the same for all the sciences. It is therefore sufficient to reflect on the discoveries already made to learn how to make new ones. The simplest would be the best for this purpose, because in them it is easier for us to observe the means that have been used; my example will therefore be the elementary notions of mathematics, and I assume that we were in the situation of acquiring them for the first time.

§28 No doubt we would first form the idea of unity, and by adding it several times to itself, we would form collections which we fix by signs. Repeating this operation, we would soon, by this means, have as many complex ideas of numbers as we wish. We would then reflect on the manner in which they have been formed; we would observe the progression, and we would not fail to acquire the means of their decomposition. From then on, we could compare the most complex with the simplest, discovering the qualities of either kind.

By this method the operations of the mind would have no other object than simple ideas or complex ideas we have formed, with their generation being perfectly known to us. We would therefore encounter no obstacle to the discovery of the first relations of magnitudes. With those known, we would easily perceive the relations which immediately follow them, which in turn could not fail to make us perceive others. Thus, having begun with the simplest, we would insensibly rise to the most compounded, creating a sequence of discrete items of knowledge so firmly interdependent that we could not reach the most distant except by those that have preceded it.

§29 Being equally within the reach of the human mind, all the other sciences are based on the single principle of simple ideas coming to us by sensation and reflection. To acquire complex ideas from them, we have no other means than, as in mathematics, to unite simple ideas in different collections. We must therefore follow the same order in the progress of ideas, and use the same precaution in the choice of signs.

A large number of preconceived opinions are opposed to this procedure, but here are the means I have devised to protect us against them.

It is during childhood that we absorb the prejudices which retard the progress of our knowledge, thus causing us to fall into error. A man created fully grown by God and with his organs so well developed that he would, from the first moment, have the perfect use of reason, would not meet the same obstacles as we do in the search for truth. He would invent signs only to the extent that he experienced new sensations and engaged in new reflections. He would combine his first ideas according to the circumstances in which he found himself; he would fix each collection by a particular name; and when he wished to compare two complex notions, he would be able to analyze them easily because he would have no difficulty reducing them to the simple ideas from which he had formed them himself. Thus, since he imagined words only after framing ideas, his notions would always be exactly determined, and his language would not be subject to the obscurities and ambiguities which prevail in ours. Let us then imagine ourselves in the place of this man, passing through all the circumstances in which he must find himself, seeing with him what he senses, forming the same reflections, acquiring the same ideas, analyzing them with the same care, expressing them with similar signs, and let us, so to speak, make an entirely new language for ourselves.

§30 By reasoning, according to this method, only with simple ideas or with complex ideas that are the work of the mind, we will have two advantages: the first is that since we know the generation of the ideas on which we meditate, we will not move forward without knowing where we are, how we got there, and how we can retrace our steps. The second is that on every subject we will clearly see the limits of our knowledge, for we will be up against them when the senses cease to furnish us with ideas so that the mind consequently can form no further notions. Nothing seems more important to me than being able to distinguish the things to which we can apply ourselves with success from those in which we cannot but fail. Not having known how to make that distinction, philosophers have often wasted their time on insoluble questions, when they might have employed it on useful inquiries. One example is provided by their efforts to explain the essence and nature of beings.

§31 All truths whatsoever are limited to the relations between simple ideas, between complex ideas, and between a simple idea and a complex idea. By the method I am proposing, we can avoid the errors we make in the study of any one of these.

Simple ideas can never cause any mistake. The cause of our errors stems from our subtracting something from an idea that belongs to it because we do not know all its parts; or from our adding something that does not belong to it when our imagination overhastily judges that it contains something that it does not contain at all. But we cannot subtract anything from a simple idea, because it has no parts; and we cannot add anything so long as we see that it is simple, for it would then lose the quality of being simple.

We can be mistaken in the use of complex notions only by wrongly either adding or subtracting something. But if complex notions are formed with the great care I prescribe, mistakes can be avoided by retracing their generation, thereby seeing what they contain, and neither more nor less. That being so, whatever comparisons we make of simple and complex ideas, we shall never attribute other relations to them than those that belong to them.

§32 Philosophers produce obscure and confused reasonings only because they do not suspect that there are ideas that are the products of the mind, or because, if they do suspect that there are, they are incapable of discovering how they were generated. Being under the false impression that they are innate or that they are well made such as they are, philosophers believe they ought not to change anything, but take the ideas just as they happen to come. Since we can effectively analyze only the ideas we have ourselves formed by a regular procedure, their analyses, or rather their definitions, are nearly always defective. They wrongly extend or restrain the signification of their terms, they change it without being aware that they do so, or they even refer the words to vague notions and unintelligible beings. I beg leave to repeat that we must then make a new combination of ideas for ourselves, beginning with the simplest ones supplied by sense, forming them into complex notions and in turn combining them to form additional ideas, and so forth. This method will save us from falling into error, provided that we assign a distinct name to each collection.

§33 Descartes was right to think that in order to gain certain knowledge we must begin with the rejection of all the knowledge we believe we have acquired; but he was wrong when he thought that it was sufficient to doubt that knowledge. To doubt if two and two are four, whether man is a rational animal, amounts to having ideas of two, of four, of man, of animal, and of rational. Thus doubt leaves the ideas subsisting such as they are; therefore doubt is no remedy, since our errors have their source in wrongly framed ideas. It can make us suspend judgment for a while, but in the end we do not escape from uncertainty except by consulting the ideas which doubt has not yet destroyed, and it follows that they will lead us astray as before if they are vague or poorly determined. So Descartes' doubt is ineffectual. That it also cannot be put into practice is within everyone's own experience, for if we compare familiar and well-determined ideas, we cannot doubt the relations that exist between them, such as in those of numbers, for example.

§34 Without the prejudice of innate ideas, this philosopher would have seen that the only way to acquire a new stock of knowledge was to destroy the ideas themselves so that they could be traced to their origin, that is to say to sensations. In that respect, we detect a great difference between saying with Descartes that we must begin with the simplest things, and, as it appears to me, with the simplest ideas supplied by the senses. For him the things that are simplest are innate ideas, general principles, and abstract notions, which he takes to be the source of our knowledge. According to the method I propose, the simplest ideas are the first particular ideas that come to us by sensation or reflection. Those are the materials of our knowledge which we combine according to the occasions in which they appear in order to form complex ideas whose relations are discovered by analysis. It must be understood that I do not limit myself to saying that we must begin with the simplest ideas, but I say with the simplest ideas *that the senses supply*; I make that addition to ensure that these ideas are not confounded with abstract notions or with the general principles of the philosophers. The idea of solidity, for example, in spite of all its complexity, is one of the simplest to come directly from the senses. In the process of decomposing it, we form ideas that are still simpler and which differ in the same proportion from those supplied by the senses. We see it diminish in a surface and in a line, and entirely disappear in the point.[56]

§35 There is still another difference between the method of Descartes and the one I am trying to establish. According to him, we must begin with the definition of things and consider the definitions as principles by which their properties are discovered. By contrast, I believe that we must begin by seeking their properties, a procedure that to me seems

[56] I take the words "surface," "line," "point" in the senses of those words as they are used by geometricians.

sound. If the notions we are capable of acquiring are, as I have shown, nothing but different collections of simple ideas which experience has made us put together under certain names, then it is much more natural to form those notions by examining the ideas in the same order as that given by experience than to begin with the definitions in order afterwards to deduce the different properties of the things.

§36 This account shows that the order we must follow in the search for truth is the same as I have already had occasion to indicate when talking of analysis. It consists in returning to the origin of ideas, to trace their generation and thereby to make different compositions and decompositions for the purpose of comparing them in all the aspects that can show their relations. I will say a word about the procedure we should follow in order to make the mind as well prepared as possible for discoveries.

§37 We must begin by examining our knowledge of the subject matter we wish to understand by tracing its origin, and by precisely determining the ideas. With a truth that is found by chance and that cannot be firmly grasped, we run the risk, when having only vague ideas, of falling into numerous errors.

Once the ideas have been determined, they must be compared; but since comparing them is not always easy to do, it is important that we make use of whatever assistance is available. In that regard, we must note that, in accordance with the habits the mind has acquired, there is nothing that does not offer aid to reflection. This means that there are no objects to which we cannot connect our ideas and which, it follows, are not well suited to facilitate the exercise of memory and imagination. What matters is to know how to make these connections in conformity with the aim we have in mind and with the circumstances in which we find ourselves. With this skill, it is not necessary for us to take the precaution, as some philosophers do, of withdrawing into solitude or entering a cave in order to meditate there by the light of a lamp. Neither light, nor darkness, nor noise – nothing can stand in the way of the mind of a man who knows how to think.

§38 Here are two experiences which may be familiar to many people. If someone withdraws into silence and darkness, the slightest noise or the faintest light will suffice to distract him if he is struck by either one at a moment when he did not expect it. The reason is that the ideas that occupy him naturally connect to the situation in which he finds himself, with the result that perceptions that are at variance with this situation cannot occur without at the same time upsetting the order of ideas. The same may be observed in an entirely different case. If in broad daylight and in the midst of noise I am reflecting on something, I will immediately be distracted if the light or noise suddenly ceases. Here, as also in the first example, the new perceptions I experience are entirely at odds with the state I was in before. Thus the sudden impression that strikes me must again interrupt the sequence of my ideas.

The second experience shows that light and noise are not an obstacle to reflection; I even believe it merely requires habit for them to promote reflection. Properly speaking, only unexpected change distracts us. I say "unexpected," for whatever the changes occurring around us, if they present us with nothing but what we would naturally expect, they only make us apply ourselves more firmly to the object of our concern. Think of all the variety of things that sometimes confront us in the same landscape: fruitful hillsides, barren plains, crags that pierce the clouds, forests where noise and silence, light and darkness alternate, etc. Yet the poets always feel inspired by this variety, which, by virtue of being connected with the most beautiful ideas that are the ornament of poetry, cannot fail to evoke these ideas. The view, for example, of a fruitful hillside evokes the singing of birds, the babbling of streams, the happiness of shepherds, their pleasant and peaceful life, their loves, their constancy, their fidelity, the purity of their manners, etc. Many other examples would show that men think only insofar as they borrow the assistance either of the objects that strike their senses or of those objects of which the imagination evokes the images.

§39 I have said that analysis is the unique secret in the making of discoveries. But what is the secret of analysis, someone will ask? The connection of ideas. When I intend to reflect on some object, the first thing I do is to notice that the ideas I have of the object are connected to those I seek but do not yet have. Next I observe that the ideas of either kind can enter into a variety of combinations and that, depending on these variations, there is more or less connection among the ideas. Thus I can imagine a combination in which the connection is the strongest possible, as well as several others with diminishing connections, until they finally cease to be perceptible. If I regard an object from a point of view that offers no perceptible connection with the ideas I seek, I do not discover anything. If the connection is slight, I discover little, since my thoughts appear to be the mere effect of forced application or even of chance; that sort of discovery affords little assistance for further discovery. But if I view an object in the aspect that has the greatest connection with the ideas I seek, I will discover everything; the analysis will occur almost without effort on my part; and with the progress I am making in the knowledge of truth, I will be able to observe the most intricate workings of my mind and thereby learn the art of making new analyses.

The whole difficulty lies in knowing how to begin in order to lay hold of ideas by their greatest or principal connection. My point is that the combination where we find this connection is the one that agrees with the true generation of things. For this reason, we must begin with the first idea which must have produced all the rest. Let us look at an example.

The scholastics and the Cartesians knew neither the origin nor the generation of our knowledge, for the good reason that the principle of innate ideas and the vague notion of the understanding, on which their thinking was based, have no connection with this discovery. Locke had greater success, because he began with the senses, while what is imperfect in his work stems from his failure to examine the early progress of the operations of the mind. I have tried to supply what this philosopher left out by going all the way to the first operations of mind, and I have, it seems to me, not only provided a complete analysis of the understanding, but also discovered the indispensable necessity of signs and the principle of the connection of ideas.

In addition, we cannot successfully use the method I am proposing without taking all sorts of precautions not to proceed except in step with the precise determination of ideas. If we pass too lightly over some, we will find ourselves facing obstacles that cannot be overcome without returning to the initial notions in order to fix them better than we did before.

§40 Everyone sometimes has thoughts that are wholly of his own making, even though they may not be new. It is at such moments that we must examine ourselves in order to reflect on what we inwardly experience. We must observe the impressions made on the senses, the manner in which the mind was affected, the progress of its ideas – in a word, all the circumstances that could give rise to a thought which we owe entirely to our own reflection. After several observations of this kind, we cannot fail to discover the natural progression of our minds. In the end, we will recognize the means most suitable for eliciting reflection, and even for making corrections along the way if we have contracted some habit that is contrary to the exercise of these operations.

§41 It would be easier for us to recognize our mistakes if we knew that the greatest men have also made similar mistakes. The philosophers would, for the most part, have remedied our inability to look into ourselves if they had left us a record of the history of the progress of their minds. Descartes did that, thereby putting us greatly in his debt. Instead of attacking the scholastics head on, he describes the time when he shared their prejudices; he openly treats the obstacles he had to overcome in order to disabuse himself of those opinions; he lays down rules for a much simpler method than any that had been in use before his time; he gives a glimpse of the discoveries he believes he has made; and by this strategy he prepares our minds to accept the new doctrines which he made it his aim to establish [see his *Discourse on the Method*]. I believe that his example in this regard has greatly contributed to the revolution in philosophy which he initiated.

§42 It is of the greatest importance to guide children in the same manner in which I have shown we ought to conduct ourselves. In playing with them, we might exercise the operations of their minds in every possible way, provided, as I have said, that every object can be used to proper effect. We could even make them assume unawares the habit of conducting these operations in an orderly way. When age and circumstances later change the objects that occupied them, their minds would be fully developed so as to possess, at an early age, a degree of intelligence which by any other method would come only much later, if ever. Thus we ought not to teach children Latin, history, geography, etc. What use are these subjects at an age when the child does not yet know how to think? For my part, I pity the children who are admired for their learning, and I foresee the moment when we will become surprised by their mediocrity or perhaps their stupidity. I say once more that the first thing we must aim for is to give their minds the exercise of all its operations; and to that end we need not run after things that are unfamiliar to them: playful talk will do the trick.

§43 Philosophers have often asked whether there is a first principle of human knowledge. Some have assumed only one, others two or even more. It seems to me that everyone can consult his own experience to be sure of the truth that is the foundation of this entire work. Perhaps people will even become convinced that the connection of ideas is, without rival, the simplest, the most lucid and most fertile principle. Even at the time when its influence was not understood, the human mind owed all its progress to it.

§44 Those were my reflections on method before I read Bacon for the first time. I was as flattered to find myself agreeing with this great man in some respects as I was surprised that the Cartesians borrowed nothing from him. No one has understood the cause of our errors better than Bacon, for he saw that the ideas which are the product of the mind were poorly formed, and that, for that reason, they had to be formed afresh if we were to make progress in the search for truth. He often repeats that advice.[57] But did he have a hearing? Being prejudiced in favor of the jargon of the schools and innate ideas, who would not treat the project of restoring the human understanding as a chimera? Bacon proposed a method that was too perfect to initiate a revolution; and Descartes' method would succeed because it left some errors standing. To this may be added that the English philosopher had other employments which did not permit him to put into practice what he advised to others; he was therefore obliged to limit himself to giving directions which could only make a light impression on minds that were incapable of seeing their solid foundations. Descartes, on the contrary, with philosophy as his only employment and with a more agile and fertile imagination, sometimes substituted even more seductive errors for the errors of others; they have contributed not a little to his reputation.

---

[57] Bacon, *Novum organum* [*1, §97].

> No one has yet been found so firm of mind and purpose as resolutely to compel himself to sweep away all theories and common notions, and to apply the understanding, thus made fair and even, to a fresh examination of particulars. Thus it happens that human knowledge, as we have it, is a mere medley and ill-digested mass, made up of much credulity and much accident, and also of the childish notions which we have at first imbibed.
>
> Now if any one of ripe age, unimpaired senses, and well-purged mind, apply himself anew to experience and particulars, better hopes may be entertained of that man. (. . .) There is no hope except in a new birth of science; that is, in raising it regularly up from experience and building it afresh, which no one (I think) will say has yet been done or thought of.

That is one of the aphorisms of which I spoke in my Introduction. [*Condillac quotes Bacon in Latin.]

4 The order to be followed in the exposition of truth

§45 Everybody knows that a work should not give the appearance of art, but it is perhaps not so well known that art can be concealed only by art. For the sake of being easy to read and natural, many writers believe they should not submit to any order, but if we take the term *belle nature* to mean nature without blemish, then it is evident that we ought not to attempt to imitate nature by being careless, and that art will appear absent only when we have the mastery to avoid carelessness.

§46 There are other writers who put too much order into their works, with meticulous divisions and subdivisions, but shocking us with the artifice that sticks out everywhere. The more they strive for order, the more they become dry, off-putting, and difficult to understand, because they have failed to find the order that is most natural for their subject matter. If they had chosen it, they would have expounded their thoughts with such clarity and simplicity that the reader would have understood them too easily to suspect the effort they were obliged to apply to the writing. We are inclined to believe that things are easy or difficult for others as measured by our own reactions to those things, and we naturally estimate the difficulty a writer has had in expressing himself by the difficulty we have in understanding him.

§47 The natural order cannot do any harm. It is necessary even in works written in the spirit of enthusiasm, as in an ode, for example. This is not because there is a need for strict reasoning, but because we must conform to the order in which the ideas that characterize each passion sort themselves out. And here indeed, so it seems to me, lie the whole force and beauty of this kind of poetry.

In a work of exposition and rational argument, only the order he puts into it can make the author aware of what he has forgotten and what he has not treated in sufficient depth. This I have often experienced myself. This essay, for example, was finished, and yet I still did not understand the principle of the connection of ideas in its full extent, only because of a passage of about two pages which was not in its right place.

§48 We are pleased by order for the very simple reason, so it seems to me, that it brings things together and connects them, thus by this means facilitating the operations of the mind so that we can easily note the relations which it is important for us to perceive in the things that affect us. Our pleasure ought to increase in proportion to the ease with which we conceive the things it matters for us to know.

§49 Sometimes lack of order may also please, depending on particular affections of the mind. In moments of reverie when the mind, being too indolent to contemplate the same thoughts for any length of time, loves to see them float around haphazardly, we are, for example, more greatly pleased by a landscape than by the most beautiful gardens; the reason is that the disordered landscape seems more congenial to the absence of order in our own ideas and that it sustains our reverie by preventing us from dwelling on the same thought. This state of mind is even rather sensuous, especially when enjoyed after long application to work.

There are also some affections of mind which favor the reading of works without order. I sometimes, for example, read Montaigne with much pleasure, while I must admit that at other times I cannot bear reading him. I do not know if others have had the same experience, but I would not myself wish to be condemned always to read authors of that kind. However that may be, order has the advantage that it is a constant pleasure; lack of order pleases only now and then, without any rules for ensuring success. It was therefore Montaigne's very good fortune to succeed, but it would be rash to attempt to imitate him.

§50 It is the aim of order to facilitate the understanding of a work. We ought therefore to avoid prolixity because it is tiresome, digressions because they distract, divisions and subdivisions because they confuse us, and repetitions because they are fatiguing to the mind. A thing said once in its proper place is clearer than when it is repeated several times in different places.

§51 In the exposition as well as in the search for truth, we must begin with the ideas that are easiest and come directly from the senses, afterwards gradually rising to more simple or more complex ideas. I believe that if we rightly understand the progress of truths, we need not look for arguments to demonstrate them, their mere statement being sufficient, because their sequence will exhibit an order which ensures that what one truth adds to its predecessor is too simple to require proof. Thus we should arrive at those which are more complex, and be surer of them than by any other means. We might even establish such a great subordination among all the discrete parts of knowledge we have acquired that we could, as we pleased, pass from the most complex to the simplest, and vice versa. They would be hard to forget, or if that happened their connection would at least make it easy to find the means of recovering what was lost.

But in order to expound the truth in the most perfect order, we must examine the order in which it could most naturally have been discovered, for the best procedure in the instruction of others is to lead them along the same route that we had to follow in our own learning. By this means we do not seem so much to demonstrate truths already discovered as to make others seek and find new truths. We would not merely convince the reader, but even make him understand; and by showing him how to make his own discoveries, we would present the truth to him in the most interesting light. In the end, we would make him capable of explaining every step to himself, always knowing where he is, where he came from, and where he is going. He would consequently himself be able to judge of the road his guide showed him, and to take a safer path whenever he anticipated any danger in following his guide.

§52 Nature itself shows the order we ought to follow in the exposition of truth, for if all our knowledge comes from sense it is evident that it is the task of ideas of sense to prepare the intellect for abstract notions. Is it reasonable to begin with the idea of the possible in order to arrive at the idea of existence, or with the idea of the point to arrive at the idea of the solid? The elements of the sciences will never become simple and easy unless we follow the very opposite method. If philosophers find it difficult to recognize the truth, it is because they are prejudiced in favor either of innate ideas or of some custom which seems to have been consecrated by time. This bias is so universal that only the ignorant are on my side. But here those who are ignorant are the judges, because the elements are made for them. In this kind of writing, what learned people look upon as a masterpiece is of little use if we do not understand it.

Even the geometricians, who ought better than other philosophers to know the advantages of analysis, often give the preference to synthesis. Therefore, we do not find in them the same clarity, the same precision, or the same reach of mind when they pass from their calculations in order to pursue studies of another nature. We have four celebrated metaphysicians – Descartes, Malebranche, Leibniz, and Locke. The last is the only one who was not a geometrician, and yet how greatly superior he is to the other three!

§53 Let us conclude that if analysis is the method we ought to follow in the search for truth, it is also the method we should follow in the exposition of the discoveries we have made; I have endeavored to follow that method.

What I have said about the operations of the mind, about language and about method, proves that the sciences cannot be brought to perfection except by striving to make language more precise. Thus it is demonstrated that the origin and progress of our knowledge depend entirely on the manner in which we make use of signs. It is with good reason, therefore, that I have sometimes not followed the conventional wisdom.

Here, finally, is what I think everything can be reduced to that contributes to the development of the human mind. The senses are the source of our knowledge. The materials of knowledge are the different sensations, perception, consciousness, reminiscence, attention and imagination, with these last two being considered as not yet subject to our control; these materials are put to work by memory, by imagination once subject to our control, by reflection and the other operations; signs, to which we owe the exercise of these same operations, are the instruments they employ, and the connection of ideas is the first spring that puts all the rest in motion. I shall close by proposing the following problem to the reader. "The work of an author being given, determine the quality and extent of his mind, and in consequence thereof, tell not only what the talents are of which he gives proof, but in addition what the talents are that he can acquire. Take, for example, Corneille's first play and show that, when this poet wrote it, he already had, or at least very soon would have, the genius which earned him such great acclaim." Only analysis of the work can reveal the operations that have made it possible and the degree to which they were practiced; and only the analysis of these operations can make us distinguish in the same man the qualities that are compatible from those which are not, and thereby give the solution to the problem. I doubt that there are many problems more difficult than this one.

Index

Cambridge texts in the history of philosophy

Titles published in the series thus far